Contingent Valuation and Endangered Species

NEW HORIZONS IN ENVIRONMENTAL ECONOMICS

General Editor: Wallace E. Oates, *Professor of Economics, University of Maryland*

This important new series is designed to make a significant contribution to the development of the principles and practices of environmental economics. It will include both theoretical and empirical work. International in scope, it will address issues of current and future concern in both East and West and in developed and developing countries.

The main purpose of the series is to create a forum for the publication of high quality work and to show how economic analysis can make a contribution to understanding and resolving the environmental problems confronting the world in the late 20th century.

Titles in the series include:

Principles of Environmental and Resource Economics
A Guide for Students and Decision-Makers
Edited by Henk Folmer, H. Landis Gabel and Hans Opschoor

The Contingent Valuation of Environmental Resources
Methodological Issues and Research Needs
Edited by David J. Bjornstad and James R. Kahn

Environmental Policy with Political and Economic Integration
The European Union and the United States
Edited by John B. Braden, Henk Folmer and Thomas S. Ulen

Energy, Environment and the Economy
Asian Perspectives
Paul R. Kleindorfer, Howard C. Kunreuther and David S. Hong

Estimating Economic Values for Nature
Methods for Non-Market Valuation
V. Kerry Smith

Models of Sustainable Development
Edited by Sylvie Faucheux, David Pearce and John Proops

Contingent Valuation and Endangered Species
Methodological Issues and Applications
Kristin M. Jakobsson and Andrew K. Dragun

Acid Rain and Environmental Degradation
The Economics of Emission Trading
Ger Klaassen

The Economics of Pollution Control in the Asia Pacific
Robert Mendelsohn and Daigee Shaw

Economic Policy for the Environment and Natural Resources
Techniques for the Management and Control of Pollution
Edited by Anastasios Xepapadeas

Welfare Measurement, Sustainability and Green National Accounting
A Growth Theoretical Approach
Thomas Aronsson, Per-Olov Johansson and Karl-Gustaf Löfgren

Contingent Valuation and Endangered Species

Methodological Issues and Applications

Kristin M. Jakobsson and Andrew K. Dragun
Swedish University of Agricultural Sciences and LaTrobe University

NEW HORIZONS IN ENVIRONMENTAL ECONOMICS

Edward Elgar
Cheltenham, UK. Brookfield US

Published by
Edward Elgar Publishing Limited
8 Lansdown Place
Cheltenham
Glos GL50 2HU
UK

Edward Elgar Publishing Company
Old Post Road
Brookfield
Vermont 05036
US

A catalogue record for this book
is available from the British Library

Library of Congress Cataloging-in-Publication Data
Jakobsson, Kristin M. , 1957—
  Contingent valuation and endangered species : methodological
issues and applications / Kristin M. Jakobsson and Andrew K. Dragun.
  (New horizons in environmental economics series)
  Includes bibliographical references and index.
  1. Endangered species—Economic aspects. 2. Endangered species–
–Economic aspects—Australia—Victoria. 3. Biological diversity
conservation—Economic aspects. 4. Biological diversity
conservation—Economic aspects—Australia—Victoria. 5. Contingent
valuation. I. Dragun, Andrew K. II. Title. III. Series.
QH75.J35 1996
  338.4'33339516—dc20   96–5824
                                                                    CIP

ISBN 1 85898 464 5

Printed and bound in Great Britain by
Hartnolls Limited, Bodmin, Cornwall

Dedication

To Asher and Haakan

Contents

PART FOUR   THE SURVEY APPLICATION TO SPECIES
             CONSERVATION

PART FIVE   CONCLUSIONS

List of Tables

List of Boxes

List of Figures

Foreword

Michael Hanemann

There are at least two reasons why it is a pleasure to contribute a foreword to this book. First, this book provides an excellent account of the contingent valuation method which is increasingly being employed to place a monetary value on items that are of value to people but are not traded in markets. As the authors explain, this approach draws on the same theory of preferences that economists use to analyze market behaviour. But, people have preferences for many things, not just consumer goods. And, given an opportunity, they make choices about many things other than just consumer goods. The contingent valuation method exploits this by confronting them with choices about possible public actions - in this case, actions to protect endangered species - that could be undertaken at some cost to themselves as citizens and taxpayers. Their responses to the survey question trace out a demand function for the public action.

Implementing this approach to valuation involves a blend of economics, statistics and survey research. This book offers a hands-on account of the design and implementation of a contingent valuation survey, combined with a clear and informative exposition of the theoretical and statistical issues associated with the analysis and interpretation of the survey responses. It gives the general reader a good feel for what is involved in a contingent valuation exercise, while providing sufficient technical detail to satisfy the needs of specialist researchers interested in the latest methodological developments. Economists sometimes have a cavalier attitude towards data collection. Data is something that other people collect and that you find in libraries. The highest prestige in economics tends to be associated with developing theoretical models, followed by econometric analysis.

Designing a measurement exercise and collecting the data tend to be regarded as inferior activities. For an empirical science - and all the social sciences are fundamentally empirical sciences - this is an unwise and short-sighted attitude. Thus, I regard it as a virtue that contingent valuation requires the researcher to pay attention equally to data collection and model building. The authors exemplify this, and in their book they provide a fine example of what can be accomplished with a thoughtful and carefully executed research design.

Second, this book is a welcome addition to the growing literature on the economics of endangered species. It surveys the economic theory of species extinction and lucidly summarizes the alternative approaches that have appeared in the literature. For those interested in public policy, it offers a comprehensive account of efforts at endangered species protection in Australia, and a comparison with current developments in the United States. It also provides a useful comparison of the empirical results in this study with those obtained in contingent valuation studies of environmental and other resources that have so far been conducted in Australia and New Zealand.

The authors conclude that the protection of endangered species and environmental amenities can have a significant social value which needs to be explicitly considered in the assessment of development projects in Australia. This conclusion applies with equal force in the United States and in many other countries. Often, one of the best ways to establish this social value is through a contingent valuation analysis like that reported here. This is an exemplary study which deserves a wide audience.

Michael Hanemann
Berkeley

Preface

The purpose of this book is to investigate the theory and methodology for appraising unpriced values in the natural environment. Markets exist for many goods and services in our societies enabling most citizens to interact and organise their day-to-day affairs in a comparatively ordered, efficient and equitable manner. However, most environmental considerations escape this order and citizens and their governments have a great deal of difficulty coming to decisions as to how the environment should be used - or conserved.

Unfortunately, it can be the case that this lack of price information on environmental goods and services can convey the impression that they have little value or are unimportant relative to the market priced alternatives and thus much environmental value can be lost.

It is clear however, that there is great interest in environmental issues in most societies, but the problem is that most interested citizens have few means to express their interests and establish their value on questions of environmental concern. Not only are there no relevant markets for the environmental goods in question, but it is often the case that the political and judicial processes are slow to respond to them.

In this setting the underlying theme of this book is to explore the theory and the means by which the value citizens might place on the environment can be identified and included in decision making. In particular, the focus of study here is on the profound environmental problem of biodiversity, where socio-economic insight seems to be lagging the pronouncements of innumerable ecologists that species conservation is a problem which is becoming more serious everywhere on the planet.

The objective is to provide an appraisal of the value of species conservation which can be related to the decisions on best use of the environment. Accordingly, the analytical focus is on the different economic methods for assessing the value people place on environment considerations, especially in relation to endangered species. Of principal interest is the relatively new methodology of contingent valuation, which is a method for asking people directly about their preferences.

The first part of the book explores the welfare economic theory concerned with the valuation of non-market goods in general and then reviews the literature on the contingent valuation method and its application. Economic issues relating to endangered species and biodiversity loss are also examined and the biological and institutional setting within which species conservation is conceived and managed is outlined.

The second part of the book is an application of the contingent valuation method to the conservation of endangered species in the State of Victoria, Australia. This application has two objectives. The primary objective is to investigate some of the methodological issues in contingent valuation identified in the first part of the study. The issues examined include the scope effect, the effect of using different valuation questions, the use of different payment vehicles and the effect of varying the information supplied to survey respondents.

The second objective is to estimate values for species conservation in Victoria, both for all endangered species and for an individual species, Leadbeater's possum, *Gymnobelideus leadbeateri*. This study is the first in Australia to estimate these values. The use of such values in the decision making process required under the Victorian *Flora and Fauna Guarantee Act* is discussed. The results also emphasise the importance of careful survey design, implementation and analysis as well as the precise definition of the environmental good being valued.

Fundamentally, this book demonstrates a rigorous and refined methodology for practitioners wishing to investigate a range of environmental issues with the contingent valuation method. It also highlights the theoretical strengths and weaknesses of the method in relation to environmental valuation generally and species conservation in particular and prepares a substantial basis by which the social problem of biodiversity might be publicly considered and ameliorated. The main conclusion of the study is that the contingent valuation method is capable of providing information that will be of assistance in the decision making process.

Parts of Chapter 2 were developed in the setting of a paper the authors presented to the Second meeting of the International Society for Ecological Economics, Stockholm August 1992, with Crosthwaite and Edmonds (1992). Otherwise, much of the research reported here was developed in the setting of a PhD dissertation by Jakobsson, which was completed in 1994 at LaTrobe University.

We wish to thank our colleagues at LaTrobe University, John Kennedy of the Department of Economics and Rob Dumsday and Anthony Chisholm both of the School of Agriculture, for their continued advice and support throughout the conduct of our research.

A range of people provided particular help at various stages of the research. Mervyn Silvapulle assisted on statistical issues, Bob Powell and David de Vaus provided advice on questionnaire design and survey techniques, Tom Voon and Ian Gatehouse helped print and mail the questionnaires, Jonas Pertoft did the graphics and Bev Tannock and staff helped with the data entry.

Specific comments on earlier drafts of the manuscript were provided by

Michael Hanemann, Bengt Kriström and John Loomis who also supplied a range of papers and information on various components of the research. Kevin Boyle, Alan Randall and Per-Olov Johansson also provided papers, information and wisdom on a wide range of issues. We would also like to thank Peter Frykblom at the Swedish University of Agricultural Sciences for his comments and helpful suggestions.

We would finally, and most deeply, wish to thank our parents and children for providing continuous moral and practical support over some considerable time. Especially, we would like to recognise the contribution of Haakan and Asher, for so often sacrificing a night time story and offering to do 'Mummy's and Daddy's work'.

Kristin Jakobsson
Andrew Dragun
Uppsala

PART ONE

Environmental Values: The Institutional and
Biological Setting for Species Conservation

1. Introduction

INTRODUCTION

Biodiversity and species conservation are among the most pressing environmental issues confronting contemporary society. In the setting that most human activities are priced in some way or other, there is a temptation in some decision circles to down play or ignore species conservation values as a function of the non-existence of prices for species. No prices equate with no value.

But most communities seem to place considerable importance on the natural environment of which species considerations are obviously an important and implicitly valuable component. The conservation of species does have value, but no easy means of interpreting that value is generally available. Consequently, the challenge for economic analysis is to establish how such value might be identified and interpreted so that the value of protecting species can be compared with the value of other human activities which adversely affect the survival of species.

There has been substantial effort applied to calculate monetary benefits for most human activities impacting on the natural environment, such as the harvesting of forests or fish, or the draining of wetlands for agriculture, but it is more difficult to calculate comparable benefits for many environmental goods, such as species survival or unpolluted waters.

This disparity has generally meant that social and political interest has focussed on enterprises with identifiable monetary costs and benefits to the detriment of environmental attributes which are treated as if they had little or no value (Mishan 1982).

ENVIRONMENTAL VALUES

Evaluation of the costs and benefits of many environmental goods presents major difficulties because of the lack of markets in which prices or values can be established. As a consequence, environmental goods have been undervalued or ignored when comparing the net benefits of conservation projects with those of development projects. The conservation of endangered flora and fauna is one of the areas in which few attempts have been made to evaluate the costs and benefits in monetary terms.

Substantial methodological innovation in the valuation of environmental goods has occurred in recent years, with a range of valuation methods being developed. Contingent valuation has emerged as a promising methodology, particularly in the valuation of non-use benefits. Application of the technique could provide a perspective on the benefits of conserving flora and fauna which could be very valuable for the formation of social policy. Evaluation of the benefits and costs of conserving flora and fauna assists in the efficient allocation of total resources to conservation programmes and also in determining priorities among programmes.

OBJECTIVES OF THIS STUDY

Although application of the contingent valuation technique is potentially very useful, it raises a range of significant methodological questions which have not been resolved. In this book, some of the methodological problems are considered in an application to species conservation to test the robustness of the methodology. In order to investigate the methodological issues, a range of hypotheses have been delineated on the respective questions. These are detailed in Chapter 8. A further objective is to estimate the values that citizens of Victoria place on the conservation of endangered species. This study is the first in Australia to estimate such values.

A motivation for considering the conservation of species as an application was the enactment of the *Flora and Fauna Guarantee Act* by the Victorian State Government in 1988. This Act provides for the protection of endangered species which have been nominated and listed through a prescribed process taking into account the social and economic consequences of protection. There is, however, no mechanism suggested in the Act for evaluating the social and economic consequences of providing protection. The substance of the Act is detailed in Chapter 2.

Two main questionnaires were used in the study. One concerned willingness to pay for the conservation of all the endangered species of flora and fauna in Victoria and the other concerned the willingness to pay for conservation of an individual species. The estimate of value for the conservation of all endangered species is useful as an indication of Victorians' attitudes to species conservation and how these attitudes relate to current policies and expenditures in this area.

The value for a single species was estimated for a number of reasons. It is likely that, as a consequence of the *Flora and Fauna Guarantee Act*, the benefits of protecting an individual species may need to be estimated for inclusion in the economic evaluation of a conservation programme where the opportunity costs of conservation are high. Comparison of the value estimates for protecting all species and for protecting an individual species enables consideration of one of the major methodological issues of contingent valuation, the issue of scope effects (Chapter 6). Most studies which have valued the conservation of endangered species have been for individual species. Valuing an individual species in this study enables some comparison with values obtained in other studies.

A number of species which are significant in Victoria were considered for study, including the Mallee fowl, helmeted honeyeater, Eltham copper butterfly and the Eastern barred bandicoot. Leadbeater's possum was selected as the subject of this study because the opportunity cost of conservation is likely to be higher than for the other species and there is the potential for considerable conflict.

Leadbeater's possum is a small, arboreal, nocturnal marsupial which is particular to Victoria and is one of the two faunal emblems of the State. It was thought to be extinct for many years, but was rediscovered in the 1960s. It has been subject to a considerable amount of research since its rediscovery and is one of the few endangered species to have a management plan, albeit still in draft form after several years. It is currently confined to the mountain ash forest in the Central Highlands area of Victoria.

The Central Highlands forest is considered by the timber industry to be a valuable timber resource. Management strategies to assist survival of the possum come at a cost to timber production and there has been some conflict between environmentalists and the forestry industry as to the most appropriate use of the area. Information on the value of the possum will assist in making a full and systematic evaluation of the social costs and benefits of management actions to protect the possum.

This book has three main objectives:

1. To establish the welfare economic principles by which biodiversity issues might better be considered as well as the biological and institutional setting within which this analysis should be set.
2. To test a range of methodological issues related to the application of the contingent valuation technique in order to establish its validity and applicability as a policy tool. This will provide a basis of analysis for practitioners wishing to apply the method in specific situations.
3. To apply the contingent valuation methodology to estimate the value Victorians place on the conservation of native flora and fauna and to consider the results in relation to policy needs and decision making processes in Victoria. Subsequently, the contingent valuation welfare economic approach is appraised in a public policy setting.

PLAN OF THE BOOK

This book is divided into five main parts. In the first part (Chapters 1, 2 and 3) the policy background in which the study is set is described. In Chapter 2 the legislation determining the decision making processes with respect to protecting endangered species is outlined.

The Victorian *Flora and Fauna Guarantee Act* is explored in some detail to provide the context in which decision making and policy setting occurs. The points in the process at which economic evaluation may be required are identified and the ways in which the evaluation may be done are discussed. The Victorian legislation is also related to national legislation as well as international conventions on biodiversity and significant other international legislation.

Some background to the status of endangered species in Victoria is given in Chapter 3. Also, the biology and habitat requirements of Leadbeater's possum are described in order to illustrate the nature of the conflicts to be resolved. The forest management that is optimal for timber production is far from optimal for survival of the possum and tradeoffs must be made between the requirements of the possum and timber output.

In part two (Chapters 4 and 5) the theoretical background to species conservation as an economic problem and to the contingent valuation technique is considered. While Chapter 4 develops a conventional welfare economic approach to species conservation, Chapter 5 consists of a review of the rationale for valuing environmental goods such as species diversity, economic approaches to the valuation problem and recent literature relating to the concept of total value of a natural resource. Methods of estimating values for non-market goods are reviewed and the choice of contingent valuation for the application is justified.

The analytical focus turns directly to the contingent valuation methodology in part three. Here the recent literature relating to contingent valuation is reviewed in Chapter 6. The use of contingent valuation has increased markedly in recent years and with it the debate concerning the validity or otherwise of the technique. The main methodological issues associated with the technique are discussed and the background is laid for the issues which are investigated in this book.

Chapter 7 completes the background and review section of the book. This chapter contains a literature review outlining the theory of welfare measurement in discrete response valuation studies. The discrete choice contingent valuation approach uses a 'take-it-or-leave-it' question of the form 'would you be prepared to pay an amount of $X to ensure a particular level of an environmental good', with a range of values for X being used. The method requires fairly complex statistical analysis. Measures of mean and median willingness to pay can be estimated in more than one way, resulting in different values. There seems to be no consensus as to which method is best. The treatment of zero responses is also discussed.

In the fourth part of the book, the application of the contingent valuation method to species conservation and the results are explained. In Chapter 8 the survey, questionnaires and hypotheses tested in the survey are described. The questions and responses to each question are detailed. Socioeconomic characteristics of the survey respondents are compared with these characteristics in the general population from which the survey sample was drawn to ascertain whether the survey estimates could be extended to the Victorian population.

Chapter 9 is devoted to analysis of the willingness to pay responses and estimation of willingness to pay values, using three approaches to estimation. This study used both discrete choice and open-ended (continuous) valuation questions which are analysed and compared. Aggregate willingness to pay is calculated from the individual value estimates.

The results of the hypotheses and their implications for the use of the technique, as well as the relevance of the estimated values to policy and decision making, are considered in the final part (Chapters 10 and 11). In Chapter 10 the survey results are applied to the hypotheses developed in Chapter 8 and conclusions drawn. The validity of the estimates is considered in relation to the presence and effect of any systematic errors resulting from the survey design and implementation. The main findings of the study are summarised.

In Chapter 11 the usefulness of the information gained is discussed in relation to the particular policy setting outlined in Chapter 2. The discussion is expanded to a more general consideration of the potential and usefulness of contingent valuation studies in both the Australian setting and the international scene.

2. The Institutional Setting: The Victorian Flora and Fauna Guarantee Act

INTRODUCTION

The initial focus in this chapter is to provide background on legislation and policy measures relating to endangered species in Victoria in particular and the national and international scene in general. The legislation reviewed is the Victorian *Flora and Fauna Guarantee Act 1988.*

The second part of the chapter explores the *Flora and Fauna Guarantee Act* in detail to establish the setting in which decision making and policy formulation on species conservation occurs in Victoria. The Act requires that the social and economic consequences of species management be taken into account when management schemes are developed, in addition to scientific and biological requirements.

There has been little experience of accounting for all the social and economic consequences of species conservation programmes in Australia and the Act gives no specific guidelines as to how it might be done. However, the legislative reference is to benefits and financial tradeoffs and this appears to necessitate considerations of economic valuation.

Economic techniques of non-market valuation will almost certainly be required because many of the benefits associated with species conservation are not exchanged in the market. The technique of contingent valuation (setting up a hypothetical market) is of special interest because it is the only method of measuring some of these benefits. An important example of such a benefit in species conservation is existence value, that is, the value gained simply from knowing a species is present. Consideration of how economic and social impacts might be identified and included in the *Flora and Fauna Guarantee Act* process was part of the impetus for choosing endangered species as an application for the contingent valuation methodology.

Finally, national and international legislation and conventions on biological conservation are considered, from the point of view of their broader impact on the Victorian initiatives. This discussion is also extended to deal with the prospects for the use of the contingent valuation methodology and the estimates derived from it, in the particular species conservation setting in Victoria and for biodiversity conservation in general.

THE FLORA AND FAUNA GUARANTEE LEGISLATION

The key legislation and major guide to policy relating to endangered species in Victoria is the *Flora and Fauna Guarantee Act*, passed in 1988. This legislation has been seen as some of the most far reaching environmental legislation in Australia and probably the world (Crosthwaite *et al.* 1992). The primary objective is to 'ensure that all species survive, flourish and retain their evolutionary potential in the wild'. It goes beyond remedial measures for already endangered species and provides for measures to prevent more species becoming threatened.

The Victorian Act provides for the listing of threatened species but separates this from the requirement to declare critical habitat. Potentially threatening processes and ecological communities can also be listed. Both listing and critical habitat declaration must be done independently of social and economic considerations; but substantial input on these matters is required in action statements, management plans and interim conservation orders. This Act builds on the US *Endangered Species Act* and sets the standard for further international developments in this area.

Setting a benchmark guarantee against which action can be judged, the *Flora and Fauna Guarantee Act* gives flexible means of taking into account the wide range of diverse social interests that might emerge in relation to species conservation. It provides a mechanism for individuals to express their conservation interests in a reasonably straightforward and democratic way. Where there is sufficient public concern, or intent within the conservation agency, as to a particular conservation issue, then a clear path for resolution of that conflict is provided.

Politically, the *Flora and Fauna Guarantee Act* may be seen as a process which accords with general democratic principles of taking into account diverse values and interests. However, the ability to pursue these interests through the Courts is limited by the failure of the *Flora and Fauna Guarantee Act* to over-ride common law tests which restrict the right to challenge administrative decisions.

Nevertheless, interests must be accounted for when planning conservation action as several provisions in the statute require consideration of relevant conservation, social and economic matters. Although the *Flora and Fauna Guarantee Act* leaves open the choice of economic model, its objectives seem to imply a multidisciplinary approach.

The *Flora and Fauna Guarantee Act* embodies an ambitious framework to achieve its goals and in this sense is also a biodiversity programme. Its introduction has already led to some debate about its impact on the Victorian economy. Although flora and fauna considerations feature highly within the planning process and this new Act has influenced individual resource development projects, it is generally seen as compatible with economic growth. Nevertheless, the already high rate of species extinction in Victoria is almost certain to continue, unless significant economic adjustments are made.

Historical Background to the Flora and Fauna Guarantee Act

The statutes and administration relating to flora and fauna prior to the *Flora and Fauna Guarantee Act* did not embody a sense of guarantee as the *Flora and Fauna Guarantee Act* seeks to do. Flora and fauna were covered by a variety of statutes, specifically the *Wildlife Act* 1975 and the *Wildflowers and Native Plants Protection Act* 1958. Only some vertebrates and some vascular plants were legally protected (Sutton 1988). Ecological communities, invertebrates and non-vascular plants were ignored.

Apart from the process of determining use of public land based on recommendations of the Land Conservation Council, there was no articulated and coordinated approach to conserving both flora and fauna and no clear objectives for flora and fauna conservation. Emphasis was on control of direct taking, particularly in the case of wildlife, rather than habitat management or control of threats. Flora management was largely restricted to reserves with no attempt to modify the common law tradition in which flora were possessed by landowners. Generally, flora and fauna conservation issues were dealt with on a species-by-species basis as particular issues arose, rather than as part of a coordinated, forward-looking conservation strategy which took threats and habitat conservation as central.

The Victorian statute must be seen in the context of the Australian federal system. As most revenue raising powers are held by the Commonwealth, the six states and two territories therefore depend on Commonwealth grants for preparation of their annual budgets. Powers relating to land management are constitutionally vested in the states. Environmental matters are not addressed by the Constitution and not being reserved for the Commonwealth, can be legislated on by the states. The Commonwealth can legitimately address environmental questions, but only indirectly through other powers such as trade, external affairs and finance. The Commonwealth may continue to use its powers to ensure conservation of internationally important ecosystems, as it has already with the Franklin River dam and Kakadu Conservation Zone cases.

In the field of endangered species, the current focus of Commonwealth funding is for preparation and implementation of Recovery Plans which overlaps with some processes followed under the *Flora and Fauna Guarantee Act*. The Commonwealth has moved slowly on biodiversity statutes, but has recently enacted the *Endangered Species Act* 1992 and ratified the Convention on Biological Diversity presented at the Rio Earth Summit in June 1992. The *Endangered Species Act* embodies powers related only to the relatively small areas of Commonwealth land, to actions of Commonwealth authorities and to situations where action is required under international treaty. Although programmes for nationally endangered species will be initiated and supported, action related to other less threatened species will be largely left to the states and territories.

The *Flora and Fauna Guarantee Act* was also introduced in the context of other attempts to better integrate conservation and land management activities in Victoria. Administrative changes led in 1984 to a new department, now the Department of Conservation and Environment, taking responsibility for national parks, public land management, land protection on private land, forestry, fisheries, as well as wildlife and flora conservation. In 1987 the Government published an all-embracing State Conservation Strategy.

The Flora and Fauna Guarantee Process

The *Flora and Fauna Guarantee Act* established a process whereby individuals or groups with particular conservation interests can nominate a species or ecological community for listing on the grounds that it is threatened with extinction in the State of Victoria. Subsequently, the conservation status is considered by a Scientific Advisory Committee established under the statute. After one public submission phase, the species or ecological community might then be listed, based solely on scientific criteria. The same process of nomination and listing can be applied to potentially threatening processes which threaten the survival, abundance and development of two or more native species.

The listing process has attracted some controversy, involving groups who believe it may slow down or prevent development. Unlike the US *Endangered Species Act*, critical habitat declaration is not required at the same time as a listing. Even though the US listing process itself involves only nature conservation considerations, concern about the impacts on particular economic interests has meant listings have been both delayed and avoided (Loomis and Helfand 1993). The Victorian *Flora and Fauna Guarantee Act* has been designed to avoid these pitfalls. The listings are recommended by a statutory body, serviced by, but independent of, any government agency. The listings process allows submissions on scientific questions. It also allows for any party to present evidence in an application for de-listing.

On listing, an action statement must be prepared in due course. For many listings, the action statement and its intended actions, will be the only step taken under the *Flora and Fauna Guarantee Act*. The action statement presents the most vital information on ecological, social and economic matters relevant to management and states what action and research will be done. Action statements are valuable because they are brief and relatively quickly prepared.

Such a mechanism is particularly important when hundreds of species are being listed, including many whose conservation needs have been previously neglected. This single-species focus is a necessary component of the flora and fauna guarantee programme. In many cases, species decline is such that habitat conservation alone is not usually adequate and pro-active management is necessary. Attention to the specifics of conservation, as an action statement makes possible, is necessary precisely because extinction is generally an ongoing process rather than a sudden event. Preparation of action statements for ecological communities and potentially threatening processes ensures a wider perspective and that, where appropriate, actions which address the needs of multiple species be taken.

In some cases, it may be necessary to prepare a more detailed management plan; public consultation is mandatory during its preparation. Both action statements and management plans require consideration of social and economic matters; this is a new parameter in flora and fauna conservation in Victoria.

Critical habitat which is essential to a species or community can be determined, whether or not a listing has occurred. Although not mandatory when a listing occurs, critical habitat determination is highly desirable because obligations on public authorities then come into play and also interim conservation orders can be made. Importantly, once a determination is in place, general exemptions for people taking protected flora from private land are removed.

An interim conservation order may provide for extensive controls over activities within and affecting critical habitat for any nominated or listed species or community. This was the most contentious power included in the *Flora and Fauna Guarantee Act*, even though it is seen as a last resort measure. Although most other decisions under the statute can be made by the Director-General of the Department of Conservation and Natural Resources, the interim conservation order is made by the Minister who must take into account social and economic consequences of the decision and any other relevant matter and consult with other relevant Ministers. Wide notice of an interim conservation order must be given and submissions must be considered in the period before the order is confirmed (or revoked). The order takes effect for up to two years while long-term protection measures, through planning controls or other arrangements, are put in place. Compensation is payable to landholders and water managers for non-speculative financial loss 'as a natural direct and reasonable consequence' of the order.

Several provisions in the *Flora and Fauna Guarantee Act* relate to other public authorities. Public Authority Management Agreements provide a formal mechanism for other agencies to make commitments towards conservation of particular species and ecological communities. Public authorities 'must be administered so as to have regard to the flora and fauna conservation and management objectives' and can be required to consult by the conservation agency if their actions are thought likely to 'threaten the survival of a listed taxon or community of flora or fauna or a critical habitat'. They cannot approve the taking of protected flora or fish listed as threatened and permits they issue can be suspended during the operation of an interim conservation order.

The statute includes powerful controls over protected flora. Once flora is declared protected, the controls require that 'a person must not take, trade in, keep, move or process protected flora' unless authorised. Exemptions relate to private land that is not part of critical habitat. Permits for taking can be issued only if this does not threaten conservation of the species or the community of which it is part.

Finally, the *Flora and Fauna Guarantee Act* is complementary to other statutes. Controls over fishing, wildlife, control of weeds and pollution remain under other acts, as does statutory backing for mechanisms such as codes of practice and planning controls. Other statutes govern management of nature reserves and National Parks as well as environmental requirements associated with activities such as water allocation and mining. The key to how a particular concern moves through the phases of the Flora and Fauna Guarantee management system depends partly on the conservation requirements and partly on the priority setting which is influenced by social interest and controversy.

The Listing Process

The listing process is driving the Flora and Fauna Guarantee programme at present, causing action statements to be prepared which in turn require additional funds, or re-direction of funding within the flora and fauna programme. The listing process has kept up well with the nominations at this stage, even though nominations began in 1988 while for technical legal reasons the listings could not begin until 1991. As at July 1992, 165 listings have been made from a total of 260 nominations and another 31 items have been recommended for listing. One de-listing has been recommended. Thirty six nominations have been rejected. Only 33 nominations have yet to be fully considered by the Scientific Advisory Committee.

The number of ecological communities and potentially threatening processes nominated and listed is small but growing. Twenty nine nominations have been made for ecological communities of which nine have been listed, two have been recommended for listing and 12 have been rejected. Fourteen nominations of potentially threatening processes have resulted in nine listings, two recommendations and only one rejection.

Action Statements

The process of preparing action statements is considerably behind the listings and did not effectively begin until late 1991. By July 1992, 32 action statements had been published with another 40 targeted by December. The result is creditable given that over the previous 10 years, only 10 wildlife management plans had been prepared.

Two action statements have been published for ecological communities and one for a potentially threatened process. Several others will be finalised this year, including the Western Plains Basalt grasslands community, predation of native wildlife by the introduced red fox and removal of wood debris from Victorian streams. The strategic perspective has been to establish the process of preparing action statements before moving onto more complex issues. Hence, increasing attention is now being given to preparation of action statements for important ecological communities and potentially threatening processes.

The quality of action statements in terms of proposing actions which can achieve demonstrable results seems generally high. There are various safety nets which help ensure that this happens. The action statement guidelines require a measurable management objective, elaboration of relevant management issues, justification for any research, monitoring and survey proposals, specification and assessment of wider conservation, social and economic issues which must be addressed, brief consideration of alternative management strategies and circulation of drafts within the managing Department.

Departmental guidelines require frequent monitoring and review within five years. Whether adequate attention is being paid to what is necessary in the long term is not yet clear. Planning for a 100-year period, let alone a 500-year period, is difficult. Mistakes will be inevitable and some species and ecological communities will be irreversibly lost because of inappropriate action taken in the next few years.

However, doing nothing is even less likely to secure them. Techniques such as population viability analysis and decision analysis, which are valuable for clarifying appropriate direction in situations of uncertainty and lack of information (Maguire 1986, Crosthwaite and McMahon 1992), have yet to be widely used in preparation of action statements. Resolving economic and social matters can be crucial to the success of recovery efforts (Reading, Clark and Kellert 1991). Within the constraints they face, compilers of action statements must identify and address social and economic matters.

The action statement process has been used successfully to resolve controversial issues associated with Tall Astelia, a lily growing in small areas of mountain ash forest. Recently, a review of the destruction of one of the plant colonies during construction work on logging roads led to extensive examination of the relevant biological issues and opportunity costs associated with buffer zones of different dimensions. Finally, an appropriate buffer size and other protective measures were agreed by biologists and production foresters and then incorporated into the action statement.

Critical Habitat Determinations

Preparation of an initial set of critical habitat determinations had a high priority in 1992-93. Attention was given first to easy cases so that the principles could be established and the process bedded in. Whether the level of controversy in the US (Salzman 1990, Yagerman 1990) can be avoided will depend on the operational definition of critical habitat that is adopted, how land management implications are perceived and the extent to which recourse is made to the court system.

Management Plans

Preparation of management plans under the *Flora and Fauna Guarantee Act* has not yet been given attention because of the necessary emphasis on action statements. Experience has shown that management plans are generally costly and that they direct energies to plan preparation rather than action and necessary research. However, the preparation of management plans in strategic cases is more likely to result in decision making based on full and systematic evaluation of social costs and benefits. In development proposals fostered by the private sector and State agencies, it should lead to a better accounting for social benefits associated with conservation.

Action statements and management plans should carry considerable weight in regard to other authorities and to development proposals. Proponents of development would have to explicitly justify any move away from the previously stated conservation requirements. A management plan is likely to carry more weight than an action statement in the legal arena because it has a formal consultation phase.

The Role of Economic Evaluation

Although the *Flora and Fauna Guarantee Act* requires consideration of social and economic matters, no evaluative framework is specifically identified.

However, the Ministerial Second Reading Speeches show that the intention is to save more species from extinction than under previous processes and 'that this would be done in the most economically and socially acceptable way that can be devised'. The Minister also stated that 'the controls contained in the Bill are designed to be flexible and targeted so that the maximum conservation effect can be achieved with the minimum level of impact on landholder and other interests'. However, in practice this could mean almost anything.

There are two main roles for socio-economic input into the *Flora and Fauna Guarantee Act* process. Firstly, ensuring that conservation programmes are carried out in the most cost effective way; that is, making the best use of the limited funding available. This relates to the guarantee aspect of the *Flora and Fauna Guarantee Act*; what is the most economically efficient way of meeting the objective of protecting all 'flora and fauna so it can survive, flourish and retain the potential for evolutionary development in the wild'? The second role is in evaluating the social and economic impacts of conservation programmes.

A third role of attempting to evaluate the total amount of funding required each year is implied by the legislative requirement to table annually an assessment of progress towards achieving the objectives of the *Flora and Fauna Guarantee Act*. This book attempts to contribute to this role through the estimation of the value Victorians have for protecting all endangered species of flora and fauna.

Cost Effectiveness

The overall aim related to cost effectiveness is to get as much conservation as possible for the money available. The preparation of action statements has already led to considerable changes to funding of threatened species management in Victoria. Their preparation helps to indicate funding requirements and monitor progress. Much more attention is being paid to previously neglected species rather than big name, cute and cuddly ones, although the three major species recovery programmes, Eastern barred bandicoot, helmeted honeyeater and Leadbeater's possum, together still account for more resources than all other action statements combined. However, all programmes associated with threatened species, whether for research, survey, monitoring or conservation, are increasingly seen in terms of the best conservation outcome.

Finding the resources to prepare and implement all the required action statements is likely to become a major problem. Tight budgetary constraints across the Victorian Government mean that this will not easily be resolved, even if the Government continues to emphasise flora and fauna as a key conservation priority.

Given the limited funds, it is important that attention is given to ensuring an effective priority setting process. In the case of species, urgency, as reflected in conservation status, whether species are rare, threatened or endangered, is only one factor taken into account. Priorities have also been based on level of complexity, with an attempt also made to ensure a spread across taxonomic grouping and regions within the State. Future priorities are likely to take account of cost of recovery, future cost of present failure to act and significance at regional, state, national and international levels. Clearly, action statements for ecological communities and potentially threatening processes will receive high priority. However, many action statements for species also have positive spin-offs for other species; capitalising on this by concurrent preparation of action statements with common elements, whether based on taxonomic grouping or ecosystem, may extend the reach of available resources.

Setting priorities by using cost-benefit analysis, safe minimum standard or other approaches discussed by Tisdell (1990) and others does not seem practical at the level of action statements where a rapid and simple approach is required. Use of such techniques would address few of the relevant criteria and those techniques that require quantification of conservation benefits would be unwieldy when fifty or more action statements are being prepared each year. There seems to be more scope in using ranking techniques which employ both cost and a range of qualitative data. The difficulties in setting priorities with regard to species conservation are discussed in more detail in Chapter 5.

By comparison to *ad hoc* programmes, the successes and failures of action statements can be monitored and compared. Over time, the most successful management combinations, involving elements such as research, planning, regulation, on-ground management, extension with landholders and community support, can be evaluated. This provides the mechanism for positive feed-back into on-going and future management decisions and more than anything else will help achieve long-term control over costs.

The Evaluation of Proposed Conservation Programmes

The compilers of all action statements are required to identify affected parties as well as conservation, social and economic effects and to briefly canvas alternative management approaches. Conservation and other benefits are not generally given in monetary terms while conservation costs are anticipated over 10 years and discounted. Depending on available data, opportunity costs are quantified. Positive and negative social impacts must also be specified. This process is useful in encouraging consideration of all relevant issues even when action statements have small implementation costs and few wider impacts.

In most cases, this process will be sufficient evaluation of the social and economic consequences of conservation. This accords with the safe minimum standard approach, in which extinction is to be avoided unless social costs are unacceptably high. Bishop (1980) found that for species in the US, social costs were generally very low. This has been confirmed with action statements prepared under Victorian statutes. Direct costs currently are less than A$100,000 in most cases and opportunity costs are usually low.

Inevitably there will be some cases where the proposed plans for conservation will have major social and economic impacts. These may well be associated with management plans and interim conservation orders. If the social costs of conservation are perceived to be large and there is a considerable amount of conflict, more comprehensive economic and social evaluation will be required.

In several cases to date (Mt Murray, Benambra, Koetong), such evaluation has been undertaken to assist in determining an optimal solution subject to the objectives of the *Flora and Fauna Guarantee Act*. In other words, economic analysis has been used to set out and minimise the social costs of meeting safe minimum standards, rather than to determine the standards. Economic and social evaluation can in such instances also aid the search for solutions which achieve the conservation, social and economic objectives of the Government. This has been an on-going role of economists in the Department of Conservation and Natural Resources.

An extended cost benefit analysis, which attempts to value all the costs and benefits of conservation and which requires non-market valuation techniques, has thus far not been used under the *Flora and Fauna Guarantee Act* in Victoria. Such evaluation will almost certainly assist in resolving complex flora and fauna cases where choices need to be made between alternative strategies which have different social costs and non-market values and different extinction risks.

The relatively high cost of such comprehensive analysis will restrict its use to issues where conservation programmes are expensive or have significant economic and social impacts. The Department of Conservation and Natural resources has attempted to value a wetland habitat using contingent valuation (Stone 1992, Sappideen 1992), but otherwise has done little by way of valuing non-market benefits. Further research may be required to assist in the implementation of the *Flora and Fauna Guarantee Act*. This book is an attempt to further understanding in this area.

Economic Adjustment and Equity

Because the declining conservation status of many of Victoria's native species results largely from human activity, considerable economic adjustment may be needed if present trends are to be reversed. Use of Victoria's natural resources has never been as intensive as in the last 40 years. Mechanisation of agriculture, forestry and fishing placed new pressures on intact native ecosystems and those somewhat modified by human activity. Construction of roads, dams and irrigation schemes and modification of streams proceeded apace. Use of chemicals in agriculture and introduced crops and pastures reduced the ability of native species to co-habitate with introduced species.

The continuation of this approach is now being questioned by all levels of government and community because the level of environmental degradation can now be readily seen and its effect on the productive base is being felt. As a consequence, considerable energies have gone into debating and developing ecologically sustainable development principles for key economic sectors of the economy dependent on and affecting the environment (Commonwealth of Australia 1991).

The *Flora and Fauna Guarantee Act* and programme fits readily into this context. Firstly, its goals are complementary to other programmes aimed at achieving ecological sustainability. Secondly, if species have survived through the last 40 years, then it is possible that their survival may require marginal economic adjustment.

The level of adjustment required can also be placed in perspective if flora and fauna conservation measures are assessed according to level of cost and impact. Actions to secure species will be cheap and have minimal social impact in a great many cases. With this group, prompt action may be important as costs will generally balloon out as conservation status worsens. A smaller number of species are likely to require moderately expensive actions which will have small social impacts. Finally, it is likely to be only a small group of species that will involve significant effects on economic activity and/or be very expensive.

Thus, it is seen that the Victorian *Flora and Fauna Guarantee Act* is an innovative and far reaching piece of legislation in terms of conservation of endangered species. It is radical in that it goes beyond an attempt to save already endangered species to preventing more species coming under threat. Its processes attempt to minimize conflict and allow for public input at various stages.

However, in some cases, it is inevitable that conflicts in land use and management will occur. In such cases the Act requires evaluation of the economic and social consequences of conservation, although there is no guidance in the Act as to what should be included in such evaluations and how they should be carried out.

Management of Leadbeater's possum, for example, has the potential to result in some controversy. Leadbeater's possum exists in a complex multi-use region where there is a wide range of activities generating both monetary and other values. Some uses may be conflicting, for example, clear felling forest and preserving Leadbeater's possum or clear fell logging and water collection. Although it should be straightforward to estimate the benefits of forestry it is not easy to determine what values or priority should be placed on the possum. Most of the value associated with Leadbeater's possum is non-use value, which makes it particularly difficult to express in monetary terms. Clearly, this is where techniques such as contingent valuation can begin to play a useful role.

THE NATIONAL LEGISLATION

In Australia, according to the constitution (*Commonwealth Constitution Act*, 1900), responsibility for such issues as biological conservation is firmly in the jurisdiction of the individual states. In this setting the *Flora and Fauna Guarantee Act* is a very powerful document.

However, that is not to prevent the Federal government presenting legislation on somewhat the same subject matter and there are many reasons why such legislation might be prepared. The Federal legislation in particular here is the *Endangered Species Protection Act* 1992 and the reasons for its introduction could include the need to provide guidelines to the states not having specific species conservation legislation, in terms of a broader national interest. In this situation it is clear that the Federal initiative did not precede the Victorian state initiative, but it has led most of the other states.

Following on in this setting, the broader national interest on such issues as species conservation, might motivate the Federal government to use national legislation to induce certain of the states to introduce conservation measures, where it is perceived that existing state management is unsatisfactory. In contrast to the apparent authority for the individual states to act with respect to domestic issues on the environment generally, it is clear after the *Franklin Dam* case (1983 46 ALR 625), that the Federal government could be decisive here, if the government of the day possessed the will to act.

The power of the Federal government is magnified with the *Franklin Dam* case to enable the Federal government to introduce the spectre of certain considerations within international conventions and agreements, such as the Rio *Convention on Biological Diversity* (1992) or the United Nations *Agenda 21,* becoming provisions for domestic management, even at the state level. In fact the Federal government has introduced specific legislation to enable this approach in the form of the *World Heritage Properties Conservation Act* 1983 as an extension of the external affairs power conferred by the Commonwealth constitution (51(xxix)). And this is the rationale for considering the matter of international conventions and the like here.

Fundamentally, this discussion would take on a great deal more meaning if the Victorian legislation were not in place, since it is clear that the *Fauna and Flora Guarantee Act*, as it was originally conceived and enforced, was probably more conserving of species matters than the Federal legislation. However, as a function of a sea change in the political management of that state it could be that the original legislation might not be enforced as intended and that the focus will turn to the taking and property rights issues raised in the setting of the *Endangered Species Act* 1973, in the US.

Accordingly, this discussion will range through the Australian Federal situation, to the major international agreements on biological conservation to a final consideration with the US legislation. The underlying focus in this discussion will be in an objective sense, emphasising the avenues for economic input within existing institutional structures, rather than the normative setting where contingent valuation methodology and the derived estimates of value might demonstrate certain courses of public action.

The *Endangered Species Protection Act*

Within the characteristic Australian perspective of legislatively derived individual entitlements, the Federal *Endangered Species Protection Act* 1992, is characterised by apparent flexibility and lack of specific management principles relating to the management of biological species within Australia.

The objectives of the legislation, as outlined in Section 3. (1) of the Act emphasise the need to promote the;

(part a) .... recovery of species...,
(part b) .... prevent other species ... from becoming endangered ...,
(part c) .... reduce conflict ...,
(part d) .... provide for public involvement ... and to,
(part e) .... encourage cooperative management ...

The measures set out to achieve these objectives are identified in the following sub-section (3.(2)) and these include essentially bureaucratic procedures such as;

(part a) ....   providing a listing of native species ...,
(part b) ....   providing protective measures ... (recovery plans, conservation agreements and orders)...,

(part c) ....   obligations, mostly relating to funding,
(part d) ....   the conferring of powers and the,
(part e) ....   establishment of ... an ... Advisory Committee.

In this setting it should be clear that there is very little economic rationale or method in the formulation of the Act, although it may be the case that economic argument was instrumental in the actual passage of the Act. As with the Victorian legislation, the role of economic input is established in a more specific manner in the latter details of the legislation.

Thus, from Section 70 of the Act:

> In considering whether to make a permanent conservation order, the Minister must be satisfied that such action for the conservation of the listed native species or ecological communities in question is justified on economic and social considerations that are consistent with the principles of ecologically sustainable development.

Such a statement, as with the Victorian legislation, seems to provide a clear avenue for the articulation of the types of financial estimate derived from contingent valuation. An economic consideration here would certainly be construed to exist in the form of a social welfare improvement of the Kaldor-Hicks compensation criterion.

Fundamentally, it would follow that a conservation order in any state might be substantiated by the estimates of value derived from an economic study although the fact that the analysis should be of any particular form, is not identified. Following the imposition of a conservation order and given the non-cooperation of a particular state, the Federal government might then introduce the *external affairs* type powers, citing the binding principles of such international conventions on biological conservation as the *Convention on Biological Diversity* or the provisions of *Agenda 21* to which Australia was a party. In this way the Federal government is obliged to act according to international agreements to which it has just imposed on itself.

While considerable guidelines are provided in the international agreements on biological conservation in each situation, it is the case that the determinant of management is the Federal legislation and the economic interpretation which might justify conservation in a particular case.

In this setting, it is clear that the international conventions provide some leverage for management but the focus and weight of economic analysis and argument is domestic. And in the light of considering economic values in a broad national way, a basis is established within the legislation to account all the costs and benefits associated with biological conservation within an orthodox Pigovian welfare function. The implications of this methodology in relation to contingent valuation are drawn in the following chapter.

The US *Endangered Species Act*

The US *Endangered Species Act* of 1973 has been instrumental in the development of the Australian legislation and the intent and Pigovian welfare economic ramifications of the US legislation mirror the Australian situation. Consequently, the expectations for economic input generally and for contingent valuation input would be expected to be quite simular.

This situation could be expected in some other jurisdictions and indeed Hanley, Spash and Walker (1995) have reported the recently introduced Department of the Environment (1991) guidelines in the UK which focus on the need to ... 'estimate the (utilitarian) value of biological conservation' (p. 254). Hanley, Spash and Walker (1995) emphasise that for the non-market benefits usually associated with biological conservation 'CV is likely to be the dominant valuation method, especially given its recent qualified approval by the NOAA panel' (Arrow *et al.* 1993 and NOAA 1994).

Consequently, it would seem reasonable to propose that the legislative and bureaucratic arrangements in many jurisdictions is not only amenable to the application of the contingent valuation methodology, but such arrangements openly encourage the use of the methodology.

Property rights and the takings issue
The prospect for Pigovian type analysis in relation to such environmental issues as biological conservation, is under substantial challenge in the US and this confrontation could fundamentally undermine the role of such social based methodologies as contingent valuation. The *re-emergence* of takings as an issue of regulatory government in the US may have far reaching effects for the management of biological diversity in that country, but there are strong parallels in other jurisdictions, including Victoria where the principle is much admired - while the concept of a taking is not yet in the popular parlance. And accordingly there is a need to consider the issue of takings for biological conservation.

Legislation such as the US *Endangered Species Act,* which has a strong species conservation intent, could be seen to be in the public interest as a function of very substantial community valuation for species conservation. This community valuation could be demonstrated by such Pigovian methodologies as contingent valuation relative to the restriction implied by the regulations of the *Act*, little justification would be found for compensating individuals whose property is restricted by such regulations.

Of course it follows that a good deal of the species conservation achieved by the *Act* would not be possible if compensation was actually paid, as required by the 5th Amendment of the US constitution. And this is the argument of Buchanan and Tullock (1962) and Buchanan and Stubblebine (1962) which is considered further in the next chapter.

The thrust on *takings* from the 5th Amendment of the US constitution, is that the taking of private property for public use without the payment of compensation is forbidden. As far as the *Endangered Species Act* is concerned, the regulation of private property without compensation could be justified on the grounds of the very large non-market benefits of conservation.

The rationale here is Pigovian in that market failure would mean that since a large component of value was not accounted (the non-market species conservation value), inefficiency would exist and social welfare could not be maximised. There would be too little species conservation and too much of most other things. Subsequently, it is better that the government become involved in individual economic affairs to correct the inefficiency with some form of regulation if necessary, rather than the inefficiency be persevered with.

In this setting contingent valuation methodology could of course play a role in establishing the order if the inefficiency and the remedial regulation necessary to establish the optimal level of species conservation. So here, if the methodology is robust, a legitimate function is established.

Implicit in this Pigovian approach is a perspective which does not place a great deal of normative import on private property rights. Property rights are simply an instrument to a transaction. And it is here that a significant reaction to the Pigovian welfare economic approach is developed focussing on, what is interpreted to be, the rights taken from the property of individuals by such legislation as the US *Endangered Species Act.*

Fundamentally, the libertarian *Public Choice* alternative to Pigovian welfare economics focuses on the rights taken and the unfreedom created by much government regulation and finds justification in the *eminent domain* principle that individuals restricted by legislation, typical of the *Endangered Species Act*, should be compensated for the intrusion.

And politically this perspective has gained much presence in the US over the last decade or so to the extent that the takings provision has become a major part of the Republican party platform and as well significant legislation in both houses of Congress has been passed to put lower limits on the extent of private loss as a consequence of environmental type regulation (H.R.9, 104th Cong., 1st Sess., Div B, §§ 202, 210, 1995 and S.605, 104th Cong., 1st Sess. § 204(a)).

As well, it is clear that the US Supreme Court is becoming more amenable to the *eminent domain* view of private property rights and regulation (*Florida Rock Indus. v. United States,* 18 F.3d 1560, 1994).

The overall implication of the shift from the accepted regulatory approach to environmental management to one putting weight in preserving private property rights is that the economic focus shifts away from the valuation of non-marketed benefits to the articulation of non-attenuated free markets. The logic here is that in such free markets it will be possible for individuals who recognise a great deal of value in such environmental considerations as species conservation, to purchase the rights to species conservation from the owners of the property where the species might reside. In this way the owners of the property would be compensated for any species rights removed and social product would be maximised.

Accordingly, in an institutional setting which puts priority on the takings issue and the eminence of private property, there is little value for Pigovian non-market valuations - and the implication should be clear for contingent valuation. In an *eminent domain* economy, the estimates are interesting but they are possibly Pareto irrelevant (Buchanan and Stubblebine 1962).

While the trend in the US seems to be towards a greater priority for private property rights and compensation for rights taken, relative to the *Endangered Species Act*, many other jurisdictions have experienced similar swings as the dominant political interests have moved towards a more libertarian stance. Such a perspective is true for most areas of the developed world where contingent valuation is practiced including Australia and particularly Victoria.

Accordingly, there might be some expectation in this private property political climate that less room and weight will be found for the estimates of value articulated from contingent valuation. The social welfare foundations and implications of this evolution will be considered further in the following chapter.

3. Endangered Species in Victoria

INTRODUCTION

In this chapter, the status of endangered species in Victoria and reasons for their potential loss are described. This is followed by a discussion of the significance and ecology of the particular species, Leadbeater's possum (*Gymnobelideus leadbeateri*), that was the subject of the study. Leadbeater's possum was chosen because it is unique to Victoria, lives in a relatively well defined area and the conflict between development and conservation of the possum's habitat is reasonably straightforward.

Leadbeater's possum has particular habitat requirements which are not compatible with all the other uses of the area in which it lives, in particular the logging activities. It has also been subject to more ecological research than most endangered species in Victoria and is one of the few species to have a draft management plan. The biology and habitat requirements of Leadbeater's possum are described in order to elucidate the nature of the conflict between competing uses.

ENDANGERED SPECIES IN AUSTRALIA

Australia (including Victoria) is unique as a modern western nation in that a large component of its native flora and fauna is still present despite significant ecosystem modification. However, since European settlement 200 years ago, there has been a high rate of species extinction and large numbers of the remaining species are in danger of being lost.

Victoria has its share of the Australian endangered and threatened species. It is estimated that about 60 species have been lost over the past 200 years. Unless current trends are changed, it is predicted that Victoria may lose up to 700, or one in six, of the remaining vertebrate animals and vascular plants over the next 50 years (Department of Conservation, Forests and Lands, undated).

Primary reasons for species loss in Australia are habitat loss and modification and marked changes in land management practices as European

26

settlement occurred and continues to expand. Since European settlement in Victoria, forest cover has been reduced by over 65 per cent, natural grasslands and grassy woodlands have been almost entirely eliminated, half the freshwater wetlands have been drained and almost all riverine systems have been modified.

Reducing or halting further species loss will inevitably require some modification of current land use and management and it is inevitable that there will need to be some trade offs between species conservation and economic activities.

LEADBEATER'S POSSUM

Leadbeater's possum, as one of the two faunal emblems of the State of Victoria, has unique value and is considered one of the most important rare faunal species in Australia. It is classified by the International Union for Conservation of Nature (Wilcox 1988) as being vulnerable, while the Council of Nature Conservation Ministers (1989) considers it endangered.

Leadbeater's possum had been thought to be extinct for most of this century and was known only from five specimens collected before 1910. Since the collected specimens had been obtained from areas which were subsequently cleared, it was not thought that the species had survived. However, the possum was rediscovered in 1961 at Tommy's Bend near Marysville in the Central Highlands of Victoria (Wilkinson 1961).

Although the species is considered to be under considerable threat of extinction over the next 50 years as a consequence of current and past management practices, it has been commonly observed at a range of sites in the Central Highlands of Victoria. At this stage the marsupial has been observed at about 300 sites, with half of the observations being in the past decade.

It is generally believed that Leadbeater's possum was distributed fairly widely throughout the State prior to the first extinction. Fossil records and the pre-1910 specimens appear to confirm this. Currently, however, there is little evidence that the possum occurs outside a limited area of about 11,000 hectares of the montane ash forests of the Central Highlands of Victoria (Kennedy 1994), although a considerably larger area is potentially suitable habitat.

The Basic Biology of Leadbeater's Possum

The Leadbeater's possum is a small, nocturnal arboreal marsupial which lives in social groups of up to about eight individuals. The possum is monogamous and matriarchal with a typical colony consisting of one breeding pair, one or several generations of young and possibly several unrelated males. Young females are driven out early by the established female.

The possum lives in territories of between one and two hectares, yielding a population density of between 1.6 to 2.9 individuals per hectare. The female produces an average of about 4.8 young over her lifetime, which is in the order of three years, while the male lives for about 7.5 years. The diet of the possum is based on exudates from plants including *Eucalyptus* manna and *Acacia* gum as well as a range of arthropods such as caterpillars, beetles, tree crickets, moths and flies and some insect honeydew.

A good deal is known of the biology and population dynamics of the possum with the main sources being A. Smith (1982, 1983 and 1984), Smith and Lindenmayer (1988), Lindenmayer (1989) and Lindenmayer *et al.* (1990a,b,c,d).

Habitat Requirements

The montane ash forest habitat of the Leadbeater's possum is characterised by *Eucalyptus regnans, E. delegatensis* and *E. nitens.* The forests in question were largely burnt out by wildfire in 1939 and there has been considerable regrowth since. This event created a habitat that has been favourable to Leadbeater's possum. The fires of 1939 killed many of the larger and older trees, encouraging the development of hollows to provide the necessary nest trees for the possums to live in and the fires also provided abundant regrowth on which the possums could feed.

Leadbeater's possums require the presence of nest trees and a food source within a relatively small area as there is a limit to how far they can travel in one night and return to the nest tree. Hollows, which are used as nests, usually only develop in trees over about 190 years of age, or in younger mature trees which are killed by fire. However, as the ash forests become more mature there is a loss of understorey and thus food source for the possums. Thus, Leadbeater's possums require forest which is diverse in age structure where both the old nest trees and regenerating areas for food are available.

Following the extensive wildfires of 1939, which killed a great many mature trees and thus produced many nest trees, it also appears that a significant level of homogeneity in the forest was generated which ironically poses a significant threat to the viability of the possum. Many of the nest trees produced by the fires are being lost through natural causes and the regenerating forest is still too young for hollows to develop. It is estimated that about 80 per cent of the forest in the area is aged 55 years or younger (Macfarlane and Seebeck 1991). Thus, the species could come under threat before the next cycle of maturing trees produces the hollows necessary for nests (Lindenmayer *et al.* 1990a).

It has been suggested that some management intervention may be necessary to provide more forest heterogeneity. Thus, controlled fires and even some logging have been suggested as potentially useful in establishing new areas of regrowth and thus food source for the possum. However, such management does not assist in the establishment of the necessary nest trees. Even if fire killed some of the more mature trees there is concern that these trees are not mature enough to have hollows created after a fire.

Land Use and Management in the Central Highlands

The Leadbeater's possum habitat occurs in the Central Highlands region of Victoria, which is a large area of public land with easy access from metropolitan Melbourne and its region and a human population of nearly 3.5 million. The forest area in question is in the order of 670,000 hectares of which 3 per cent is set aside for parks and recreation, 1 per cent is reserved as reference areas, 20 per cent is included in water production reserves and 75 per cent is designated State Forest where logging is permitted under license (an additional 1 per cent is uncommitted).

The Central Highlands region is a valuable multi-use area which is important for a range of reasons:

1. The region has valuable recreational and educational facilities within the close proximity of 3.5 million people.
2. The region provides significant water catchment for the Melbourne metropolitan area (where domestic water is provided without filtration or chlorination - as a consequence of high natural quality).
3. The forestry industry considers the Central Highlands to possess some of the most valuable mountain ash (*Eucalyptus regnans*) forests in the State. Royalty value to the State Government for the *E. regnans* has been estimated in net present value terms to be in the order of $25,000 per hectare (for an 80 year rotation), while wood value has been estimated to be in the order of $0.5 million per hectare at the point of consumption (Squire *et al.* 1987), gross of all costs.
4. The Central Highlands region contains a wide and rich range of important flora and fauna.

The Authority for Management

According to the Australian constitution the principal authority for the control and management of public lands constituted as State Forest, National Parks and the various other forms of reserves is the State Government.

In Victoria the primary managing authority for such public lands is the State

Department of Conservation and Natural Resources which is responsible for such activities as the day-to-day management of forests to produce optimal supplies of timber as well as to protect conservation values, provide licences to exploit timber from State forests, collect the royalty revenue from timber harvesting and to maintain and manage recreational resources and facilities within the same areas.

The Department of Conservation and Natural Resources took its new name on the election of the Liberal Government in 1992 and had such titles as Department of Conservation, Forests and Lands and Department of Conservation and Environment under the previous Labour Government. Other State authorities such as Melbourne Water and the Alpine Resorts Commission and the Environmental Protection Authority also manage certain environmental considerations or particular areas set aside by the Government for given uses.

Habitat Threats to the Possum

In relation to the categories of land use described in the section above, very little concern has arisen as to the survival of Leadbeater's possum as a function of water management, recreational use or the management of other species within the region. Principally, the major threat to the species viability emerges in relation to the extensive scale of private logging on public land. Approximately 75 per cent of the current distribution of Leadbeater's possum occurs in areas designated for timber production (Macfarlane and Seebeck 1991). However, it is also clear that the species could be threatened as a consequence of natural phenomena.

The principal human threat to the long term viability of Leadbeater's possum appears to be clearfelling logging operations with rotations of less than 150 to 200 years. Although regeneration of clearfelled areas, if it occurs, provides some of the food base for the possum, the problem of clearfelling is the elimination of nest trees. The number of nest sites is a key factor limiting the population of Leadbeater's possum (McKenney and Lindenmayer 1994).

Efficient clearfelling logging operations would not normally leave any trees on site. Additionally, the tendency within the industry to move towards pulp wood and woodchips results in pressure for much shorter rotations with no possibility of generating mature nest trees.

Where mature trees are deliberately left in logged areas to enable the generation of sufficient nest trees, it is found that a combination of factors including the high degree of exposure of isolated trees makes them less than desirable nest sites for the possum as well as subjecting the trees to high rates of natural decline. It is unlikely that the current forest management practices will enable the survival of Leadbeater's possum.

CONCLUSIONS ON MANAGEMENT

The current thinking on the conservation management of Leadbeater's possum is discussed in the 'Draft management strategies for the conservation of Leadbeater's possum, *Gymnobelideus leadbeateri*, in Victoria', authored by Macfarlane and Seebeck (1991). This report is not a management plan under the *Flora and Fauna Guarantee Act* since it was completed before the Act was passed, but it should produce a similar result.

Apart from the establishment of a Leadbeater's management team, the development of educational programmes and the initiation of further research, the focus of management involved the establishment of particular reserves for the possum based on known rates of occurrence and the zoning of logging forests according to the production of nest trees.

In this last setting, mature forests (120 years +) with twelve or more live or dead hollow bearing trees per 3 hectares, would be protected from all types of timber harvesting except for 'low intensity selective logging' (Macfarlane and Seebeck 1991, p. 25). Less mature forests with fewer hollow bearing trees would then be accorded a lower priority for Leadbeater's possum conservation and thus enabled for greater timber exploitation.

The question of how less mature forests are to become more mature forests with more nest trees is not addressed. Otherwise, a range of forest management strategies is suggested such as providing wildlife corridors, streamside reserves, unmerchantable areas and the like (Macfarlane and Seebeck 1991, p. 26) as well as specific conditions for logging coupe size, site and management. A captive breeding programme is also underway. However, there is no agreement that the provisions of the Draft Management Plan is sufficient to preserve the possum in the face of threats from forestry operations, nor is it clear that the plan will be implemented and enforced.

Some research has been done into the possibility of providing nest boxes, but it is too early to know if this would be successful and it appears to be a costly alternative. McKenney and Lindenmayer (1994) compared the cost of a nest box programme (which would allow continuation of logging) with estimates of the value of timber production from the forests inhabited by Leadbeater's possum. 'In most scenarios the nest boxes cost more than logging bans even under a variety of discount rates' (McKenney and Lindenmayer 1994, p. 2012).

In the current setting, the focus of forest management in the Central Highlands of Victoria is the extraction of timber, albeit under highly subsidised conditions (Dragun 1994). According to the ongoing management approach, the Leadbeater's possum seems to have little or no value and issues relating to its conservation are not taken seriously. It is to redress this oversight that the following chapters are concerned.

PART TWO

Welfare Economic Principles
of Species Conservation

4. Welfare Economic Principles and Issues

INTRODUCTION

The social welfare foundations of the contingent valuation methodology are framed in the problem situation of a social decision on the best use of certain environmental resources. Basically, the society has a choice on the use of given environmental resources over a range of different activities or alternatives. The choice problem here is exacerbated in that the prices of the competing alternatives are inferred in different ways.

Thus, while some activities are priced directly from existing markets, other activities have no price or market analogy. For such activities contingent valuation may be used to simulate a hypothetical market to obtain prices which can be accounted in the traditional welfare calculus to then establish the welfare implications of alternative environmental use.

The general approach is that an environmental alternative will be socially desirable as long as those who gain from the implementation of the alternative receive more than is sacrificed by those who lose. The gainers then could *in principle* compensate the losers and still come out ahead, thereby improving the welfare of all and the option should proceed. This theoretical foundation and the implications will be explored in the following sections.

METHODOLOGICAL ISSUES

There has been considerable debate and research into the validity of the contingent valuation method involving a range of theoretical and operational issues. In the contingent valuation literature itself there is much focus on the actual preference measure and whether it should be willingness to pay or willingness to accept, but the whole issue of preference needs to be considered. Additionally, contingent valuation identifies estimates of value which might be identified in an ordinal utility setting and thus the issues of compensation criteria and ultimately Arrow's impossibility theorem need to be raised.

Public Choice theory portends an alternative to ordinal social welfare theory which would render contingent valuation redundant, but it in itself does not seem immune from the dilemmas confronting ordinal welfare theory. The Arrow theorem raises profound issues for social choice which inevitably mean that the practitioner needs to be cautious in terms of the interpretation of particular contingent valuation estimates, but on the other hand the valuation estimates can still be fundamentally important in highlighting the scope and importance of a problem and providing a focus for further informed public debate on indelibly complex social issues.

CHOICE OF WELFARE MEASURE

The basis of economic benefit measurement is individual preferences. For market goods, these preferences are indicated by the prices people are prepared to pay for goods and services. The demand curve represents peoples' willingness to pay, although they have to pay only the market price. Market prices alone underestimate the total benefit as there are people who would be willing to pay more than the market price and hence they secure a surplus of benefit over expenditure, or consumer surplus. The total benefit is the sum of the total expenditure and the consumer surplus, the area under the demand curve bounded by the quantity sold.

This approach assumes that income is held constant with movement along the demand curve (known as a Marshallian demand curve). The strict requirement to measure benefits from the area under the demand curve is that individual's welfare (utility) rather than income is held constant. To hold utility constant, the demand curve must be adjusted (Pearce and Markandya 1989). This gives the four possible measures of consumer surplus derived by Hicks in 1941; equivalent variation and surplus and compensating variation and surplus (Hanley 1987). A full exposition of the theory of measuring welfare changes is given in Ng (1985).

The compensating measures relate to the initial level of utility, that is maintaining the level of utility prior to any change. The equivalent measures relate to the level of utility subsequent to any change. Surplus measures are appropriate in cases where the consumer is unable to adjust the quantity of the good consumed and variation measures are appropriate where consumers are able to adjust quantity in response to a price change.

Generally, for a change that decreases an individual's welfare, compensating variation is measured by asking a willingness to accept compensation question and equivalent variation is measured by asking a willingness to pay question. For a change that increases an individual's welfare, compensating variation is measured by asking a willingness to pay question and equivalent variation is measured by asking a willingness to accept compensation question (Hanley 1987). Thus, use of a willingness to pay to prevent a loss question (for example, willingness to pay to prevent the loss of Leadbeater's possum) results in a Hicksian equivalent measure and willingness to be compensated for a loss results in a Hicksian compensating measure.

WILLINGNESS TO PAY AND WILLINGNESS TO ACCEPT

There has been much discussion in the contingent valuation literature as to which welfare measure should be used. The choice between a willingness to accept compensation and willingness to pay question can be considered as a question of property rights (Mitchell and Carson 1989). If the individual had the right to sell the good then willingness to accept compensation would be the appropriate measure, whereas if the individual had to buy it to enjoy it willingness to pay would be the correct measure.

In the case of most public goods however, it is often not clear what the property rights are and who holds them. Nevertheless, there has been general agreement in the literature that in cases of environmental loss willingness to accept compensation is the theoretically correct measure (Hanley, Spash and Walker 1995, Hoevenagel 1990, Knetsch 1993, Loomis and White 1995 and Pearce and Markandya 1989).

Although willingness to accept compensation has been regarded as the appropriate measure theoretically, in practice willingness to pay measures are usually used because of the difficulty in getting valid willingness to accept compensation results. It is often difficult to ask willingness to accept compensation questions in a way that realistically simulates a market. Contingent valuation studies using willingness to accept compensation elicitation questions have 'consistently received a large number of protest answers such as 'I refuse to sell' or 'I want an extremely large or infinite amount of compensation for agreeing to this' and have frequently experienced protest rates of 50 per cent or more', although these problems diminish when money is offered as compensation (Mitchell and Carson 1989, p. 34). Valid willingness to accept compensation results have been obtained for some use values but seldom yield usable results in studies of non-use values.

Initially, use of willingness to pay rather than willingness to accept measures was not seen as a problem because the theory predicted relatively small differences between the four Hicksian welfare measures (Freeman 1979, Hoevenagel 1990). This was taken to mean that in practice either measure would be acceptable (Hanley 1987). Willig (1976) showed that for price changes and for consumers with well-behaved utility functions the bounds between willingness to pay and willingness to accept were small and the Marshallian consumer surplus lay between these measures. Randall and Stoll (1980) extended the Willig-type bounds to general quantity changes.

As more contingent valuation studies were carried out, empirical evidence accumulated that showed the difference between the measures was consistently large. Willingness to accept measures were in the order of 3 to 20 times or more greater than willingness to pay (Pearce and Markandya 1989 review a range of studies). One explanation suggested for the disparity was that the willingness to accept compensation scenario is too hypothetical and the idea of compensation is rejected as implausible, or that respondents reject the property right implied by the willingness to accept question (Mitchell and Carson 1989).

Monetary compensation may not be seen as an appropriate response to the loss of some environmental goods, for example the loss of an endangered species (Gregory and Bishop 1986). This explanation is supported by the high rate of protest bids compared with the rate when willingness to pay questions are used and the high compensation amounts claimed in some studies (Mitchell and Carson 1989).

However, evidence of large and persistent disparities came from experimental studies conducted in laboratory and field conditions using real goods and real dollars (Bishop and Heberlein 1979, 1980, 1986; Bishop, Heberlein and Kealy 1983; Knetsch and Sinden 1984, 1987; Knetsch 1989, 1990, 1993 and Gregory 1986). Thus, the explanation of hypothetical bias does not explain all the difference in the two measures.

An alternative explanation for the disparity is that people value gains and losses asymmetrically; that is, the value function for losses is steeper than for gains (Kahneman and Tversky 1979). Knetsch (1993, p. 5) points out that the disparity is a well known behavioural finding and gives 'recognition to people's common attachment of greater weight to losses than to otherwise commensurate gains'.

Hoehn and Randall (1987) have suggested that respondents who are uncertain, who lack time to optimise their valuation and are risk averse, may initially give a high willingness to accept compensation estimate and a low willingness to pay estimate but that the estimates will converge as respondents gain familiarity with the procedures. There is some evidence that willingness to accept amounts decrease after repetitions (Mitchell and Carson 1989) but generally it appears disparities will persist even after repeated valuations (Knetsch 1990).

A further reason for disparity is that in general the goods considered in contingent valuation studies do not meet the conditions required for Willig's as well as Randall and Stoll's bounds to hold. Brookshire, Randall and Stoll (1980) show that the equivalent and compensating variation measures are equal for a given welfare change for perfectly divisible goods with zero transaction costs in infinitely large markets. In contingent valuation studies, however, there are usually large, discrete (lumpy) changes in quantity, invalidating these conditions (Hanley 1987). The conditions specified by Willig (1976) also do not apply in cases when the quantity of the good being valued may change as in the case of the extinction of a species. When the conditions specified by Willig and by Randall and Stoll do not hold, willingness to pay and willingness to accept measures need not be close. Krutilla (1967) clearly expected the two measures to be different in the case of unique natural assets which may be irreversibly lost.

Hanemann (1991a) extended the theory to show that large differences could be expected, depending on the availability of substitutes. For quantity changes, Hanemann (1991a) showed that the difference between willingness to pay and willingness to accept measures depends not only on an income effect but also on the ease with which other commodities could be substituted for the given public good. Holding income effects constant, the fewer the substitutes, the greater the disparity. With no substitutes, the two measures could differ greatly.

Adamowicz, Bhardwaj and Macnab (1993) found experimentally that the presence of substitutes reduced but did not eliminate the disparity. Shogren *et al.* (1994) also tested Hanemann's proposition and found that for readily available market goods with close substitutes and low transaction costs, willingness to pay and willingness to accept measures converged. For a non market good with no close substitutes the two value measures were different and the difference persisted even after repeated valuations.

The disparity in measures poses a problem for contingent valuation studies. At present for many environmental goods it seems only possible to get valid results using a willingness to pay measure, but as Knetsch (1993, p. 10) points out, use of willingness to pay where willingness to accept is the correct measure will produce 'systematic and on current evidence, very serious, underestimates of value'.

Mitchell and Carson (1989) suggest that in some cases willingness to pay is in fact the correct measure. They argue that in cases of public goods for which the consumer is already paying on a regular basis, the Hicksian compensating surplus is the appropriate measure. In this case, the Hicksian compensating surplus is the 'amount the consumer is willing to pay to forgo the reduction in the level of the good and still be as well off as before' (Mitchell and Carson 1989, p. 41).

In practice, willingness to pay measures will continue to be used because considerable further research is required before willingness to accept compensation valuations can be used with confidence for non-use values. The procedural guidelines proposed by Arrow *et al.* (1993, p. 4608) in a recent review of the contingent valuation method, strongly recommend that 'when aspects of the survey design and the analysis of the responses are ambiguous, the option that tends to underestimate willingness to pay is preferred. A conservative design increases the reliability of the estimate by eliminating extreme responses that can enlarge estimated values wildly and implausibly'. They go on to recommend use of the willingness to pay format instead of compensation required because willingness to pay is the conservative choice.

This recommendation is clear if individual preferences are acceptable and it is now necessary to consider the foundations of preference theory.

THE ISSUE OF PREFERENCE

The dilemma in considering management issues in relation to species biodiversity is that it is, by definition, not possible to observe the welfare consequences of peoples behaviour with respect to biodiversity because the necessary markets for individuals to express their values do not exist. Consequently, there is a difficulty in measuring the welfare of individuals here and the need is to take the individual preferences with respect to biodiversity conservation to be an indicator of their actual welfare.

In practice however, there are a wide range of reasons why preferences might not be an indicator of welfare, as explored by Sagoff (1994).

Probably most importantly here, individual preferences may not only be affected by an individual's own welfare for the conservation of a given species, but may also be influenced by the welfare of other persons. Thus, a person when confronted with an issue of species conservation might prefer an alternative situation which yields less direct individual welfare because the welfare of other persons is greater in that situation.

In the setting of biodiversity and species conservation, where a good many persons respond to survey questions expressing concern that their children might experience the species in the future, the possibility here is not hard to see. This consideration relates to the broader issue of intergenerational equity which seems to be irremovable from the analysis and discussion of species management over time.

Additionally, given the complex technical settings of many biodiversity issues it could be the case that individuals are ignorant of certain of the possibilities or otherwise their perspective is incorrect. In terms of some recent controversy on the nature and meaning of the extinction of species by many eminent and learned biologists (Lawton and May 1995), it would not be unreasonable to expect that most citizens would have considerable difficulty in identifying all the scientific information relevant for the conservation of a particular species and then actually coming to some meaningful analytical assessment of such information. Consequently, it would be reasonable to expect that the preferences that individuals might have on species conservation issues could be based on ignorance and imperfect consideration and foresight.

It is notable that the general biodiversity issue has ignited deep fundamental passions from some individuals, special interest groups and communities. As a function of certain customs, habits, traditions and principles certain individuals appear to take particular positions on biodiversity issues and environmental issues generally, which seem to run counter to their own welfare. Thus, preferences for certain biodiversity outcomes could include an element of irrationality.

Further, given the great temptations of wealth and pleasure, which might often be associated with the frontier lands where many sensitive ecosystems might be found - and thus endangered species - there is again the basis that individual preferences for species conservation (or alternatively development) might be irrational.

In conclusion, as Sagoff (1994) has observed, there is a good deal of reason to suggest that the preferences that individuals might express on a particular issue, even biodiversity, could actually mean a multitude of other things. Of course the actual values derived in this setting could be construed in either direction according to the weight of the other things. However, if it is considered that preferences are acceptable, the need is then to consider some fundamental issues of ordinal welfare functions.

ORDINAL SOCIAL WELFARE FUNCTIONS

The evidence of a great many empirical studies on environmental issues has demonstrated a strong link between willingness to pay for environmental considerations and ability to pay. At the same time there is little evidence to suggest that the marginal utility of environmental considerations is the same for all persons in a community (Kanninen and Kriström 1992).

As a function of the inability to make interpersonal comparisons of utility, it is generally accepted that there is very little justification for using other social welfare forms (such as a cardinal social welfare function) other than the traditional ordinal form, known as the Samuelson-Bergson ordinal social welfare function.

However, the application of the Samuelson-Bergson form of social welfare function raises several classes of issues. The first considered here, relates to the actual application of the social welfare function, while the second focuses on the consistency of the results obtained from the application.

Compensation Criteria

Even if the social welfare function is well defined in relation to individual utilities, it is not clear that such a function will be well defined in connection with different social states (Little 1949 and 1957). Where it emerges that some persons might be made better off whilst others are rendered worse off, the only recourse seemed to be the unsatisfactory one of adopting some form of cardinal welfare function where a direct comparison of utilities could be made. In this setting Kaldor raised the possibility of conceiving of compensation to establish a socially desirable outcome (Kaldor 1939).

Kaldor, contrasting the Paretian insight where 'everybody could be made better off without making anybody worse off', with a reality that some persons were going to suffer, suggested that if;

> all those who suffer as a result are fully compensated for their loss, the rest of the community will still be better than before. (1939, p. 550)

The result here is that a social improvement would occur if the beneficiaries of some alternative could remain better off even if they fully compensated the losers. This criterion was strengthened by Hicks (1939) who added the dimension that the losers in turn could not bribe the beneficiaries to oppose the change.

If the compensation in the Kaldor-Hicks criterion were real there would in fact be little need for the criteria and reference to the Pareto criterion would be sufficient to establish the desired alternative. This hypothetical character of compensation in the Kaldor-Hicks setting, led to Scitovsky (1954) identifying a contradiction where a reverse change might be possible which was also permissable on the grounds of the original Kaldor criterion.

Extending his analysis Scitovsky proposed a compensation criterion which in effect satisfied both the Kaldor and the Hicks criterion (the Scitovsky reversal test) to achieve apparent unambiguous results. However, cyclicity still seems to remain with this criterion, as with the precursors, after repeated application.

In this setting, Little proposed an additional criterion which focused on the distributional implications explicit in rendering someone worse off whilst others are made better off - and where the criterion should deal with actual improvements rather than the potential improvements suggested by the previous criteria (Little 1949 and 1957). Little's criterion incorporates the Kaldor and Scitovsky criterion with an additional consideration establishing if any redistribution was good so that an improvement could be identified if the Paretian consideration were achieved at the same time as the income distribution were improved.

But again the Little criterion has been found to suffer reversal contradictions, which led Samuelson (1950) to respecify a criterion which is effectively the original social welfare function - the Samuelson-Bergson social welfare function. And of course we have begun this discussion by considering the limited applicability of this alternative, so the cycle is complete. The

Samuelson-Bergson social welfare function does not handle states of Paretian non comparability and the compensation tests devised to avoid this lacuna inevitably lead us back to the original as a function of their own contradictions.

This indecisiveness on social welfare rules is especially important in the setting of biodiversity issues where it is fundamentally clear that any social change will make some persons worse off whilst others are made better off. Here, as Little (1957) has observed, the intractable issue is how to deal with or incorporate the distributional consequences of the social policy into a meaningful social welfare statement.

In that the contingent valuation methodology relies on improvement which seem to be based on the Kaldor-Hicks criterion, it cannot be considered that distributional issues have been avoided. Although, there is some considerable evidence that absolute willingness to pay for environmental considerations increases with income, it is the case that the relative willingness to pay seems to diminish so that the overall distributional affect of a social change which preserves biodiversity is indecisive.

Irrespective of the issue of the ambiguity of the compensation criteria, the ordinal social welfare function suffers a more consequential dilemma in terms of consistency as demonstrated by Arrow (1950).

The Arrow Impossibility Result

Once we have established that some structure of social choice is necessary for individuals to realise their interests - say with respect to biodiversity - the need is to establish *which* structure of social choice provides the best results.

Unfortunately, we can establish that no social choice mechanism, including those involving the various social welfare functional forms can provide us with a consistent result. The circumstances are portrayed by the Arrow impossibility theorem.

Considering the process of passing from individual preferences to a social choice, Arrow observes that no mechanism exists which does not impose or is not dictatorial.

Thus from Arrow:

> If we exclude the possibility of interpersonal comparisons of utility, then the only methods of passing from individual tastes to social preferences which will be satisfactory and which will be defined for a wide range of sets of individual orderings are either imposed or dictatorial. (1950 p. 342)

Given certain reasonable conditions of social choice, the implication is drawn that it is possible to identify circumstances where social decisions are inconsistent with the individual preferences that were instrumental in generating the social decision in the first place.

The insight of the impossibility theorem is that such individual freedom is compromised relative to reasonable conditions of social choice. Another way of expressing this result is that social welfare functions are inconsistent and incapable of aggregating individual preferences to social choices. The key to this statement is that the inconsistency of social welfare functions is usually perceived as a loss of individual freedom.

The traditional interpretation of the impossibility theorem is that the Samuelson-Bergson type social welfare function, which is generally assumed in the contingent valuation methodological setting, is inconsistent in aggregating individual preferences to social choice. Other forms of social welfare function which are relevant to social choice are the market mechanism as well as majoritarian democracy. The implication of the impossibility theorem can easily be seen with reference to democracy. With individual freedom articulated as the significant social principle, a good many economists have been forward in observing the tyranny of majoritarian decisions (Buchanan and Tullock 1962 and Mishan 1969).

Social Choice and Paretianism

Given the intractability of social welfare functions on social choice, the range of options is observed to be decidedly small. While a good deal of economic attention has been directed to circumventing the impossibility theorem - with little apparent success - the more positive alternatives include deriving social choice rules from the conditions of the impossibility theorem or discarding the theorem altogether. Both possibilities will be considered in turn.

In terms of the current debate on social choice the most crucial condition of the impossibility theorem is possibly the weak Pareto principle. This condition specifies that if all individuals rank one alternative higher than another, then that alternative would rank higher in the social ordering. If it is expected that individuals will not prefer alternatives which render themselves worse-off, it would appear that Pareto safety remains the only non-imposing criterion of social choice (Buchanan 1959). Consequently, if social choice situations can be recognised which do render some persons better-off, whilst no other individual is made worse-off, it is clear that a social choice rule in Pareto safety can be invoked which does not impose on the general freedom of individuals in the society. Otherwise it would appear that the process of social choice is hamstrung. Subsequently, the resultant question for practical social choice is to establish the relative importance of social decisions which, while making some persons better-off, do cause some other persons to be worse-off.

The Impossibility of a Paretian Liberal

That the Paretian approach is not inviolable to the very principles which provide its strongest justification has not gone unobserved (Sen 1970). In essence Sen has established that Pareto safety can be inconsistent with minimal conditions of liberalism. The strength of Sen's analysis is that the arbitrariness of individual freedom relative to various status-quo rights distributions can be readily observed.

The implication is that whilst the Arrow impossibility theorem finds social welfare functions inconsistent as social choice mechanisms - with the recourse seen to lie with the Paretian criterion - that Paretian criterion is itself found to be inconsistent in terms of the value - freedom - which was originally considered to be its virtue. Despite this, a substantive alternative to orthodox welfare economic theory has been developed in the setting of Public Choice theory and the implications of this approach for policy on biodiversity will be briefly considered.

Paretianism and Public Choice

Relative to the problems of inconsistency and interpersonal comparisons of utility, the Public Choice approach is a fundamental change in direction from the traditional welfare economic perspectives. The Public Choice approach emphasises the pure Paretian interpretation and then focuses on the process implied by a free market - rather than being constrained by the results of some process (Sen 1995).

The general inspiration for Public Choice theory, besides the difficulty of ordinal social welfare functions evident in the orthodox neoclassical method, appears to have arisen in connection with what is perceived as the failure of the neoclassical orthodoxy to confront or even recognise certain institutional issues that seemed to be irremovable from the application of economic theory to a range of problem situations.

Two crucial issues emerge in this institutional context. The first, being a fear that government interference in certain economic inter-relationships could impede free and mutually beneficial trades and in some cases generate inefficiency and the second, involving the recognition that an inadequate property rights structure could be seen as the root of a wide range of economic problems.

In that the explicit consideration of property rights is a precondition for recognising particular economic breakdowns, such as in an externality situation, the focus of Public Choice theory then turns to the activity of government in resolving such breakdowns. This view is highlighted by Buchanan's (1959) concern that too much government involvement in society will impede genuine trades that would normally lead to mutual gains for all parties.

Subsequently, the Public Choice perspective on such issues as biodiversity conservation is that such problems are only relevant when the benefited (damaged) parties have a desire to modify the behaviour of the parties that might be causing a threat to biodiversity (Buchanan and Stubblebine 1962). The crux here is that where gains from trade are recognised in the Paretian sense, it is expected that individuals who value biodiversity conservation can and will initiate genuine trades of mutual benefit and establish the economy at a Pareto optimum. Paretian gains from trade are realised in an externality situation where affected parties can be made better off without others being made worse off (Buchanan and Stubblebine 1962, p. 480).

In this setting the trades are realised within the existing economic institutional structure without any direct government direction or involvement. Fundamentally, if individuals do not have an incentive to bargain to a mutually beneficial Pareto optimum, then the issue is irrelevant. It follows that government involvement in such a context, must necessarily conduce a loss of utility and as well as generating further inefficiency as a consequence of the transaction cost of government (Buchanan and Stubblebine, 1962 p. 480).

Public Choice and Biodiversity Policy

The essence of the Public Choice theory on biodiversity would be that a range of problems might exist due to a break down in the property rights structure. A combination of factors including the notions of transactions costs and government interference contribute to the general malaise.

In this setting a Pigovian approach which utilises the valuations obtained from contingent valuation for a policy which favours biodiversity conservation would be seen as arbitrary in terms of both the transaction costs of government intervention and the implicit assignment of right implied by the Kaldor-Hicks criterion. An additional concern would be that the property rights structure created by government would not necessarily be conducive to negotiation and change if some more beneficial reallocation was possible.

However, despite the characterisation of externality situations according to a breakdown of the property rights structure and recognising that property rights might be created with a Pigovian policy solution, a pervading theme exists in the Public Choice literature that some individuals do in fact have rights to act even in externality situations. Such a perspective is exemplified in an externality situation where government interference is recognised as initiating an attenuation of rights or more generally a taking of property rights. In a similar vein requirements for the payment of compensation to individuals restricted in externality circumstances appears to imply a right taken.

The conclusions here are then twofold, either a normative bias is introduced in favour of certain types of individual behaviour with clear and obvious distributional implications for *status quo* interests, or alternatively the class of economic inter-relationships which have generally been referred to as externalities in the Public Choice literature are misconceived and are in fact institutionally analogous to formal market transactions in that property rights must always exist for this methodology to be consistent. The consequence in an economic policy setting is that Public Choice prescriptions on externality must either introduce normative bias according to an arbitrary description of individualist behaviour or otherwise propose remedial action to an existing problem by assuming that the problem doesn't exist in the first instance.

In addition, in the context of resolving existing externality problems the Public Choice rationale requires that the involved individuals, realising the mutual gains from trade, would bargain amongst themselves as to the conditions of inter-relationship of the particular externality activity. It follows here that the Pareto-Wicksellian bargaining procedure would conduce to a final property rights assignment which is purportedly Pareto preferable and also consistent with Wicksellian unanimity - it would also be expected that such a bargained agreement would finally be the subject of a binding legal contract that resolves the pre-legal state to one of *de jure* economic transactions.

Whilst questions of efficiency have been raised in this context previously - especially in the setting of common property problems and large group affects (Mishan 1971) - the crucial issue here appears to revolve around the use of the Pareto criterion and purported efficiency improvements to decide straightforward distributional questions.

The Public Choice blending of efficiency and distributional criteria is exemplified in the application of the standard Coasian dictum. According to Coase (1960) we are led to believe that from the perspective of economic efficiency the initial allocation of property rights is irrelevant. The usual interpretation of Coase's major contribution to economic irrelevance is that irrespective of the initial assignment of property rights, the final distribution of property rights will always be such that the value of social product will be maximised, since individuals perceiving a greater value to specific rights will always be prepared to bargain for such rights provided that a suitable medium of transactions is available.

However, if economic efficiency can be achieved from all of a range of initial property rights assignments, as Coase suggests, then preoccupation with economic efficiency is in fact irrelevant, since it can be expected that economic efficiency will always be established from all the possible initial property rights assignments. What is of course most relevant to social welfare in this context then is the actual interpersonal assignment of the involved property rights and the inevitable consequences for such an assignment for the distribution of income and wealth, the distribution of economic power in society, market structure and also environmental quality.

To neglect the explicit issues of property rights assignment in this setting is to presume a sanctity in the *status quo* distribution of property rights - a position which even Buchanan does not see fit to justify (Buchanan and Samuels 1975, p. 27). The implicit issue on the other hand is that the medium of transaction is indeed satisfactory and socially acceptable.

Of course, the core of the consideration of the actual assignment of property rights revolves around the questions of how the property rights are to be assigned and to whom the property rights are to be assigned, and it is in this context that the inherent and irremovable normative content of Public Choice theory becomes manifest.

The conclusion here is that Public Choice does highlight that the *distribution* of property rights is fundamental to such issues as biodiversity conservation and this is also a natural conclusion from a consideration of compensation criteria in conventional welfare economic theory.

The issue now is to contemplate how contingent valuation and the propositions of welfare economic theory can better determine economic policy for biodiversity and the distribution of property rights and wealth that are inherent to such policy.

BIODIVERSITY AND DISTRIBUTION

Fundamentally, the various economic social choice processes considered here, from contingent valuation and its implicit ordinal social welfare foundations to Public Choice, reduce the social issue of biodiversity to one of the distribution of the property rights to biodiversity.

If a society were egalitarian and the distribution was even, it would appear that the benefits of biodiversity and species conservation could be distributed along all segments of the community and any negative impact on the basic distribution of income might not be that great.

But in practice the problem of income distribution inherent in preserving species is very great as a function of the income disparities in most societies and the non existence in entitlements or property rights in most species at risk. Thus, public decisions on species conservation will create a new structure of entitlement and income and the distributional consequences could be quite marked. This is especially the case at an international level where most of the willingness to pay for species conservation will be seen to originate from the more developed countries, whilst most of the species at risk are actually located in less developed countries. Also there is a need to consider the question of the distribution over time (Norgaard and Howarth 1991).

Thus, according to the Kaldor-Hicks criteria the more wealthy individuals residing in the developed world would obtain the entitlements to species existing in the less developed nations, according to principles of potential compensation - because they appear to be willing to pay more - while the poor citizens could be deprived of the basic sustenance for their day-to-day survival. Ironically, the Public Choice approach would have the poor people of the less developed countries actually pay the wealthier citizens of the developed world for not taking the species away.

While some issues of biodiversity occur at a national level, it is not clear that many citizens in most nations would support some form of auction of biodiversity rights to the highest bidder, especially if the high bidder was subsequently excused payment.

Alternatively, the prospect of compensating the presumptive rights of all persons negatively affected by biodiversity conservation, would probably attract even less support. But at a national level, entitlements will be created and income will be distributed as part of the accepted political process. And this is the political setting underlying this study of contingent valuation as applied to biodiversity conservation in Victoria, Australia.

But probably the more substantive issues of biodiversity occur with an international dimension, where the willingness to pay for species conservation resides in the wealthier developed nations while much of the biological material at risk resides in the poorer less developed nations. Here, the possibilities for redistributions are not so clear.

Overall, it is clear that while the values derived by contingent valuation may not actually enable the description of the optimum use of biodiversity, the values at the same time will provide valuable input and information on an indelibly complex social issue and should provide the font of explicit social discussion and deliberation.

This conclusion on the application of modern welfare economic theory is consistent with the conclusion of Sen (1995).

Thus, according to Sen:

Arrow's impossibility theorem does indeed identify a profound difficulty in combining individual orderings into aggregate social welfare judgements. But the result must not be seen as mainly a negative one, since it directly leads on to questions about how to overcome these problems. In the context of social welfare judgements, the natural resolution of these problems lies in enriching the informational base. .... Many of the more exacting problems of the contemporary world - varying from famine prevention to environmental preservation - actually call for value formation through public discussion. (1995, p. 18)

5. The Economics of Species Conservation

INTRODUCTION

The initial theme of this chapter, drawing on the previous discussion of welfare economic theory, is to outline the main issues of biodiversity and species loss. Subsequently, alternative economic approaches to these problems are considered. Because there is an extensive literature on biodiversity issues, the intention here is to review the main themes.

The extent of biodiversity and species loss is discussed and reasons for the increasing rate of species extinction are given. The types of benefits provided by species are considered and methods by which values associated with species existence and biodiversity conservation can be estimated and included in decision making are identified.

BIODIVERSITY LOSS AND SPECIES EXTINCTION

Biological diversity (or biodiversity) is a widely used term, although it appears to have no precise definition, nor clear means of measurement (Solow, Polasky and Broadus 1993 and Solow and Polasky 1994). A good working definition is that 'biodiversity is the array of populations and species of other organisms with which *Homo sapiens* shares Earth and the communities, ecosystems and landscapes of which they are component parts' (Ehrlich and Daily 1993, p. 64). Biodiversity is reduced by the loss of species, populations and genetic variability. However, the most easily observed manifestation of biodiversity loss is species extinction, which is a main focus of this book.

Biological species are becoming extinct at a rate unprecedented in the earth's history (Myers 1993 and Lawton and May 1995). Extinction is usually an unintended consequence of human development activities (McMichael 1982). The main causes of species loss are habitat modification or destruction, direct killing or taking, direct and indirect effects of pollutants and environmental changes and the effects of introduced and exotic species.

These factors have also caused the rate at which new species evolve to become considerably less than the rate at which species are being lost.

Estimates of the rate of net species loss vary, but the consensus is that there will be between 10 to 25 per cent fewer species than the present numbers at the end of the century (Ehrlich and Ehrlich 1981, Langner and Bishop 1982, Lawton and May 1995, Myers 1979, Oldfield 1981 and Wilson 1988) and 50 per cent fewer by the end of next century. Raven (1994) gives around 50,000 species a year as a moderate estimate of loss. Myers (1993) estimates the present rate of extinction is at least 120,000 times greater than before the human era. There is little doubt that this process will continue under the present system of economic growth (Tisdell 1979).

The loss in biological diversity from this mass extinction has wide ramifications for many values associated with wildlife and plant resources in such areas as agriculture, medicine, amenity and recreation, absorption of wastes and ecosystem stability in general (Swaney and Olson 1992). Many of the benefits in these areas are undervalued or not accounted for at all by existing institutions and policies (Folke *et al.* 1993), resulting in a faster than optimal rate of depletion of species. Better estimates of the values associated with wildlife and plant resources will lead to a better allocation of all society's resources and should lead to a greater appreciation of wildlife resources generally.

THE ECONOMIC LITERATURE RELATING TO SPECIES

The economics of species conservation received very little attention in the literature up to the last 20 to 30 years. Until the 1970s almost exclusive attention was given to the economics of conserving species which contribute to material production (Tisdell 1990). Bishop (1980) reports some other aspects of the problem which have received attention are the inability of the market system to cope with the species extinction problem (Amacher, Tollison and Willett 1972 and Bachmura 1971), the open access problem (Berck 1979), the possibility that profit maximisation might result in extinction for some species (Clark 1973) and the economic implications of uncertainty in relation to extinction (Smith and Krutilla 1979).

Miller (1981) and Miller and Menz (1979) considered the irreversibility of extinction and the possibility of an existence value for a stock of species. Swanson (1994) provides a generalised framework for the analysis of the problems of endangered species and biodiversity losses. The economics of biodiversity and landscape are considered in Kim and Weaver (1995).

Since the early 1970s there has been an increasing number of studies which have attempted to value some or all the sources of benefit from species conservation, including both use and non-use values. For example, see Bishop, Boyle and Welsh (1987), Boyle (1985), Bowker and Stoll (1988), Brown and

Goldstein (1984), Brown and Henry (1989), Gregory, Mendelsohn and Moore (1989), Norton (1986), Stoll and Johnson (1984), Stevens *et al.* (1991) and Whitehead (1992, 1993) among others. Most studies were concerned with conservation of single species, but attention is now turning from single species evaluations to attempts to value all the endangered species in an area or biodiversity as a whole (Barrett 1988, Hampicke *et al.* 1991, Pearce and Moran 1994, Polasky and Solow (in press), Randall 1991, Swaney and Olson 1992 and Walsh *et al.* 1987).

BENEFITS DERIVED FROM SPECIES AND ECOSYSTEMS

Species and ecosystems are valued for a variety of uses and reasons (Barrett 1988, Brown 1985, Pearce and Moran 1994 and Randall 1986). The benefits derived from environmental goods such as species are generally recognised to include both use values (direct and indirect) and non-use values. Ciriacy-Wantrup (1952) and Leopold (1966) recognised the idea that one source of economic value of species is the present and potential productive knowledge to be derived from them. This idea has been taken up and explored further by Krutilla (1967) and Brown (1986).

The terminology and categorisation of benefits within the use and non-use classes varies from author to author, for example see Brown and Moran (1993), Cicchetti and Wilde (1992), Mitchell and Carson (1989), Pearce (1987) and Stevens *et al.* (1991), and not all agree with the concept of option value (Johansson 1993).

This book follows the categories used by Blamey and Common (1992). These are:

1. *Use value* - value which arises from the individual's present or planned use of the species.
2. *Existence value* - value which arises from knowledge that the species exists and will continue to exist, independent of any actual or possible future use by the individual.
3. *Option value* - the value to the individual of knowing the species will be available for use in the future, over and above expected use value (Cicchetti and Wilde 1992).
4. *Quasi-option value* - the value of preserving options, given uncertain outcomes from decisions and an expectation of gaining more information with time. For example, for a decision to preserve a species there is a positive probability that a new use with a positive value will be discovered (Randall 1986). With a decision leading to extinction, the probability of discovering a new use drops to zero. Conrad (1980) considers quasi-option

value to be the expected value of information gained from delaying an irreversible decision. Quasi-option value can also be thought of as 'the value of information conditional on undertaking a particular action'. (Mitchell and Carson 1989, p. 70)

The total economic value of a species or group of species will thus consist of use value plus existence value plus option value plus quasi-option value. Existence, option and quasi-option values are often classed together as non-use values. These categories of benefit are outlined in the following sections.

Use Values

Use values derive from actual use of a species and include both consumptive and non-consumptive considerations. For example, a species may be a source of raw materials, pharmaceutical products, recreational use and/or aesthetic satisfaction. Use values may be differentiated into groups, for example (after Barrett 1988):

1. Direct productive values where certain species are harvested for the sale of their products.
2. Direct consumptive values such as recreational fishing, hunting, plant collecting and so on.
3. Indirect productive values where some species provide services for productive species, for example are a source of food or provide pollination services.
4. Non-consumptive uses such as bushwalking, camping, viewing or photographing and other categories such as the knowledge obtained to improve agricultural crops.

Existence Value

The origin of the concept of existence value is attributed to Krutilla (1967) who suggested that people may still value a resource even if they do not use it (Kerr and Sharp 1987). This value is independent of any current or expected future use. For example, the knowledge that species such as blue whales and giant wetas exist may provide value, even if the possibility of seeing one is very small or non-existent.

Barrett (1988) suggests people may also derive value from knowing that a certain level of biodiversity exists. Fredman (1995) defines existence value as a non-use value limited to the existence of the resource and links it to the concept of a minimum viable population size, that is, it will not change with increasing population.

Krutilla suggested two sources for this non-use value; bequest value, which is a desire to leave the resource to future generations and existence value, which is related to simply knowing the resource exists (Kerr and Sharp 1987). Generally, these two values are aggregated and the aggregated value is referred to as existence value, which is considered to be motivated by some form of altruism. Randall (1986) lists three altruistic motives which might account for existence values, *viz*:

1. *Philanthropic* - the resource is valued because contemporaries may wish to use it. Also sometimes known as vicarious value.
2. *Bequest* - current generations may wish to provide an opportunity for future generations to enjoy or use some resource.
3. *Intrinsic* - individuals care about nonhuman components of ecosystem.

Barrett (1988) considers existence value reflects an individual's ethical values towards biological resources and Bishop and Welsh (1992) consider that part of the motivation for existence values may be feelings of environmental responsibility. There is some variation in the literature as to the exact motivations for existence values (Mitchell and Carson 1989 and Cicchetti and Wilde 1992), but there is considerable agreement that such values are real and are quite compatible with economic theory (Bishop and Welsh 1992, Boyle and Bishop 1987, Hanemann 1989a and Randall 1986).

The presence of existence values is supported by some empirical evidence. Empirical studies on existence values of wildlife indicate that values may be significant (Boyle and Bishop 1987, Cummings, Brookshire and Schulze 1986, Fredman 1995 and Whitehead 1992, 1993). Even relatively unknown species such as the Wisconsin striped shiner may have some existence value (Boyle and Bishop 1987). Madariaga and McConnell (1987) and Diamond and Hausman (1993) cite donations to conservation organisations as evidence of existence values.

The concept of existence value is particularly important for species issues as humans use only a fraction of species at present. Most species have no immediately obvious direct uses so most or all of their benefit is existence value. This applies, for example, to the species chosen for study in this book, Leadbeater's possum. A small amount of eco-tourism is associated with the possum and it can be seen in captivity, but its predominant value is that of knowing it exists. The largest component of value may be existence value even for species which do have use value (Stevens *et al.* 1991).

Option Value

The concept of option value was first introduced by Weisbrod in 1964

(Cicchetti and Wilde 1992 and Kerr and Sharp 1987). Subsequent key papers in the literature are those by Cicchetti and Freeman (1971), Schmalensee (1972), Bishop (1982), Freeman (1985) and Fisher and Hanemann (1990). 'Option values are an adjustment to resource values to reflect uncertainty' (Boyle and Bishop 1987, p. 944), that is, option value can be considered as a risk premium when there is uncertainty about the future demand or supply of environmental services, where expected consumer surplus would underestimate value.

The sum of option value and the expected consumers' surplus, where consumers' surplus is either the Hicksian compensated or equivalent variation measure, gives what is known as option price (Brookshire, Eubanks and Randall 1983, Barrett 1988). Option price is 'the maximum an individual is willing to pay now to ensure future provision of the resource with a given probability' (Kerr and Sharp 1987, p. 89). It represents the largest sure payment that will be made to secure an option for future use (Bishop 1982 and Brookshire, Eubanks and Randall 1983). Simply estimating expected consumer surplus in situations of uncertainty will underestimate the benefits of a resource.

The uncertainty associated with option value may occur on both the demand side and the supply side. Demand side option value occurs when there is uncertainty about future demand. For example, an individual may be uncertain about visiting Africa to view wild rhinoceroses. Demand side option value can be either positive or negative (Schmalensee 1972 and Bishop 1982). Intuitively, it could be expected to be positive for many endangered species, such as rhinoceroses, pandas, possums and so on, but it is possible to think of instances where people would like to avoid the species, such as poisonous snakes or the small pox virus.

Supply side option value exists when there is uncertainty about the supply of the resource. For example, will there be any rhinoceroses left in the wild to view by the time the individual goes to visit them? Again the sign of this option value can be either positive or negative (Freeman 1985 and Smith 1985).

The sign of option value when there is both supply and demand uncertainty cannot be determined theoretically; it can be either positive or negative depending on the circumstances. It seems likely that the overall option value will be positive when uncertainty on the supply side is large and the resource is unique (Chisholm 1988), as is the case with many endangered species.

Gallagher and Smith (1985) have proposed a further concept of option value, that of access option value, which 'reflects willingness to pay for an increase in the probability of gaining access to the resource'. Supply side option value is a special case of access option value in which the probability of access to the resource is equal to one if a conservation programme is undertaken. This concept may be particularly applicable to endangered species as it is almost impossible for any conservation programme to guarantee a species will be saved. It is possible only to increase the species' probability of survival.

Option value is one means of adjusting for uncertainty. There are also several other means of accounting for risk and uncertainty and there is considerable debate as to which means is most appropriate in what circumstances.

Measurement of option value is difficult. Because it is a public good it is not possible to organise an options market as occurs with some other goods (Kerr and Sharp 1987). It is usual to estimate instead option price, that is, option value plus consumer's surplus. Option price can be estimated from survey techniques.

Quasi-option Value

The notion of quasi-option value was first advanced by Arrow and Fisher (1974) and independently by Henry (1974). Quasi-option is relevant in valuing the expected outcome of a decision which leads to the opportunity for further decisions in the future to be made in the light of future events (Fisher and Hanemann 1987). Expected values calculated without recognising the scope for future decisions made in the light of future events are incorrect. The correction amount is quasi-option value.

Quasi-option value is a different concept to option value, although some authors refer to it simply as this (for example, Henry 1974, Fisher and Hanemann 1986 and Hanemann 1989a). Hanemann (1989a) distinguishes option value as a risk premium in an uncertain situation and quasi-option value as time dependent which does not involve any assumption of risk aversion.

Quasi-option values arise in situations where one of the choices under consideration is irreversible, for example preserving a wilderness area which contains endangered species or flooding it with the construction of a hydroelectric dam. If the area is preserved, it is still possible to build a dam, but if the area is flooded it will never be possible to discover potential uses of the species that were there. Formal theoretical models of quasi-option value can be found in Arrow and Fisher (1974), Kerr and Sharp (1987) and Hanemann (1989a).

It was generally concluded that delaying a development choice where there were irreversible consequences would result in a positive quasi-option value. However, Freeman (1984) has shown that there are some circumstances where it may be negative. Whether it is positive or negative for conservation depends on 'the nature of the uncertainty, the opportunities for gaining information ... and the structure of the decision problem' (Freeman 1984, p. 292).

WHY ARE SPECIES THREATENED?

While individual species and biodiversity may generate considerable benefit to society, this benefit is rarely reflected in the market or in government policies with an appropriate rate of wildlife resource use (Brown 1985, Tisdell 1990). Perrings *et al.* (1995, p. 13) identify the central policy problem in biodiversity loss as the fact that 'the private value of biological resources ... is not equal to the social opportunity cost of these resources'. Swanson (1994) attributes many extinctions to the diversion to human uses of the resources species need for survival, because the value of these resources in supporting species is not recognised.

For the social benefits of species to be fully accounted for in a market structure, they need to be firstly demonstrated and measured. Secondly, the values need to be captured. These two processes have been described as demonstration and appropriation (Brown and Moran 1993). It is only in the last few decades that non-use values for environmental amenities have been suggested and shown to exist theoretically, for example, option value and existence value. Attempts to measure these values are even more recent. The problem of capturing or appropriating the benefits has also received some attention (Barrett 1988, Brown and Henry 1989, Goodland 1988 and Pearce and Moran 1994).

In addition to the fact that there are no markets for many of the benefits associated with species, a 'set of institutional, market and information failures have ensured that biodiversity remains not only undervalued ... but also that its value is not captured' (Brown and Moran 1993, p. 18). The general conclusion is that the market will consistently undervalue species benefits compared to the benefits of a development that will cause extinction. This is because not all species benefits are included and those that are may be undervalued (Tisdell 1979).

There are several considerations which account for the inadequate conservation of species and maintenance of biodiversity by both the private and public sector.

Public Good Aspects

Some of the benefits associated with species conservation exhibit the characteristics of pure public goods, with the consequence that no efficient price can be found and no markets can be established. Existence value for a species or for a given level of biodiversity, for example, is clearly a public good. It is non-rival and non-excludable and no market exists (Bishop 1978).

Access to a distribution of species for research into new uses can also be considered an undepletable public good as exploitation by one researcher does not preclude exploitation by others. The issue of the potential scientific and productive value of species is explored in some detail by Brown in several papers (Brown 1985, 1986, Brown and Goldstein 1984 and Brown and Swierzbinski 1985). In these papers, the authors consider the effect of various market structures on the level of species conservation. The conclusion is that the market will conserve too few species in relation to the socially optimal level. 'Even with perfect patent rights to established ideas, access to the pool of genetic resources enables competitors the opportunity to create substitute products ... which corrode the profitability of the earlier discoveries' (Brown 1985, p. 7).

Open Access Problems

The conservation problems of many species are characterised by open access problems in which individual users have little incentive to conserve the species because, although the users collectively may benefit from managing the resource in a sustainable manner, any individual user can be made better off by cheating and increasing their own use (Barrett 1988, Clark 1973). Collective management may be a solution in situations where it is possible to prevent cheating and control poaching by individuals outside the collective.

Generally, the transaction costs of establishing and enforcing property rights to species appear to be high. The extent of global wildlife trafficking especially in birds and reptiles, the illegal taking of elephant ivory and rhinoceros horn and illegal logging in many tropical rainforests provides ample evidence of these difficulties (Barbier *et al.* 1990, Barbier *et al.* 1994, Barbier and Schulz 1995, Milner-Gulland and Leader-Williams 1992, Rabinowitz 1995 and Swanson and Barbier 1992).

The issue of property rights is important in another context. If the indigenous forest dwelling people of the world held recognised and enforceable property rights in the land where they lived, the forests most likely would be preserved. In general, indigenous people are not recognised to have any rights and the cost to them of the forest loss is not considered (Swaney and Olson 1992). As they have no 'economic' endowments, they have no means of negotiating for a different solution. These are moral aspects of the species conservation problem which economic approaches may not be able to resolve.

Capturing the Benefits

Not all species values are easily captured (if at all) because of a lack of markets for benefits with public good characteristics. An additional problem is the distribution of the costs and benefits, at both a global and local level.

For example, most of the genetic resource material for the common agricultural crops is found in poor countries, but most of the benefits go to the developed countries. Similarly, subsistence farmers can capture the benefits from clearing and farming forest areas. They cannot capture the (possibly large) benefits of preserving the species in those forests which go to the affluent first world, but bear the cost of not being able to grow food.

Ways of overcoming these difficulties are central to resolving the problem of excessive species extinction and biodiversity loss at a global level. These issues have been the subject of much discussion (Abramovitz 1991, Barrett 1988, Brown and Moran 1993, Goodland 1988, Goodland and Ledec 1987 and McNeely *et al.* 1990). Although there might be considerable transaction costs involved in overcoming some of these problems, there have been some successful initiatives such as debt-for-nature swaps and changes in World Bank lending to recognise environmental conservation (Ledec and Goodland 1988, Pearce and Moran 1994).

The same problems occur at a local level except that with lower transaction costs it may be possible to provide compensation to those who bear the costs. If, for example, logging native forests in Victoria was halted to help preserve both the forests and species such as Leadbeater's possum, the logging industry suffers the immediate loss while the conservation benefits go to the whole community. The logging industry in this case could be compensated, if they are considered to hold the property rights to the forests. This is an issue open to debate since the allocation of property rights to many natural resources in Australia has not been clearly resolved.

Uncertainty and Irreversibility

A fundamental problem in determining what level of species conservation is adequate is the large degree of uncertainty which characterises this issue, on both the supply and demand side. The main issues of concern involve the sources of uncertainty, irreversibility and responses to uncertainty and irreversibility.

Sources of uncertainty

There are two main sources of uncertainty (Bishop 1978). Social uncertainty occurs where there is a lack of knowledge about future time paths for income levels, technologies and other variables that will determine which species become useful and which do not. Natural uncertainty exists where there is a lack of knowledge of the flora and fauna and of the consequences of its loss or reduction. Gradual changes in resource use can produce discontinuous and catastrophic effects. The information base for species is small; at least 70 per cent of the world's species are uncatalogued and there is little knowledge of the links between species and the services they provide (Norgaard 1985).

Even if it is decided to preserve a species or a particular level of species diversity, there is uncertainty about how to achieve this goal at a practical level. Very little is known about the best management strategies for conservation of a species. How will a given programme affect the probability of survival? How much habitat is required and in what locations?

What is the best mix of captive and wild programmes? What is the likelihood of a catastrophic event such as fire or failure of a food source and what effect is this likely to have on the species? What is the minimum viable population size? What does viable mean? Is it to ensure survival for 100 years or 1000 years? In most cases these questions cannot be answered even for well studied species and certainly not for less well known ones.

There is an extensive literature on the biological aspects of species conservation and the issues raised above, but few solutions. McNeely *et al.* (1990) provide a overview. Other key references include Lehmkubl (1984), Shaffer and Samson (1985), Soulé (1986, 1987), Reid and Miller (1989), Terbough (1974) and Wilson (1988), while Groves and Ride (1982) note the Australian situation.

Irreversibility
Species extinction is irreversible. Once a species has been lost, it is not possible to substitute for all or any of the services provided by that species. In general it is easier to find substitutes for the products of the development which destroys the species than for the species (Norton 1986). For example, there are no close substitutes for elephants or blue whales, but there are many substitutes for ivory and whale meat.

The irreversibility of species extinction becomes a problem when future generations value species more than the present generation (Saddler *et al.* 1980), which seems likely as the number of species diminishes, the populations of individual species decline and the human population increases (Krutilla 1967 and Tisdell 1979). Unless some account is taken of future generations, conservation benefits are likely to be undervalued.

Allowing for future generations is of course very difficult, as it is not possible to know what their preferences will be and what technology they will possess. It seems unlikely, however, that they will be able to do without the 30 to 50 per cent of current species that will be lost in the next 100 or so years without a significant loss in welfare.

Myers (1993, p. 77) asserts that by our present actions 'we are implicitly deciding that at least 200,000 future generations can certainly do without large numbers of species', as the genetic impoverishment caused by present extinction rates will not be replenished for about 5 million years (Myers 1993).

Responses to uncertainty and irreversibility

The presence of uncertainty and irreversibility is a rational argument for retaining flexibility, even at a cost and assuming risk neutrality (Chisholm and Clarke 1992). Existing markets, however, do not allow for this with respect to species conservation, partly because of excessive transaction costs (Brown and Swierzbinski 1985).

Governments are faced with the task of establishing public preferences for the level of conservation - the demand - and also the costs of providing this level - the supply - and making an appropriate allowance for uncertainty. At a practical level this involves constructing benefit functions for conservation and development options, identifying the uncertainties and finding means of dealing with uncertainty (Fisher and Hanemann 1985).

There would seem to be two main approaches to dealing with uncertainty. The first is based on expected utility theory which provides the conventional framework for rational choice under uncertainty (Chisholm and Clarke 1992). This approach requires that either an objective probability can be attached to different states of the world (for example the presence or absence of a species) or that people can make subjective assessments of probabilities to be incorporated in the choice model (Johansson 1990, Whitehead 1992).

An example of this approach is the concept of option value as an adjustment to expected consumer surplus because of uncertainty. An alternative is quantifying the probability distributions for uncertain components and estimating the benefits from the expected outcome. Other concepts are the willingness to pay locus (Graham 1981) and the expected value of the fair bet (Cory and Saliba 1987).

There is a large and controversial literature concerning the best measure to use in different situations which is beyond the scope of this book to cover. Meier and Randall (1991) provide a useful review of the four main measures and the circumstances in which they are most appropriate. Other key references are Bishop (1986) and Smith (1990).

There is also a large literature on the way in which people perceive and assess the risk and probabilities of certain events (Pearce and Markandya 1989, Smith 1990 and Viscusi 1993). There are systematic biases in the way individuals perceive risk which affects the valuations they will make in the light of changes in probability. For example, it is well documented that individuals tend to overestimate low probability events and underestimate risks of high probability events (Viscusi 1993). Johansson (1989) found an interesting difference in responses to risk between men and women.

The way in which risk probabilities are presented in a questionnaire may be expected to affect respondents' perceptions. Loomis and du Vair (1993) used pie charts and a risk ladder to present the same change in risk and obtained statistically different valuations. Smith and Desvousges (1987) found that changing the level of the baseline risk also changed the marginal valuation of the risk change.

A second approach to uncertainty has been proposed for situations in which the uncertainty is so large that it is not possible to attach probabilities to possible states of the world (or even to be sure of the states of the world). This would appear to be the situation with many species and biodiversity problems. There is often inadequate information to put probabilities on the effect of conservation programmes other than to say they will increase or decrease the probability of survival, even for quite well studied species such as Leadbeater's possum. Similarly, there is no means of knowing which species will prove to be of use or benefit to future generations.

In these circumstances, the second approach may be more appropriate. This approach places greater weight on risk conservatism and proposes decision rules which err on the conservative side, for example, setting some kind of minimum standard which must be met before projects can be considered. Alternative theories include the strategy of safe minimum standards (Ciriacy-Wantrup 1952 and Bishop 1978, 1979 and 1980) and the closely related precautionary principle (Chisholm and Clarke 1992 and Folke *et al.* 1993). These approaches are considered further below.

DETERMINING CONSERVATION PRIORITIES

Where the resources are not available to preserve all species, which is the usual case (Gregory, Mendelsohn and Moore 1989), there must be some decision criteria to determine which species are given priority. Should some parts of the environment be saved according to ecological value, to human preferences or to some other criteria? How should species that are unknown be dealt with? What are the relevant trade-offs?

Several approaches to decision making may be identified. Some are biologically based and some use economic principles (Tisdell 1990 and Kennedy 1994). The basis of the US endangered species list has been an assessment of the imminence of the threat to the species' continued existence (Sparrowe and Wight 1975). Diversity theory (Weitzman 1992) is one biological system, with priority given to conservation programmes that conserve more rather than less diversity.

The World Conservation Strategy implies that priority should be given to species which are 'more unique ..... in relation to the biological classification system and the more imminent the loss' (Tisdell 1990, p. 80). Maguire (1986) describes the use of decision analysis in managing endangered species and assessing alternative conservative programmes. In decision analysis the consequences at each step of choices under uncertainty are considered using a payoff matrix (Pearce and Markandya 1989).

The two main economic approaches are the efficiency-based cost benefit analysis approach or the risk averse safe minimum standard strategy. A very simple 'maximum number of species' or cost effectiveness system has also been proposed.

Maximum Number of Species

In this approach, species are ranked by the cost of their conservation and funds are allocated from the least costly to the most costly until the budget is exhausted. However, this method implicitly assumes the benefits of preserving all species are the same, which gives results inconsistent with both current conservation practices and peoples' preferences (Brown 1985).

There must also be some means of deciding what the total budget for species conservation will be. Chisholm and Moran (1993) have suggested using survey techniques such as contingent valuation to set the total budget based on peoples' willingness to pay for species conservation. However, they propose that priorities within this budget should be determined by scientists and wildlife managers.

Safe Minimum Standard

The safe minimum standard (SMS) approach was originally developed by Ciriacy-Wantrup (1952) and has been further developed by Bishop (1978, 1979 and 1980). The safe minimum standard stems from the idea that it is not really possible to measure the benefits of conservation or to estimate the socially optimal level of conservation because of the large uncertainty about species benefits, although failing to preserve enough species may have serious consequences. Uncertainty is treated as pure uncertainty, that is probabilities cannot be estimated for the possible states of the world under consideration.

Bishop (1980) presents the choice that society faces as bearing the cost of conservation of a species, or avoiding conservation costs now by permitting extinction and creating the possibility that large future economic losses will be incurred because an important resource has been lost. This is largely an ethical and distribution problem which Bishop argues cannot be adequately addressed by the use of efficiency approaches such as cost benefit analysis.

Krutilla (1967, p. 785) described the safe minimum standard as the 'minimum reserve [of habitat, number of individuals of a species, biodiversity and so on] needed to avoid potentially grossly adverse consequences to human welfare'. Bishop (1980) gives the practical decision rule from the safe minimum standard as avoiding extinction unless the social costs of doing so are unacceptably large. The problem is in deciding what is 'unacceptably large'; in effect, what costs the present generation will bear for future generations (Brown 1985). Economists can contribute some information on the opportunity costs of preserving a species, but the decision as to whether the costs are acceptable or not must be left to society (Bishop 1980).

In practice, it has been found that often the net social costs of preserving species are low or negligible (Bishop 1980). Studies have been made of many species using the safe minimum standard approach, for example, the Californian tule elk, Californian condor, leopard lizard, snail darter and the mountain gorilla (Langner and Bishop 1982). Environmental conservation may also bring other benefits, such as recreation or watershed protection.

Allied to the safe minimum standard approach is the idea of 'sustainability criteria', that is setting minimum ecological criteria for development projects and maximising the benefits of development once these criteria have been satisfied (Goodland and Ledec 1987, Norgaard 1985 and Pearce 1987). The World Bank has begun to apply such criteria to projects the Bank funds and has found that for many projects, the cost of meeting the environmental standard is low or even negative and forms a small part of total project costs (Goodland 1988).

But, although conservation costs for individual species are usually small, cumulative costs may be more significant. Bishop (1978) considers cumulative costs are not likely to be large in North America, but they may be a serious problem in tropical and less developed countries. Myers (1985) however, considers significant worldwide progress in species conservation could be made for an estimated US$200 million a year.

The idea of sustainability criteria is closely related to the precautionary principle. This may be defined as the principle that:

> If it is not certain that a specific action will impose severe costs on future generations, but there is reason to believe that it may do so (even if the probability that it will do so is unknown and currently unknowable statistically) then the action should not be undertaken. (Folke *et al.* 1993, p. 63)

Both the safe minimum standard and the precautionary principle have been described theoretically using game theory, being interpreted as a two person game with humans and nature. Bishop's (1978) decision rule was that of avoiding the maximum possible loss, that is, a minimax loss criteria. Ciriacy-Wantrup (1952) and Bishop (1978) argue that 'since the cost of conserving a species is usually low and the possible or potential benefits are extremely high, almost always the optimal minimax loss strategy will be SMS, to conserve the species at a safe minimum standard' (Tisdell 1990, p. 83).

Tisdell (1990), Hohl and Tisdell (1992) and Chisholm and Clarke (1992) show that although in most cases the minimax loss rule will favour conservation there are circumstances in which this decision rule will not give this result. If it is known with certainty that, for example, allowing a species to become extinct will result in large losses, but the success of the conservation programme to save the species is not known, the minimax loss rule will result in no conservation programme and the extinction of the species.

As an alternative, Ready and Bishop (1991) propose the use of the minimax regret decision rule. This is a strategy in which society seeks to 'minimise its regrets for not having, in hindsight, made the superior choice' (Chisholm and Clarke 1992, p. 8). This can be interpreted as a decision now 'which the current generation believe future generations would least regret' (Chisholm and Clarke 1992, p. 8). Moyle (1995) has applied game theory to the conservation of species.

There are still difficulties with the safe minimum standard and precautionary principle approaches. One problem is in setting the safe minimum standard. The questions of what are the minimum habitat requirements of a species and what is the minimum viable population size to ensure survival are not easy to answer (Soulé 1987 and McNeely *et al.* 1990).

Another difficulty is in making the decision on what an unacceptably large cost may be. However, these principles do shift the burden of proof to developers (Tisdell 1990). Developers must show that the costs of conservation are unacceptably large as opposed to the usual situation now where conservationists must prove that the benefits of conservation outweigh those of development.

Cost Benefit Analysis

The essence of the cost benefit approach is to compare costs and benefits of different development or conservation alternatives over time and attempt to maximise the value of society's resources. As many of the costs and benefits as possible are expressed in monetary terms and further impacts are identified and quantified as well as they can be. Impacts on environmental goods from a particular project, for example, a change in water quality, loss of a species or ecosystem damage from an oil spill, have been in the past often identified but not valued in monetary terms because there were no methods with which to value them.

There has been a great deal of research in recent years into methods of valuing non-market goods and services in order to include them in cost benefit analysis and damage assessment claims following environmental accidents. Much of the work on option value, quasi-option value and existence value has been an attempt to improve cost benefit evaluations and take account of the irreversibilities associated with environmental problems such as species extinction (Smith and Krutilla 1979).

Tisdell (1990, p. 81) comments that the usual approach to uncertainty in cost benefit analysis of projects is to 'characterise uncertainty by probability distributions and to use expected gain or utility characteristics as a deciding factor .... whether such precision is possible or desirable is debatable'. In many species conservation situations the necessary information is not available and may be prohibitively costly to obtain in terms of the decision which is being made.

Another issue pertinent to cost benefit analysis, although not confined to it, is choosing an appropriate discount rate (determining intergenerational distribution) which will influence the outcome of any cost benefit analysis and thus the decisions based on it (Norgaard and Howarth 1991).

There are situations where cost benefit analysis will provide considerable assistance in decisions involving species conservation. For example, when the opportunity costs of conservation are high, information on the benefits of conservation is crucial to the decision. It is also useful to have some estimate of the costs and benefits of conservation if scarce resources have to be allocated among species. Simply considering the conservation costs of species may result in the wrong priorities.

Combination of Methods

Randall (1986) suggests a two-tiered system for setting priorities, using a cost benefit approach for species on which there is some information and a safe minimum standard approach for species for which there is very little or no information. Tisdell (1990) notes that this recognises but does not solve the mixture of decision problems concerning species as there is not such a clear cut distinction in knowledge in reality. For some species the payoff matrices may involve probability and in others pure uncertainty and for some species extinction may be a certainty without some action.

The two-tiered system does, however, fit reasonably well into the processes of, for example, the *Flora and Fauna Guarantee Act*, where it is anticipated that most species will have a small opportunity cost for conservation and would fall under the safe minimum standard approach and a few will have high opportunity costs and require more exhaustive economic evaluation.

VALUING SPECIES CONSERVATION

A range of methods are available by which the benefits and costs of environmental goods may be evaluated. A key issue when considering these methods is the ability to capture existence value, which is crucial to species conservation because for many species it is the primary (or even only) source of value. Considerable progress has been made in the past 20 to 30 years in developing techniques for placing monetary values on benefits which are not exchanged in markets. There are a number of main approaches.

Opportunity Cost Based Approaches

With cost based approaches no attempt is made to estimate the benefits. The actual or potential costs of a proposed conservation activity are estimated using market prices and a judgement is made as to whether the benefits could be expected to be greater than the costs. There are several such approaches (Sinden 1991, Pearce and Markandya 1989).

1. *The opportunity cost approach,* in which the foregone income from the best alternative use is measured, that is, what would be given up to ensure conservation of a particular species. For example, what is the opportunity cost of prohibiting forestry in Leadbeater's possum habitat areas?
2. *The cost effectiveness approach,* in which the least cost means of achieving a particular objective is determined. This relates to the safe minimum standard approach in which the standard of species conservation is set and then the most efficient way of achieving this is ascertained.
3. *The replacement value or alternative cost approach,* in which the benefit is assessed at the cost of replacing or restoring the environmental asset. For a species this may involve the cost of an alternative site if an area of habitat is under question or the cost of synthetically producing a drug instead of collecting it from the species. If it is decided to replace the asset at a cost of $X, this reveals a value for the species of at least $X.
4. *The cost saving approach,* in which the benefits of conservation are valued as the costs of damage which are avoided. For example, the benefits of a flood mitigation scheme may be valued as the reduction in flood damage.

Physical Linkage or Dose Response

Physical linkage or dose response methods are also known as indirect valuation. These methods attempt to link physical information with some kind of market information. Some examples of these methods are linking the level of air pollution with the cost of damage to building surfaces and the reduction in the life of a hydro-electric dam due to sedimentation from erosion caused by deforestation upstream. There is also the 'loss-of-earnings' approach, for example the loss of working days and medical costs due to smog may be used to estimate part of the benefit of reducing air pollution.

These methods are not applicable to many species conservation problems, although Ragozin and Brown (1985) estimated the economic loss associated with a reduction in the population of a species that is preyed on by a commercially harvested predator (Barrett 1988). This type of approach again may significantly underestimate the true benefits of a species because only use benefits (and perhaps not even all of those) can be estimated.

Revealed Preference Techniques

In some circumstances, individuals' preferences for environmental goods such as species conservation can be revealed or estimated from market data for private goods and services that are either produced or consumed in conjunction with that good (Barrett 1988 and Bateman 1993). For example, contributions to private conservation organisations, media coverage of a species or protest action may give some indication that particular species or habitats have a positive value.

However, the techniques used most widely for evaluation of environmental goods are the travel cost method and hedonic (or implicit) pricing. An review of both these methods is given in Bateman (1993).

Hedonic pricing

The hedonic price method is a procedure to estimate the value of a characteristic of a good from the market price of a good. The most common application of the hedonic price method is in relation to property values where different environmental attributes in different locations will be reflected in property values. For example, the price of houses may be influenced by noise level, air pollution levels, access to parks and so on.

Hedonic pricing attempts to identify how much of a property value differential is due to a particular environmental difference. This information is used to infer how much people are willing to pay for an improvement in the environmental quality that they face and then calculate the consumer surplus.

There are some problems with the hedonic price approach (Pearce and Markandya 1989).

1. Data requirements for an hedonic pricing study are unusually exacting. All relevant characteristics must be controlled to ensure that the characteristic of interest is the one causing the difference. Sufficient market data for reliable estimations are difficult to obtain.
2. The functional form of the true underlying equation is unknown and the assumptions made about its form may affect the value estimated.
3. Observations on implicit price and quantity of the characteristic may not enable identification of marginal willingness to pay functions if the implicit price function is linear in the quantity of the characteristic (Freeman 1979).
4. The market for the good must be efficient (Hoevenagel 1990).

5. People must be aware of the actual physical differences in the levels of environmental characteristic being valued or the differences will not be reflected in property values.

The hedonic pricing method is not applicable to species conservation in most cases because there is seldom a suitable related market. If hedonic pricing could be used the benefits of species would be underestimated because the non-use values such as existence value are not captured.

Travel cost method

The travel cost method was proposed in a letter by Hotelling in 1949 (Bateman 1993). The first applications were by Clawson in 1959 and Clawson and Knetsch in 1966 (Bateman 1993). The method has been used most frequently to value site specific recreation benefits. The underlying idea of the travel cost method is to use information on the amount of money and time people spend in getting to a recreation site to estimate their willingness to pay for the use and facilities of that site.

The first step is to determine zones at different distances from the recreation site and then to survey visitors to determine the average number of visits to the site from each distance zone (people further away could be expected to make fewer visits). These data are used to estimate a demand curve for the recreation site.

The second step is to assign a monetary cost to each kilometre travelled to estimate the travel costs of reaching the site. Consumer surplus is then calculated by measuring, for each zone, the area below the demand curve and above the price (travel cost) line (Hoevenagel 1990). This method provides an estimate of Marshallian consumer surplus. The demand curve may also be estimated using data from each individual rather than using zones.

Some strong assumptions are required in order to specify a travel cost model. Firstly, what sites or activities are substitutes for the one being valued and how should they be included in the model? The travel cost method works best for unique or isolated sites. The question of how to value the time spent getting to the site is also important. How much should be considered as a cost to recreation and how much should be considered as part of the recreation activity? The method is also very sensitive to the functional form used to estimate the demand curve.

The travel cost method has been used successfully for studies of the recreation and hunting values of wildlife, for example, Pearce valued big game hunting in Canada in 1968 (Barrett 1988) and Brown and Henry (1989 and 1993) valued elephant viewing in Kenya. However, the travel cost method is not capable of estimating the total economic value of a resource as it cannot estimate non-use values such as existence value. Again this method will result in an underestimate of species value if existence values are an important component of total value.

Survey Methods

A further approach to determining the values that individuals place on improvements in environmental quality, such as improving the probability of species survival, is simply to ask people through surveys and direct questioning (Freeman 1979). The most commonly used method is known as the contingent valuation method.

The contingent valuation approach uses survey methods to measure benefits directly, rather than to infer them from a demand curve. The underlying idea of this technique is that individuals have true, hidden preferences for environmental goods, such as species conservation, which they will reveal if they are asked the appropriate, specific questions. This method results in estimates of Hicksian welfare measures, where it is assumed that utility remains constant when calculating a monetary value.

A contingent valuation survey creates a hypothetical market for the environmental good and asks people directly what they would be willing to pay (or willing to accept as compensation) for a specified change in the quantity or quality of that good. The willingness to pay amounts given by respondents are contingent on the information presented in the questionnaire. The 'contingent market is taken to include not just the good itself ..., but also the institutional context in which it could be provided and the way in which it would be financed' (Pearce and Markandya 1989). Because a contingent valuation survey is conceived to mimic a real market, the hypothetical market must be as realistic as possible. A contingent valuation suvey may also be framed as a referendum on, for example, a proposed change in the level of provision of a public good.

A contingent valuation questionnaire consists of three main parts (Mitchell and Carson 1989). The first part gives a detailed description of the environmental change to be valued and the hypothetical circumstances under which it will be available to the respondent. The description and the proposed market should be as realistic, plausible and meaningful as possible. The second part requests the respondent's maximum willingness to pay for (or willingness to be compensated for losing) the environmental change of interest. There are various techniques of eliciting this information (Sellar, Chavas and Stoll 1986). In the third section of the questionnaire, information about the respondent's characteristics (for example age, income), their preferences for the environmental change and past use of the environmental good in question is requested. This information is used to help assess the validity of the willingness to pay responses and interpret the variation in responses to the valuation question across respondents (Arrow *et al.* 1993)

The major attraction of the contingent valuation method is that it should, technically, be applicable to all non-market goods. Unlike the hedonic pricing and travel cost methods, the contingent valuation technique is the only method which can measure non-use values such as existence and option values. Such non-use values can form a significant component of the total value. For example, Walsh *et al.* (1987) found that non-use public conservation values accounted for two-thirds of the benefits from preserving endangered species in Colorado and recreation accounted for the other third.

The greatest disadvantage of the contingent valuation method is that its measures are based on responses to hypothetical markets, rather than observed market behaviour. There is some controversy about what the estimates produced by contingent valuation surveys measure. The two main concerns are whether individuals actually know the surpluses they derive from environmental assets and if so, whether they will reveal these values truthfully.

Because of these concerns, there has been considerable research into the contingent valuation methodology over the last 20 to 30 years. Comprehensive reviews and comparative studies of contingent valuation methodology can be found in Bishop and Heberlein (1979), Brookshire *et al.* (1982), Cummings, Brookshire and Schulze (1986), Cummings and Harrison (1992), Hanley (1987), Johansson, Kriström and Mäler (1995), Mitchell and Carson (1989), Rowe and Chestnut (1983) and Arrow *et al.* (1993).

Much of the earlier debate occurred in academic fora and focussed on the technical aspects of contingent valuation (Blamey and Common 1992). In more recent years the debate about the validity of contingent valuation values has become more public, at least in the US, as the business community has been faced with the possibility of large compensation payouts following Court acceptance of the inclusion of non-use values in natural resource damage assessment cases (Larson 1992). An enormous amount of research and debate occurred following the Exxon Valdez oil spill, because the contingent valuation method was used to assess losses in non-use values caused by the spill. However, eventually a settlement was reached without using information from the contingent valuation studies. The general contingent valuation methodology is discussed more fully in the following chapter.

CONCLUSIONS

Biodiversity loss and species extinction are among the major environmental problems facing present and future societies. The current rate of species loss will result in considerable impoverishment of the biological resources available for both present and future generations. Although biological species provide humans with a wide range of benefits, the nature of many of these benefits has meant they have been inadequately accounted for (if at all) in most resource allocation decisions. Open access problems and the public good nature of many benefits provided by species have resulted in a rate of species extinction that is greater than that which would be socially optimal.

The species conservation issue is also characterised by enormous uncertainty, both in terms of what benefits a species might provide (as well as what species actually exist) and in terms of what future demands may be. This uncertainty, coupled with the irreversibility of species and ecosystem loss, is a strong argument for retaining flexibility and erring on the conservative side when making decisions which may involve species extinction.

Key developments in economic theory which relate to environmental goods such as species conservation have been firstly, the recognition of both use and non-use values of resources and secondly, the development of techniques enabling the valuation of these benefits. There has also been considerable research into ways of dealing with uncertainty and irreversibility.

The adoption of a safe minimum standard approach, as suggested by Ciriacy-Wantrup (1952), or the related precautionary principle approach gives the practical decision rule that extinction, with its uncertain and potentially grossly adverse consequences, should be avoided unless the social costs of doing so are unacceptably large. This removes the need to value the benefits of a species unless the opportunity costs of conservation are high. For many species the net social costs of conservation are low and the conservation decision should be straightforward.

For species where the opportunity costs of conservation are high, however, valuation of the benefits of conservation for comparison with the opportunity costs becomes necessary. The development of economic techniques for the valuation of non-market goods in the past few decades has enabled comparison in monetary terms of both the costs and benefits of species conservation projects. The technique most applicable to species conservation programmes is contingent valuation because it is the only method capable of estimating non-use values such as existence value, which may comprise the major or only benefit of a particular species.

There has been criticism of non-market valuation techniques such as the contingent valuation method by those who believe that environmental 'goods' such as species cannot be measured in monetary terms, or that it is morally unacceptable to do so (Ehrlich and Daily 1993). However, species are being implicitly valued anyway. Swaney and Olson (1992, p. 8) point out that 'we *are* valuing biodiversity. We can choose to continue to undervalue it, or we can change our valuations, but we cannot choose to not value it'. Myers (1993) asserts that current decisions imply that species are being undervalued to the extent that at least a third or more have been judged to be unnecessary in the future. Explicit recognition and valuation of species benefits should result in an improved allocation of resources between conservation and development. Excluding non-use values from damage assessments and cost benefit analyses of projects involving environmental resources such as species will result in serious resource misallocation (Randall 1993).

PART THREE

The Contingent Valuation Method

6. The Contingent Valuation Method

INTRODUCTION

The concept of the contingent valuation method seems to have originated in 1947 when Ciriacy-Wantrup considered the question of how to obtain economic values for public goods and proposed the use of surveys for obtaining such values. Ciriacy-Wantrup (1947 and 1952) considered five possible objections to this survey procedure (including strategic behaviour) all of which, in his view, could be overcome with careful design of the questionnaire (Hoevenagel 1990). However, Samuelson (1954) published an article on the theory of public expenditure which concluded that because of free riding and strategic behaviour it would not be possible to obtain reliable values of individual preferences for public goods. As a result, little was reported about valuing public goods with survey methods until the 1960s.

The first recorded contingent valuation study was conducted in 1961 by Davis, who had independently conceived of the idea of using surveys to value public goods (Mitchell and Carson 1989). Davis used a contingent valuation questionnaire to estimate the benefits of outdoor recreation in the Maine woods, US (Davis 1963). The next major study appears to have been conducted in 1969 (Hammack and Brown 1974).

This study involved a contingent valuation questionnaire mailed to a sample of hunters asking for their willingness to pay for the right to hunt water fowl or willingness to accept compensation to give up their right to hunt water fowl. Since these early beginnings, the contingent valuation method has been used extensively and there are now more than 1,600 documented works on the contingent valuation method (Carson *et al.* 1994a).

The earlier contingent valuation studies generally estimated use values but, as the theory of non-use values developed, contingent valuation was extended to estimate these values as well (Randall, Ives and Eastman 1974). Initially, many authors attempted to measure the components of non-use values separately, but the recent emphasis has been on measuring the total economic value, which is usually more relevant for decision making purposes. There is some doubt that individuals can in fact differentiate between the components of non-use values when considering their willingness to pay for a non-market good (Cummings and Harrison 1995).

Since the early 1970s the contingent valuation method has been used to measure the benefits of a wide range of environmental goods (Mitchell and Carson 1989), including recreation, amenity value, scenery, wetlands, air and water quality, forest conservation and wildlife. Early contingent valuation studies related to species include big game hunting in the Maine woods (Davis 1963), water fowl hunting in North America (Hammack and Brown 1974), hunting Canadian geese (Bishop and Heberlein 1979), the value of viewing whooping cranes (Stoll and Johnson 1984) and option and existence values for grizzly bear and bighorn sheep populations (Brookshire, Eubanks and Randall 1983).

As well as valuing environmental goods, many contingent valuation studies were designed to either test for potential biases of the method or the results obtained were compared with the results of other studies as a means of external validation of contingent valuation (Mitchell and Carson 1989). More recently, there has been a trend to include expertise from other disciplines such as market research, survey research, social psychology and cognitive psychology, in order to improve the methodology (Gregory, Lichtenstein and Slovic 1993, Harris, Driver and McLaughlin 1989 and Peterson 1992). The use of experimental economics is becoming increasingly important in investigating the various methodological issues (Harrison, Harstad and Rutström 1995).

METHODOLOGICAL CONCERNS

There has been considerable debate and research into the validity of the contingent valuation method involving a range of theoretical and operational issues. The major issues are discussed in the following sections. Other recent reviews of the practical problems of the contingent valuation method include Arrow *et al.* (1993), Bateman and Willis (forthcoming), Hanemann (1994a), Hoevenagel (1994), Johansson, Kriström and Mäler (1995), Kriström (1994) and Mitchell and Carson (1989).

The issue of whether willingness to accept or willingness to pay questions should be used, and in what circumstances, has been discussed in Chapter 4 in the section on choice of welfare measure.

Embedding or the Problem of Scope

An issue in the contingent valuation literature that has received a large amount of attention is the issue of embedding or the effect of the scope and sequencing of the good to be valued on the willingness to pay estimates. The term 'embedding' has been used to describe several different effects (Carson and Mitchell 1995, Hanemann 1994a) which has resulted in some confusion over the extent and occurrence of the problem.

Kahneman and Knetsch (1992a, p. 58) introduced the term embedding (Hanemann 1994a). They define embedding as occurring when 'the same good is assigned a lower value if WTP for it is inferred from WTP for a more inclusive good than if the particular good is evaluated on its own'. They distinguish perfect embedding, which occurs when directly elicited values for a good are equal regardless of the degree of nesting or scale the good is defined over and regular embedding (Kahneman and Knetsch 1992b and Loomis, Lockwood and DeLacy 1993). That is, perfect embedding would occur if willingness to pay was the same for one, two or a dozen endangered species. To demonstrate regular embedding, 'it is sufficient to show that WTP for a particular commodity varies depending on whether it is assessed on its own or as part of a more comprehensive inclusive commodity' (Kahneman and Knetsch 1992b, p. 91). That is, the value for species A would be different if species A was valued on its own, than if it was valued as part of a group of species.

The term embedding has also been used for the phenomena known as symbolic bias, part whole bias or mental account bias. Mitchell and Carson (1989) regard these as forms of amenity mis-specification bias, which results when respondents value a larger or smaller environmental change than the one intended by the researcher (Hoevenagel 1990).

Symbolic bias occurs when respondents react to an amenity's general symbolic meaning instead of to the specific level of provision described (Mitchell and Carson 1989), for example treating conservation of a single endangered species as a proxy for all endangered species.

Part whole bias occurs as a result of the supposed tendency of respondents to treat public goods as global symbols without paying attention to the specific good in the survey. Part whole bias may be geographical, for example, giving similar valuations for improving fishing in one river and for improving fishing in several rivers, or benefit part whole bias, where respondents are unable to differentiate between benefit sub-components such as option value and existence value (Mitchell and Carson 1989).

Mental account bias follows the idea that people focus on groups of commodities (such as food, entertainment, charity) when making allocative decisions (Tversky and Kahneman 1981). Thus a question on an endangered species may result in an answer that is really most or all of the respondent's 'mental account' for environmental goods (Hoevenagel 1990, Willis and Garrod 1993).

Carson and Mitchell (1995) also include 'probability of provision' bias which occurs when the perceived probability that the good will be provided differs from the researcher's intended probability. If respondents are not convinced the good will be provided in the manner or quantity described, they will undervalue it. This is a particular problem when large changes in quantity are being valued.

The 'amenity mis-specification' biases described above can generate serious problems for particular contingent valuation studies. However, it should be emphasised that such biases are usually a function of poor survey design or specification of the good to be valued, rather than being an inherent fault of the contingent valuation method.

Another issue which has also been confused with embedding is what is known as the 'adding up' problem, or independent valuation and summation (Hoehn and Randall 1987). For example, if each endangered species in Victoria is valued separately, it is almost certain the sum of the valuations will be greater than if all the endangered species in Victoria were valued together. Similarly, if separate studies of many environmental goods were done and the results were added up for any individual, the result may be implausibly large. However, this will also occur with market goods if the substitution or complementary effects are ignored (Bishop and Welsh 1992) and it is a problem that has long been recognised in the cost benefit literature (Hoehn and Randall 1989). Simply adding up the values for endangered species separately will result in an overestimate of their combined value if some of the species are substitutes for each other, which would seem to be fairly likely, especially for less well known and less attractive species.

Carson, Flores and Hanemann (1992) and Hanemann (1994a) have substantially clarified and redefined the terminology and concepts relating to 'embedding' into three main effects; the scope effect, the sequence effect and the subadditivity effect. The scope effect exists when respondents do not distinguish differences in quantity or scale of a good, for example, valuing three wetland areas the same as only one wetland area. The sequencing effect occurs when, for example, a given species is valued differently if it is placed early in a list of species to be valued than if it is placed near the end. The subadditivity effect is the 'adding up' problem. If a number of species were valued individually and the values added together, the total value will be greater than if they were valued collectively.

Sequencing and subadditivity effects have clearly been to occur (Carson and Mitchell 1995, Cummings, Ganderton and McGuckin 1994 and Samples and Hollyer 1990). But, as noted above, these effects are expected and can be explained in terms of substitution effects and diminishing marginal returns (Hanemann 1994a). Carson, Flores and Hanemann (1992) show that for strict Hicksian substitutes willingness to pay for an increase in a given public good decreases the further out in a sequence of goods it is valued, with the opposite being true for willingness to accept compensation for the loss of a public good. Thus, the sequencing and subadditivity effects are part of the general problem of valuing a number of goods or projects and are not a problem particular to the contingent valuation method.

Two studies have been particularly influential in raising concerns that the issue of scope (or perfect embedding as defined by Kahneman and Knetsch 1992) could be a serious problem for the contingent valuation method; Desvousges *et al.* (1993b), Boyle *et al.* (1994) and Kahneman and Knetsch (1992). Knetsch (1993) also reports some studies which show embedding. However, these studies have been criticised on many aspects of survey design, implementation and data analysis (Carson 1994, Carson and Mitchell 1995, Hanemann 1994a and Smith 1992) which throw doubt on their evidence of embedding.

Numerous other studies have found that willingness to pay does vary significantly with scope, for example, the meta-analysis of recreation studies by Walsh, Johnson and McKean (1992) and a review of air quality studies by Smith and Osborne (1994).

Desvousges, Smith and McGivney (1983, cited in Mitchell and Carson 1989) and Mitchell and Carson (1984) have reported surveys of fresh water quality improvements in which 'more geographically extensive water improvements were valued several times higher than the local improvements, as would be expected if respondents' values were contingent on the amount of water involved' (Mitchell and Carson 1989, p. 252).

Loomis, Lockwood and DeLacy (1993) designed a contingent valuation study to test for embedding that attempted to meet the design criteria Smith (1992) developed to improve the Kahneman and Knetsch (1992a and 1992b) study. Evidence from this study was inconclusive. An embedding effect was demonstrated at one level, but not at another and when it did occur 'there was a reduction in value much smaller than that found by Kahneman and Knetsch' (Loomis, Lockwood and DeLacy 1993, p. 45).

Whitehead (1993) conducted a contingent valuation survey to value a coastal non game wildlife programme, which included a sea turtle programme, and also to value the sea turtle programme alone. Whitehead considered that embedding was not a problem, as the sea turtle values were significantly different from the total coastal wildlife values (about 70 per cent):

> Option price for a coastal nongame wildlife program, which would include a sea turtle program, is larger than that for the sea turtle program. This increases confidence in the validity of the option price estimates since embedded values are not found. (1993, p. 130)

Imber, Stevenson and Wilks (1991) found significantly different valuations for avoiding major and minor impacts of mining near a national park. Fredman (1995) compared the mean value he estimated for preserving the white-backed woodpecker in Sweden (about 20 SEK per household per year) with a mean willingness to pay of 1200 SEK per household per year for environmental improvements in general estimated by Johansson and Zavisic (1989, cited in Fredman 1995). Carson (1994) reviewed over 30 studies which used split-sample tests of sensitivity to scope which all clearly rejected the hypothesis that respondents are insensitive to the scope of the good being valued.

The empirical evidence so far seems to support the fact that willingness to pay does change with the scope of the good and that contingent valuation survey respondents do consider the characteristics of the particular good they are asked to value (Carson 1994, Carson and Mitchell 1995 and Hanemann 1994a), although there is room for further research. Provided care is taken with survey design and implementation the issue of scope does not seem to be an inherent problem of the contingent valuation method.

The main strateg recommended to minimise the likelihood of scope effects is to describe both the larger entity and the good being valued, with a clear warning not to confuse the good with the larger entity and to include clear descriptions of the good with the use of maps and diagrams as required (Willis and Garrod 1993).

Potential Biases

A major implementation problem occurs in contingent valuation studies when defining a realistic context for a hypothetical market so that responses reflect peoples' preferences without biases or inaccuracies. Survey design is also important in eliciting accurate unbiased responses. There is a large literature concerning potential biases and inaccuracies in contingent valuation (Mitchell and Carson 1989).

Strategic bias and hypothetical bias are the most often discussed biases and are the most difficult to deal with. There are also many factors related to questionnaire design and implementation, question format and the provision of information that will affect the responses obtained from contingent valuation surveys. Some of these biases are endemic to social survey work in general, for example interviewer bias, sampling bias and non-response bias and are well covered by the literature in that field (Dillman 1978 and de Vaus 1985). Other biases are particular to the contingent valuation method.

Evidence on the significance and direction of particular biases is often inconclusive. Some biases are no longer considered as biases, for example, it is now expected that differences in the information provided or differences in the provision of the good will result in different estimates of value.

The major sources of potential bias or error are discussed in the following sections. There are two questions of interest, firstly, do people know their willingness to pay for environmental goods such as species conservation and secondly, do they reveal their preferences truthfully?

Strategic bias

Strategic bias is present if survey respondents intentionally mislead the researcher (Bishop and Heberlein 1987). Respondents may understate or overstate preferences depending on whether or not they think their answers will influence policy and depending on how much they expect to have to pay in reality. There may be some aspect of joint goods associated with environmental goods. For example, people expressing their view or willingness to pay for one issue may believe that this will influence policy on related issues. Thus, preventing the Franklin Dam in Tasmania may make subsequent similar issues easier for environmentalists to influence. Consequently, people may have incentives to overstate or understate their true preferences.

The concern with strategic bias stems from the free rider problem associated with public goods (Samuelson 1954). The problem here is to persuade individuals to reveal their true preferences 'in contexts where, by not telling the truth, they will still secure a benefit in excess of the costs they have to pay' (Pearce and Markandya 1989, p. 36).

There have been three approaches to testing for the presence of strategic bias in contingent valuation surveys (Mitchell and Carson 1989). The first is to provide additional information to respondents to allow them to behave strategically (for example, the mean bid of other respondents) and offer them the chance to revise their bids.

The second approach is to assume the distribution of bids follows a distribution such as the normal distribution, or one consistent with the distribution of income. If the distribution of actual bids differs significantly from the assumed distribution, it is probable that strategic bias exists.

The third approach uses a split sample with two groups valuing the same good but with different incentives for engaging in strategic behaviour. Little evidence for strategic behaviour has been found in laboratory or field experiments with any of the three approaches (Pearce and Markandya 1989, Mitchell and Carson 1989).

In 1972 the Swedish economist Bohm conducted a contingent valuation experiment in which he asked respondents their willingness to pay to see a preview of a popular Swedish television show. In this experiment he explicitly tested and rejected Samuelson's strategic behaviour hypothesis (Bohm 1972). Other contingent valuation studies have also tested and rejected the existence of strategic behaviour (Rowe, d'Arge and Brookshire 1980). Milon (1989) found some evidence of weak free riding behaviour in an experiment he conducted.

There has been one experiment, by Throsby and Withers (1986), in which large strategic effects were identified, although this behaviour was exhibited by only a minority of respondents (Milon 1989). Milon postulates that this may be because the good valued in this survey (cultural arts) accounts for a much larger share of a respondent's total budget than the goods usually valued in contingent valuation surveys.

Overall, the evidence suggests that strategic bias is not a serious problem but is not conclusive (Rowe and Chestnut 1983). Milon (1989, p. 306) concludes that there is 'little evidence to reject the hypothesis that ... contingent valuation survey respondents try, to the best of their ability, to provide truthful information about their preferences'. Hoehn and Randall (1987) and Mitchell and Carson (1989) show that incentives for strategic behaviour in most contingent valuation studies are weak and that if any such behaviour does occur it is likely to have little effect on mean values.

In addition, contingent valuation studies usually contain behavioural and attitudinal questions which are used to check for inconsistencies between attitudes and willingness to pay answers. It is usual to delete inconsistent answers and outliers (very high willingness to pay amounts), which will further remove the possible effects of any strategic behaviour.

Hypothetical bias
Hypothetical bias is defined as the difference between the stated payments in response to a hypothetical opportunity to pay and actual payments when individuals are presented with the opportunity in reality. It is one of the most troublesome biases in contingent valuation because it is very difficult to test for except by comparison with actual payments. But clearly, if it was possible to obtain actual payments for the good in question, contingent valuation would not be necessary.

Inaccuracies or biases may occur because respondents are trying to predict what their behaviour would be in a hypothetical situation. Respondents may not be able to visualise the situation, or it may not seem realistic enough to spend time thinking it through. Also they may not believe their answers will have any effect on policy. However, attempting to reduce hypothetical bias by making the contingent valuation scenario as realistic as possible may induce strategic bias.

The question of concern is whether the hypothetical nature of contingent valuation surveys generates a systematic error (bias) in one direction or another. The main test of this question has been to compare responses to a hypothetical survey with actual payments. There have been a number of studies which do this, with mixed results (Hanemann 1994a and Mitchell and Carson 1989 provide comprehensive reviews).

Bishop, Heberlein and Kealy (1983) obtained higher willingness to accept responses from hypothetical questions than from actual payments. Seip and Strand (1992) obtained very poor correspondence between hypothetical intentions and actual payments to an organisation for preserving wildlife, with the hypothetical responses being substantially higher, but there were shortcomings to the survey itself which leave the results open to question (Hanemann 1994a). Duffield and Patterson (1991) found that a greater number of respondents stated they would pay for maintaining stream flow than actually did, but the size of contributions were not very different between those who said they would pay and those who did pay.

More recently, hypothetical bias has been the subject of several experimental studies, for example, Cummings, Harrison and Rutström (1995), Harrison, Harstad and Rutström (1995) and Neill *et al.* (1994). This work has found significant divergences between hypothetical and actual payments. The extent of the divergence appears to vary with price level, being less at low and high prices (Frykblom 1994 and Nape *et al.* 1995).

Other studies provide considerable evidence that hypothetical bias may not be a problem. Sinden (1988a) conducted 17 empirical experiments comparing hypothetical and actual money donations to a fund for soil conservation or for controlling dieback of eucalyptus trees and found that there was no statistical difference between the two markets in any of the experiments. Hanemann (1994a) lists further studies which found no significant differences in hypothetical and actual willingness to pay estimates. These include Bishop and Heberlein (1990) (deer hunting permits), Bohm (1972) (television viewing) and Dickie, Fisher and Gerking (1987) (strawberries).

Some studies have found hypothetical estimates may even be slightly less than actual payments. Bateman *et al.* (1993, p. 39) cite experiments which 'clearly show that stated willingness to pay in a hypothetical market may be below actual willingness to pay in a real market' and Randall, Hoehn and Brookshire (1983) obtained lower willingness to pay responses from hypothetical questions.

Other studies have compared actual and intended behaviour, with encouraging results. Navrud (1991) conducted a study comparing stated support for the World Wide Fund for Nature (Norway) and actual payment of membership fees and found the correspondence between actual and intended behaviour was in the order of 47 to 64 per cent. Carson, Hanemann and Mitchell (1986) tested voting intentions with a contingent valuation survey and found a close correspondence between predicted and actual voting. Mitchell and Carson (1989) report on the literature from social survey and political polling work where at the aggregate level there is a very close correspondence between intended actions and actual behaviour.

Mitchell and Carson (1989) and Freeman (1986) contend that there is little evidence suggesting a systematic error due to the hypothetical nature of contingent valuation questions, but it may increase the variability of responses. The poor explanatory power of many contingent valuation models is sometimes taken as an indication of presence of hypothetical bias.

Rowe and Chestnut (1983) suggest that the large disparities between willingness to accept values and willingness to pay values may be due in part to hypothetical bias reflecting property rights problems or problems with the hypothetical nature of the questions. Feenberg and Mills (1980, cited in Hoehn and Randall 1987) expect hypothetical effects to lead to high levels of pure noise, that is, a random directionless error which is unlikely to affect mean estimates of value but will increase variability. Bennett (1981) and Sinden (1988b) concur with this view.

Generally, the response to the problem of hypothetical nature of contingent valuation is to make both the hypothetical situation and the payment vehicle as credible and realistic as possible (Arrow *et al.* 1993 and Mitchell and Carson 1989). It is obviously easier to do this for studies trying to elicit use values than for those trying to elicit non-use values as use values are more familiar and more closely related to market type situations. For example, being asked to pay for recreational fishing through a licence is more familiar than being asked to pay for species conservation through a tax increase.

Design biases
The early contingent valuation literature was concerned with issues such as information 'bias' and vehicle or instrument 'bias'. The valuation process of respondents was assumed to concern only the value of the good in question, with all other elements of the hypothetical market being neutral (Hoevenagel 1990). The influence of different amounts of information and different methods of financing the proposed project on valuation responses was interpreted as bias. However, it is now recognised that the valuation process will depend on all the elements of the contingent valuation scenario, including the payment mechanism, information, likelihood of actual provision and so on (Randall 1986). These features (for example, the system of payment) are arguments in the individual's utility function (Hanley 1987).

It could be expected that variations in information would produce different estimates of value (Boyle 1989). It is, quite obviously, easier to make a valuation of a 'red car' if information is also available about its age, mileage, size, make and so on, than to make a valuation of a 'red car'. Empirical evidence from contingent valuation studies supports this contention (Bergstrom, Stoll and Randall 1989 and Rowe and Chestnut 1983).

Samples, Dixon and Gowen (1986) tested the proposition that an individual's reported willingness to pay to preserve a particular species would be significantly influenced by information about the species and its endangered status, with the expected result that the estimated values of wildlife conservation were indeed dependent on the information given. Hanley, Spash and Walker (1995) found that willingness to pay to preserve biodiversity increases significantly as the level of information provision increases, but at a decreasing rate.

The fact that responses vary with the information provided raises the question of how much information should be provided in a contingent valuation questionnaire. In general, the more fully informed respondents are, the better the valuation they should be able to make, but the need for information must be balanced with the need to keep surveys to a reasonable length and for the information to be easily comprehensible.

Enough information must be provided to enable the respondents to make sound choices (Fischhoff and Furby 1988). Bishop and Welsh (1992, p. 408) see a goal of contingent valuation as obtaining from a representative sample of the population 'the values that the population as a whole would express if it was more fully informed'. A well informed group of respondents should be better able to form and express preferences for the good in question.

Careful and extensive pretesting of the information to be presented in a contingent valuation field survey is recommended to ensure that respondents will be able to understand the material and interpret it as is intended (Arrow *et al.* 1993 and Kennedy 1994). Arrow *et al.* (1993) also recommend that there should be some evidence from the final survey that respondents have understood and accepted the contingent valuation scenario. This may, for example, involve intensive follow up questioning of a sample of the respondents.

It is generally considered that the more information there is and the more realistic a scenario is the more valid the responses will be (Gregory, Mendelsohn and Moore 1989). However, Kennedy (1994) suggests that in some cases it may not be realistic to expect respondents to be able to accurately differentiate between the many, complex policy options which are available. It may be better to construct a simpler scenario and adjust the estimated values obtained as appropriate for the different policy options. Carter (1992) found through focus group testing that respondents did indeed have difficulty in comprehending several forest management options and the resulting field survey used fewer and simpler scenarios.

Form of payment question

The way in which the willingness to pay (or willingness to accept) question is asked also appears to influence valuation results. One of the methods of questioning used is iterative bidding, where respondents bid up or down from a given starting point. There may be a problem of starting point bias here where respondents reassess their valuation to be more in line with the expectation of the interviewer as indicated by the starting point (Bennett 1981). Alternatively, if respondents are uncertain as to their valuation the starting point may be used as an indication of what an appropriate value is. Iterative bidding is now less commonly used than it was because of the starting point problem. However, the advantage of this method is that respondents are forced to reflect on their true value and are given the opportunity to revise their bids as they consider their value for the good.

The willingness to pay question may be asked directly, as in 'how much would you pay to ensure the survival of the takahe'? A variation on this is to provide a card with a range of values (a payment card) which the respondent is asked to use as a guide in choosing the amount they would pay. Payment cards may be unanchored, simply a range of values, or anchored, where tax or household expenditure items are indicated against the range of values. The anchored card is designed to make people consider their budget constraints. Boyle (1985) found payment cards anchored to household expenditure resulted in higher valuations than unanchored cards.

Direct elicitation of willingness to pay is also known as open-ended questioning or continuous valuation. Questions may also be closed; for example 'would you be prepared to pay $10 per year to preserve giant wetas?' This type of question is known variously as dichotomous choice, discrete choice, closed questioning or the take-it-or-leave-it approach. It is also known as the referendum approach when the payment question is presented as a yes or no vote to a proposed tax increase.

Discrete choice questioning is now the most commonly used format in contingent valuation studies. It is now often extended to a 'double-bounded' format by asking a second discrete choice price, depending on the response to the first price.

Significant differences have been found between the various approaches such as between discrete as opposed to continuous responses (Sellar, Stoll and Chavas 1985, Bennett 1981 and Hanley 1987) and iterative versus non-iterative bidding. In general, open-ended questions tend to give lower estimates of mean willingness to pay than the discrete choice approach (Dubgaard 1994, Kealy and Turner 1993, Kriström 1993, Li and Fredman 1995, Sellar, Stoll and Chavas 1985 and Walsh, Johnson and McKean 1989) although Kealy, Dovidio and Rockel (1988) find no difference.

Discrete response value estimates have been found to be comparable to those derived from other methods. Sellar, Stoll and Chavas (1985) obtained similar estimates from the discrete choice method and a travel cost evaluation and Heberlein and Bishop (1986) found similar results from a discrete choice format in both contingent markets and a simulated market with actual cash transactions. Walsh, Johnson and McKean (1989), in a meta-analysis of non-market valuation studies, found that benefit estimates from discrete choice contingent valuation studies are closer than estimates from open-ended contingent valuation studies to estimates from behaviour-based travel cost studies.

Hanemann (1994b) suggests that estimates from open-ended questions may be lower because even if people can state an amount they would be willing to pay, it is much more difficult to state the maximum amount, resulting in an underestimate of the maximum willingness to pay.

Payment mechanism or instrument bias

The method of payment specified in a contingent valuation survey may affect willingness to pay. If the respondent has a particular like or dislike for the method of payment chosen, or perceives it as unrealistic, they may not bid or may present an untrue bid. For example, people may object to paying for species conservation through increased taxes, but would be happy to pay a donation.

Many studies have found some instrument effect. For example, Bateman *et al.* (1993) tested two donation and one tax payment mechanisms in a study of an English wetland area and found the taxation method produced the more consistent results and had significantly fewer zero responses. They postulate that the taxation mechanism reduces the incentive to free ride. The presence of free riders may partly explain the lower mean estimates from the donation mechanism in this survey. A study by Rowe, d'Arge and Brookshire (1980) found respondents were willing to pay more to prevent deterioration in landscape values if payment method was an increase in income tax, rather than an entry fee to the particular site.

Hampicke *et al.* (1991) found that respondents were willing to pay more for general conservation of species if there is a general payment obligation, but found that respondents preferred to pay a private foundation rather than a public sector agency.

The difference in estimates from different payment mechanisms is not an unexpected result. It is well recognised that the way in which a good has been provided and paid for will affect willingness to pay.

Thus, from Mitchell and Carson:

> Respondents in a CV survey are not valuing levels of provision of an amenity in the abstract; they are valuing a policy which includes the conditions under which the amenity will be provided, and the way the public is likely to be asked for it (Arrow 1986, Kahneman 1986, Randall 1986). The notion that a public good does not have a value independent of its method of financing goes back at least to Wicksell, and is fully consistent with economic theory. (1989, p. 124)

It is important that the payment mechanism should be credible and, where possible, similar to payment systems used in practice. It should be appropriate to the institutional arrangements of the country or region where the contingent valuation survey is being carried out.

Questionnaire design and method

The way a survey is designed and presented, the way questions are framed and the method of survey used (for example, mail, face-to-face or telephone) can have a significant effect on both the quality of responses and the response rate (Dillman 1978, Hanley 1987 and Rowe and Chestnut 1983). Mail surveys tend to have a lower response rate, but have the advantages that there is no interviewer bias and that respondents can take as much time as they wish to consider their responses. Face-to-face interviews allow for the presentation of more complex information and a better assessment of how well the respondents have understood the scenarios presented.

Dillman (1978) provides detailed information on designing mail and telephone surveys, from questionnaire construction to the size of envelope which should be used. This method is known as the Total Design Method and is intended to elicit well thought out responses and maximum response rates. These issues are dealt with in depth in the literature on social surveys and market research (Mitchell and Carson 1989).

Non-response bias and aggregation

In any contingent valuation survey, not all the people who receive a questionnaire or those who are contacted for an interview will respond, which leaves open the possibility of non-response bias or sample selection bias. Non-response bias may arise if the respondents and non-respondents differ in the observable characteristics that influence willingness to pay (Whitehead, Groothuis and Blomquist 1993). Sample selection bias may occur if individuals who feel strongly about the amenity being valued are more likely to answer than those who do not (Fredman 1995). If such biases are present, simply aggregating the mean or median value estimates over the population will not give the correct result.

Mail surveys, particularly those designed to value off-site public good values, based on samples of the general population tend to have low response rates and are regarded as having a strong potential for non-response bias (Mitchell and Carson 1989). Loomis (1987a) records general population responses to contingent valuation mail surveys as low as 25 per cent with an average of 40 to 60 per cent in the US. Whitehead, Groothuis and Blomquist (1993) cite response rates of 20 to 60 per cent. European reponse rates tend to be higher (Kriström 1990).

Personal and telephone interviews get higher response rates than mail surveys, but these may still have non-response bias problems. Mail surveys of a select population, for example, hunters or recreators also tend to have higher response rates and as the population is more homogeneous than the general population aggregation is less likely to be a problem.

With less than a 100 per cent response rate, the problem becomes one of how to treat the non-respondents and how respondents differ from non-respondents. Various researchers using contingent valuation surveys have adopted different approaches including; firstly, to treat all non-respondents as zero value (Bishop and Boyle 1985); or alternatively to generalise directly from the sample to the whole population (assuming respondents reflect the general population). These extremes may give values either side of the 'true' value. Another approach may be to adjust sample values to account for differences between the sample population and the general population, using weighted least squares (DuMouchel and Duncan 1983, cited in Loomis 1987a).

More recently, several researchers have specifically tested for non-response and sample selection biases. Knowing if such biases occur and to what extent would enable correction of the aggregate estimates. However, the results of this research have been mixed so far. Whitehead, Groothuis and Blomquist (1993) used a combination telephone and mail survey to value conservation of a wetland area. They found no sample selection bias but there was some evidence of non-response bias. Dalecki, Whitehead and Blomquist (1993) also found a non-response effect.

Fredman (1995) and Mattson and Li (1994) used mail surveys with follow up surveys to test for non-response bias. Fredman (1995) concluded that there was no non-response bias and that people failed to respond because of general rather than survey specific reasons. Bostedt and Boman (1995) also concluded non-responses were largely due to general reasons. Mattson and Li (1994) found the value inferred from the individuals who responded was representative for the whole population.

A further issue with respect to aggregation is the 'extent of the market', that is, what population should the estimates be aggregated over. This is a particular problem with existence values as contact with a species or resource is not necessary to hold existence values for it. In the survey described in this book, for example, the population surveyed was adult Victorians, but it is quite likely that Australians in other states and even people overseas may have existence values for Victorian species. Restricting the survey to Victorians may well underestimate the value of protecting species in Victoria.

ESTIMATE RELIABILITY AND VALIDITY

The questions of validity and reliability have emerged as crucial issues in the debate about the usefulness of the contingent valuation method. 'Valid and reliable estimates of Hicksian surplus are essential for contingent valuation to be a useful method for estimating non-market values' (Reiling *et al.* 1990). The method is valid (or accurate) if it measures true willingness to pay and reliable if the estimates of value for the same good remain similar over repeated applications.

The validity of contingent valuation is very difficult to determine because the true values of any commodity, even those bought and sold in the market, is unknown (Smith 1992). The main way of inferring validity for contingent valuation studies has been to compare values derived from a contingent valuation survey with values for the same good derived from other valuation methods (hedonic pricing, travel cost models and simulated markets). These are presumed to give more valid estimates than the contingent valuation method as they are based on observed behaviour rather than hypothetical questions, but questions may also be raised about their validity (Carson *et al.* 1994b). Estimates from the travel cost and hedonic price methods can vary depending on the assumptions in their calculation, for example, functional form and how time is valued (Pearce and Markandya 1989).

There have been numerous examples of comparative studies. A selection of these studies includes Adamowicz and Graham-Tomasi (1991), Bishop, Heberlein and Kealy (1983), Brookshire and Coursey (1987), Kealy, Dovidio and Rockel (1988), Knetsch and Davis (1977), Sellar, Stoll and Chavas (1985) and Smith, Desvousges and Fisher (1986). Walsh, Johnson and McKean (1989) in a meta-analysis of studies of natural resource use for outdoor recreation compared results from travel cost and contingent valuation studies and found that in general contingent valuation results were slightly less than those from the travel cost method. Brookshire *et al.* (1982) obtained similar results from a hedonic price study and a contingent valuation survey of air quality. Carson *et al.* (1994b) reviewed 83 studies from which they made 616 comparisons of contingent valuation and revealed preference estimates. In general, the contingent valuation results were similar to but slightly lower than the revealed preference estimates and highly correlated with them.

Overall, these comparative studies show similarities in the values estimated from contingent valuation surveys and other methods. They are considered to support the contention that contingent valuation can provide reasonable estimates of the value of environmental goods, despite reservations about the validity of the other methods. A further check on the validity of contingent valuation is to compare contingent valuation estimates with actual markets, which has been discussed in the section on hypothetical bias above.

Internal validity can be assessed by regressing some form of the willingness to pay amount on the group of independent variables believed to be the determinants of the willingness to pay amount. If the sign and size of the coefficients are consistent with *a priori* expectations from the theory, the validity of the study is supported.

A second issue of concern is the reliability of contingent valuation studies. A contingent value 'is valid when it measures the correct theoretical construct, but it may not be reliable' (Reiling *et al.* 1990, p. 128). If contingent valuation studies are unreliable, considerable variation could be expected if a study were to be repeated several times. Few studies have investigated the issue of reliability (Reiling *et al.* 1990), with examples found in Kealy, Montgomery and Dovidio (1990), Loehman and De (1982), Loomis (1989, 1990) and Reiling *et al.* (1990). The conclusion from these studies is that the estimates of value produced from contingent valuation studies can be reliable.

THE STATE OF CONTINGENT VALUATION

The development of the contingent valuation technique has enabled the measurement of non-market values such as option and existence values. The addition of these values to the cost-benefit analysis of social programmes involving aspects of environmental conservation and conservation will improve the allocation of resources between development and conservation projects.

The contingent valuation method of estimating non-market values has now been applied for several decades. Some issues associated with its use have been resolved, but there is still controversy over its application. In particular, the use of contingent valuation to estimate passive use losses in damage assessment cases, where more precision is required than for most policy choices, has engendered considerable criticism (Desvousges *et al.* 1993a). Recent critical reviews of the contingent valuation technique include Cambridge Economics Inc. (1992), Cummings and Harrison (1992), Hausman (1993), Kahneman and Knetsch (1992a and 1992b) and Knetsch (1993).

In response to the controversy, the US National Oceanic and Atmospheric Administration (NOAA) 'convened a panel, headed by Nobel Laureates Kenneth Arrow and Robert Solow, to review the use of contingent valuation techniques for determining non-use value' in assessing natural damages under the US Oil Pollution Act 1990 (Larson 1992, p. 1114). The NOAA Panel reviewed all the major criticisms of the method. These were identified as:

1. The difficulty of external validation of contingent valuation results
2. Results that are inconsistent with the tenets of rational choice
3. Results that seem implausibly large in view of the many environmental goods which may need to be paid for
4. The few contingent valuation applications that remind respondents of budget constraints and substitute goods
5. Difficulties in communicating complex scenarios to respondents so that they understand and answer the question intended by the researchers
6. Issues of what population value estimates should be aggregated over
7. The 'warm glow' effect where respondents are expressing willingness to pay for the good feeling from giving rather than payment for the good in question.

After considering many submissions from both critics and proponents of the contingent valuation method, the NOAA Panel released a report (Arrow *et al.* 1993) with the Panel's findings and recommendations. The Panel concluded that the drawbacks of contingent valuation could be overcome sufficiently to provide information adequate for use in damage assessment cases, provided the studies followed a comprehensive set of guidelines spelt out in the Appendix to the report. Some of the conditions specified in the report are as follows:

> These require that respondents be carefully informed about the particular environmental damage to be valued, and about the full extent of substitutes and undamaged alternatives available. In willingness to pay scenarios, the payment vehicle must be presented fully and clearly, with the relevant budget constraint emphasised. The payment scenario should be convincingly described, preferably in a referendum context, because most respondents will have had experience with referendum ballots with less than perfect background information. Where choices in formulating the CV instrument can be made, we urge they lean in the conservative direction, as a partial or total offset to the likely tendency to exaggerate willingness to pay. (Arrow *et al.* 1993, p. 4610)

Arrow *et al.* also recommended careful and extensive pretesting and use of focus groups to ensure respondents would understand and interpret the survey questions as the researchers intended. Where these conditions are met, Arrow *et al.* make a strong recommendation in support of the use of contingent valuation methods in estimating non-use values.

In general, it can be concluded that contingent valuation methods will produce results which can be replicated, are consistent with demand theory and are consistent with results from other methods such as travel cost and hedonic pricing. Bishop and Heberlein (1986) argue that although a number of methodological issues remain to be resolved, contingent valuation is capable of providing policy relevant information in many environmental and conservation circumstances.

Most contingent valuation research to date has focussed on methodological issues. However, in recent years an additional school of criticism has been emerging which is concerned with whether individuals respond to contingent valuation questions as 'consumers' or as 'citizens' (Blamey and Common 1992 for an overview of this literature, also Cicchetti and Wilde 1992, Sagoff 1988 and Stevens *et al.* 1991).

Contingent valuation literature to date has regarded respondents as consumers, with the assumption that they will maximise their own utility and generally behave in a 'rational' economic manner. It is, however, entirely possible that respondents may support a proposed change that will reduce their personal welfare if they believe it will benefit the community as a whole. That is, they will act as 'citizens' in the public interest, rather than as selfish individuals. If this is the case, it is inappropriate to compare 'citizen' contingent valuation values with 'consumer' values for the alternative possibilities (Blamey and Common 1992). Stevens *et al.* (1991) present the same kind of argument but with different terminology. They propose that respondents may have egoistic (consumer) and ethical (citizen) preferences. They suggest their contingent valuation study 'may have asked people to choose between ordinary goods (income) and a moral principle' (Stevens *et al.* 1991 p. 399).

If respondents to contingent valuation surveys do respond as citizens, it does not mean such surveys will not give meaningful and useful results, but it may not be appropriate to use the results in conventional cost benefit analysis and damage assessment evaluations (Blamey and Common 1992). It would be a useful area of future research to follow up this line of argument and to examine respondents' motivations for their answers to willingness to pay questions and to examine the quality and nature of their decision making processes (Blamey and Common 1992).

If the 'citizen' hypothesis holds it may explain some of the problems of contingent valuation such as the apparent inconsistency with the usual assumptions on preference ordering (Stevens *et al.* 1991). It may also contribute to the growing preference for referendum style contingent valuation studies, which are perceived to produce more accurate preference revelations.

Spash and Hanley (1995) and Spash (1993) suggest that a significant proportion of individuals hold what are termed as lexicographic preferences, that is, they 'refuse to make trade offs which require the substitution of biodiversity [or a species] for other goods' (Spash and Hanley 1995, p. 191).

In a contingent valuation study on biodiversity, Spash and Hanley (1995, p. 191) defined respondents 'who stated that animals/ecosystems/plants should be protected irrespective of the costs and who refused to give a WTP amount' as having lexicographic preferences. About one quarter of their respondents fell into this category. Stevens *et al.* (1991) found a similar proportion of respondents had such preferences. If significant proportions of the population do hold lexicographic preferences, the use of benefit cost analysis in decision making could become problematic.

CONCLUSIONS

The development of the contingent valuation method over the last thirty years has been one of the major theoretical innovations in the field of resource and environmental economics. The developments in this field promise much for species conservation policy, an area characterised by hard to value benefits.

However, a range of methodological issues remain to be resolved and much of the recent research in contingent valuation has focussed on these rather than on the values of particular goods. This book is intended to add to the methodological research.

7. Estimating Changes in Welfare from Discrete Choice Surveys

INTRODUCTION

This chapter deals with the theoretical and empirical issues underlying the contingent valuation approach known as discrete choice, which is used in this study. This method is also known as dichotomous choice, closed-ended questioning, the take-it-or-leave-it approach or the referendum approach.

The discrete choice valuation format is described in this chapter and its advantages discussed. Issues relating to survey design and the estimation of welfare measures from the data obtained from such surveys are reviewed.

DISCRETE CHOICE RESPONSE ANALYSIS

In the discrete valuation format, the attributes of an environmental good and the anticipated changes in the good are described to the respondent. The respondent is then asked whether or not they would pay (or accept) a specified sum for the described change. A range of prices is specified, chosen to include the expected maximum willingness to pay of most respondents. These sums are randomly assigned to respondents so that each sum is given to an equivalent sub-sample (Mitchell and Carson 1989).

The discrete choice method of contingent valuation, which has become increasingly popular, was first used by Bishop and Heberlein (1979, 1980) to estimate the value of goose hunting in Wisconsin. Subsequent studies have included those by Boyle and Bishop (1989), Loehman and De (1982), Loomis (1987b) and Sellar, Stoll and Chavas (1985). Comprehensive reviews of the technique and particular applications are given in Cummings, Brookshire and Schulze (1986) and in Mitchell and Carson (1989).

Hanemann (1984) developed the link between economic theory and the discrete choice approach. Establishment of this utility-theoretic foundation contributed a great deal to the increasing use of the technique. Cameron and James (1987) and Cameron (1988) offered an alternative approach to estimation which focuses directly on the distribution of willingness to pay.

There are several advantages with the discrete choice method that help account for its application to a wide range of environmental issues. It is simple to administer and is particularly suitable for mail and telephone surveys. Respondents have to answer only 'yes' or 'no' to a specified dollar amount, a situation similar to most day-to-day market transactions. It is probably easier for respondents to decide if a particular value for an environmental good is too high or too low than to come up with a precise monetary estimate themselves (Boyle 1985, Hanemann 1994a and Loomis 1990). Bateman *et al.* (1995) conclude that respondents experience less uncertainty answering discrete choice questions than open-ended ones. Loomis (1990) concluded willingness to pay estimates from discrete choice studies are at least as reliable (that is, can be replicated) as when respondents directly state their willingness to pay.

The discrete choice method is considered to be not as prone to strategic bias as open-ended (continuous) valuation methods (Kriström 1990a, Loomis 1987b, Mitchell and Carson 1989 and Zeckhauser 1973). Hoehn and Randall (1987) show theoretically that discrete choice willingness to pay surveys can be designed so that there are no incentives for respondents to misstate their preferences. Harrison (1993) believes that the discrete choice format provides incentives to respond truthfully in real situations, but that in hypothetical situations it provides no incentives at all, either to lie or to tell the truth. Although strategic bias is generally not considered to be a problem in discrete choice surveys, Mitchell and Carson (1989) note that this method may be subject to a 'non zero background level of yea saying'.

According to Mitchell and Carson, 'yea' saying is the tendency of some respondents to agree with an interviewer's request regardless of what they, the respondent, believe. Thus, in the discrete choice format there may be an indeterminate percentage of those who accept the price only because their tendency to yea saying overcomes their unwillingness to accept that price. 'It is the discrete choice analogue of starting point bias but is somewhat harder to detect' (Mitchell and Carson 1989, p. 101). This is akin to compliance bias, that is, trying to 'please' the interviewer. It is unlikely to be a great problem in mail surveys where the respondent is not faced by an interviewer.

Another disadvantage of the discrete choice method is that it is inefficient relative to other methods in that many more observations are needed for the same level of statistical precision, because only a discrete indicator of maximum willingness to pay is obtained instead of the actual amount (Mitchell and Carson 1989). However, although a single discrete choice question is statistically inefficient, the use of a second linked discrete choice question (double bounded) can substantially improve efficiency (Hanemann, Loomis and Kanninen 1991).

The statistical procedures required to analyse discrete choice data are more complicated than for other methods (Boyle 1985 and Sellar, Stoll and Chavas

1985). There is also no clear consensus on the best way to derive summary statistics, such as mean and median values, for willingness to pay (Kriström 1990a). A further difficulty is the design of the bid vector, that is, the range of prices given to respondents and the intervals within that range.

The most serious difficulty with the discrete choice method is the selection of a general model for analysis and the functional specification of that model, in particular the necessity to make assumptions about how to parametrically specify either the valuation function or the indirect utility function to obtain mean willingness to pay (Mitchell and Carson 1989). These issues are discussed further in the following sections.

DESIGN OF THE BID VECTOR

In discrete choice contingent valuation surveys a range of bids or prices is used, with each respondent being given one price. Thus, it must be decided how many bids to use, the lowest and highest bids, how the bids should be spaced and what proportion of respondents should be offered each bid.

Most studies seem to use about ten bid amounts (Loomis *pers. comm.* 1993), although some use 15 to 20, chosen in an *ad hoc* way (Kriström 1994), with each price offered to an equal proportion of respondents.

It has been found that the range, intervals and number of prices offered in a discrete choice survey can affect the estimates of value of the good (Cooper and Loomis 1992). Specifying the upper range is important. If the range of bids does not cover most of the values respondents are likely to hold, it becomes difficult to determine how the bid function approaches the asymptote at high values and estimates of mean value may be difficult to make. Boman and Bostedt (1995) conclude that if less than 10 per cent of respondents answer yes to the highest bid, then the bid vector has captured the range of willingness to pay distribution well.

Cooper and Loomis (1992) investigated the effects of varying bid design on the estimates of value from three studies. They studied the effect of removing bid values from the upper and lower ranges of the bid vector and specified wider bid intervals. All the changes had some effect, but other than a reduced mean estimate with removal of upper bids, there was no clear *a priori* direction of change. Duffield and Patterson (1991) found that the estimate of mean willingness to pay was sensitive to how the total sample size was allocated among the different amounts.

Kanninen and Kriström (1993) found that the bid values in the tails increased the variances of the estimators and hence of the willingness to pay estimates. They concluded that if the true distribution is logistic, any bias would be fairly small provided the middle of the distribution is adequately covered and more than 50 per cent of the distribution is covered.

There is an increasing focus in research on more formal means of finding an optimal bid design, for example Cooper 1993 and Kanninen (1993). Nyquist (1991) and Johansson, Kriström and Nyquist (1994) provide some methodology to improve bid design. Johansson, Kriström and Mäler (1995) and Kriström (1994) present a range of design criteria based on biometric techniques. In the absence of formal statistical design, pre-testing of questionnaires in order to establish the range of values likely to be held by respondents can do much to assist in setting a reasonable range of bids.

UTILITY MAXIMISATION AND DISCRETE CHOICE ANALYSIS

Hanemann (1984) first addressed the issue of how to formulate models for the analysis of discrete choice surveys which are consistent with the hypothesis of utility maximisation. Hanemann's work drew on the random utility model developed in the transportation literature (Boyle 1985, Cameron 1988, Kriström 1990a and McFadden 1976). Hanemann's methodology 'explicitly recognises the utility-maximising choice underlying the individuals' responses to the experiment' (Hanemann 1984 p. 332). The portion of Hanemann's methodology which is relevant to the analysis in this book is described below. Hanemann derived measures for both Hicksian compensating and equivalent surplus measures, but as the survey here is concerned with estimating willingness to pay to avoid a loss, only the equivalent measures are presented.

Essentially, discrete choice responses can be interpreted as a utility maximising process. Thus, the individual will choose the outcome (out of the two offered) which will give the greatest amount of satisfaction. 'A crucial assumption is that, although the individual knows his utility function with certainty, it contains some components which are unobservable' to the analyst (Hanemann 1984, p. 338). These are given by a random error term with expected value of zero (Bowker and Stoll 1988 and Hanemann 1984).

The following theoretical framework has been developed from Hanemann (1984). Individuals are assumed to have utility functions which include arguments such as: income y; state of nature with (z^1) or without (z^0) endangered species z; and a vector of household characteristics s. It is assumed that individuals know which state they prefer. The utility function is:

$$U(z,y;s) \text{ so that } \Delta U \text{ is } U(z^1,y;s) - U(z^0,y;s) \qquad (7.1)$$

where ΔU is the change in utility following a change in the state of nature.

Since some components of the utility function are unobservable to the analyst, it is rewritten:

$$U(z,y;s) = V(z,y;s) + \varepsilon \qquad (7.2)$$

and

$$U(z^1,y;s) - U(z^0,y;s) = (V(z^1,y;s) + \varepsilon_1) - (V(z^0,y;s) + \varepsilon_0) \qquad (7.3)$$

Here ε_1 and ε_0 are independent and identically distributed random variables with zero means. Utility is treated as a random variable with a parametric probability distribution having mean $V(z,y;s)$ and a stochastic component ε.

A respondent will agree to pay a price A to avoid a change in z $(z^1 - z^0)$ if:

$$V(z^1,y-A;s) + \varepsilon_1 \geq V(z^0,y;s) + \varepsilon_0 \qquad (7.4)$$

and refuse it otherwise.

The individual respondent knows with certainty which choice maximises utility, but for the researcher the individual's response is a random variable with a probability distribution given by:

$$P_1 \equiv \Pr\{\text{individual willing to pay}\}$$

$$= \Pr\{V(z^1,y-A;s) + \varepsilon_1 \geq V(z^0,y;s) + \varepsilon_0\} \qquad (7.5)$$

and

$$P_0 = \Pr\{\text{individual unwilling to pay}\} = 1-P_1$$

Defining $\eta = \varepsilon_1 - \varepsilon_0$ with $F\eta(.)$ denoting the cumulative distribution function (c.d.f.) of η, the willingness to pay probability may be defined as:

$$P_1 = F\eta(\Delta V) \text{ where } \Delta V \text{ is the utility difference:}$$

$$\Delta V \equiv V(z^1,y-A;s) - V(z^0,y;s). \qquad (7.6)$$

It is necessary to assume a distribution function for the random variable η. The most common approach is to assume the two variables ε_1 and ε_0 are independent and identically distributed random variables with a Weibull distribution (Boyle 1985). The difference between two Weibull random variables has a logistic cumulative distribution function (Domencich and McFadden 1975). The alternative is to assume a normal distribution where $F\eta(.)$ is the standard normal cumulative distribution function, which requires analysis using a probit model (Hanemann 1984).

The logistic model was preferred because it is computationally simpler (Cameron 1988 and Sellar, Stoll and Chavas 1985), but this is no longer a problem with the many acceptable computer packages available. It also seems that in empirical applications there is little difference between the two models (Boyle 1985, Cameron 1988 and Maddala 1983).

The linear probability model could be used, but is not because of the possibility of probability predictions outside the zero to one range (Pindyck and Rubinfield 1976, Sellar, Chavas and Stoll 1986 and Wohlers and Vlastuin 1990).

Assuming a logistic distribution, the probability of a yes response can be written as (Hanemann 1984, p. 334):

$$\Pr\{yes\} = (1 + e^{-\Delta V})^{-1} \text{ which also equals } F\eta(\Delta V) \qquad (7.7)$$

This formulation can be used for calculation of expected willingness to pay following specification of the utility difference.

An equivalent formulation for the probability of a yes answer is to consider the cumulative distribution function of the random willingness to pay variable itself, written as $G_{WTP}(A)$. This function gives the probability that $WTP \leq A$. Therefore, $1-G_{WTP}(A)$ gives the probability that $A < WTP$ and the respondent will accept the suggested price A (Kriström 1990a, p. 64).

Equating the two definitions for the probability of acceptance gives:

$$\Pr\{yes\} \equiv F\eta(\Delta V(A)) = 1-G_{WTP}(A) \qquad (7.8)$$

This formulation indicates that the fitting of the binary response model: $P_1 = F\eta(\Delta V)$ can be interpreted as estimating the parameters of the distribution function $G_{WTP}(A)$ (Hanemann 1984, p. 336). It also aids with the interpretation and graphical illustration of the two welfare measures, mean (E+) and median (E*) (Figure 7.1).

Pr (probability of a yes response)

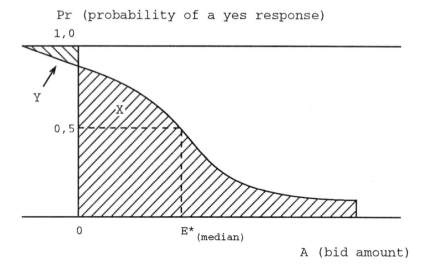

Figure 7.1   *Cumulative distribution function when willingness to pay can take positive and negative values, E^+ (mean) = area X - area Y.*

Pr (probability of a yes response)

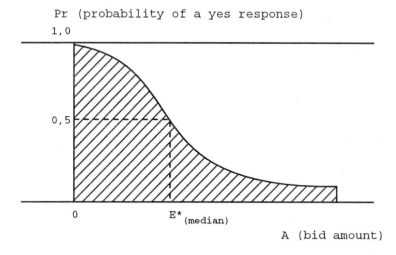

Figure 7.2   *Cumulative distribution function when willingness to pay takes non-negative values only, E^+ = area under the c.d.f.*

WELFARE MEASURES

Hanemann (1984) discusses the possible welfare measures from discrete response surveys in detail. Essentially in the willingness to pay situation there are two utility theoretic measures of equivalent surplus, the mean (E+) and the median (E*).

The Mean

The mean is calculated as the expected willingness to pay. Following Kriström (1990a), willingness to pay of the ith individual is defined as the cost A_i that satisfies equation (7.9), that is, the cost A_i that turns the inequality in equation (7.4) into an equality.

$$V(z^1,y-WTP;s)+\varepsilon_1=V(z^0,y;s)+\varepsilon_0 \tag{7.9}$$

Equations (7.10), (7.11) and (7.12) are derived from Boyle, Welsh and Bishop 1988, Johansson, Kriström and Mäler 1989, Hanemann 1989b and Kriström 1990a. To compute the expected value of willingness to pay it is necessary to use the fact that for any random variable X belonging to the set of real numbers with cumulative distribution F, it can be shown that:

$$E(X)=\int_0^\infty(1-F(X))dX-\int_{-\infty}^0 F(X)dX \tag{7.10}$$

so that:

$$E(WTP)=\int_0^\infty(1-G_{WTP}(A))dA-\int_{-\infty}^0 G_{WTP}(A)dA \tag{7.11}$$

and

$$E(WTP)=\int_0^\infty F\eta(\Delta V(A)dA-\int_{-\infty}^0(1-F\eta(\Delta V(A))dA \tag{7.12}$$

Thus mean willingness to pay values are calculated by integrating the area under each estimated logit function over the range - ∞ to ∞ or 0 to ∞ (Figure 7.1).

Equation (7.12) and Figure 7.1 apply when the willingness to pay variable can take both positive and negative values. This is quite plausible in many situations, for example, forestry companies and their employees may face an economic loss if forestry activities are restricted to preserve species. In other cases, such as Bowker and Stolls' study of the whooping crane (1988), and Boyle's study of bald eagles (1985), it does not seem likely that people would pay to remove the species.

In cases where willingness to pay can take only non-negative values the appropriate formula is:

$$\int_0^\infty (1 - G_{WTP}(A))dA = \int_0^\infty F\eta(\Delta V(A))dA \qquad (7.13)$$

That is, the second term of equations (7.11) and (7.12) is not required. This is illustrated in Figure 7.2.

The Median

The median is represented by E* in Figure 7.1. The median is a cost such that the probability of acceptance is 0.5. That is, the median individual is indifferent between the choice of paying E* to stay at z^1 and the occurrence of state z^0: or

$$\Pr\{V(z^1,y-E^*;s) + \varepsilon_1 \geq V(z^0,y;s) + \varepsilon_0 \} = 0.5 \qquad (7.14)$$

The Mean Versus Median Controversy

There is some debate in the literature as to which is the appropriate welfare measure to use in aggregating discrete choice contingent valuation results, the mean or the median. There are advantages and disadvantages to both.

Statistically the median has some advantages as it is a much more robust measure of central tendency. The mean is very sensitive to perturbations caused by errors in the data or unusual observations (Hanemann 1984), to different specifications of the function $F\eta$ (Kriström 1990a) and even to minor differences in the method of estimating the structural model, such as generalised least squares or maximum likelihood (Hanemann 1989b, p. 1060).

Truncation of the range of integration of the cumulative distribution function at a maximum less than infinity may also have a large effect on the estimate of the mean, but much less on the median. Bowker and Stoll (1988), Hanemann (1989b) and Kriström (1990a) give illustrations of variations in mean estimates.

On the other hand, although the median may be less sensitive with respect to skewness in the distribution, one can expect the distribution of willingness to pay values to be skewed and thus the median may not be the ideal measure of central tendency (Boyle, Welsh and Bishop 1988).

From the standpoint of economic theory, the choice between the mean and median represents a 'value judgement' (Hanemann 1984, p. 337). Bowker and Stoll (1988) and Boyle, Welsh and Bishop (1988) argue that the use of the median does not reflect the values of those individuals who have the most to gain or lose. Using the median ignores the 'small proportion of the citizenry who legitimately value the good highly. This arbitrary choice is akin to throwing out outliers which are not in fact outliers, a procedure which would lead to undervaluation of the item being considered' by deleting legitimate high values (Bowker and Stoll 1988 p. 375).

Kriström (1990a, p. 71) notes that aggregating a median estimate does not have 'the natural interpretation available for the mean estimate. Multiplying the mean estimate with the population size gives the total value, but no such interpretation can be given to the median'. Johansson, Kriström and Mäler (1989) argue that the mean should be the preferred measure because the mean is consistent with Pareto efficiency, whereas, in general, the median is not. If the final objective is to aggregate costs and benefits for a cost benefit analysis, then the mean value is the appropriate measure, implying adoption of the Kaldor-Hicks potential compensation criterion (Harrison and Kriström 1995). The median would be the relevant concept if the outcome is to be interpreted as the result of a referendum (Johansson, Kriström and Mäler 1989 and Imber, Stevenson and Wilks 1991).

Hanemann defends the choice of the median measure on both statistical grounds and also for aggregation over the population. Use of the median for aggregation gives a social choice rule corresponding to majority voting. Other percentiles, for example, two thirds, could also be used. Conventional economic practice is to use the mean, but the choice of welfare measure (social choice rule) is an ethical judgement (Hanemann 1989b).

Hanley (1987) notes that use of either the mean or median estimate for aggregation implies an equal weighting of bids, which in turn implies use of a social welfare function which places equal weight on the utility of all individuals. This procedure is consistent with common practice in cost benefit analysis.

TRUNCATION AT HIGH VALUES

It is common in discrete choice contingent valuation studies to truncate the range of values over which the cumulative distribution function is integrated, either at the highest price offered (Bishop and Heberlein 1979 and 1980, Bowker and Stoll 1988 and Sellar, Stoll and Chavas 1985) or at some other level such as the 90th percentile (Bowker and Stoll 1988, Boyle 1985 and Boyle and Bishop 1988).

The reasons for truncation and the level at which it is chosen to truncate are seldom articulated. Truncation appears to be justified on the grounds that since the tail of the estimated distribution is an artifact of the range of offers, it is not possible to predict how fast the tail actually approaches the axis beyond the highest data point (Boyle 1985 and Boyle and Bishop 1988).

The upper tail may not approach the axis as fast as expected, giving rise to a fat tail which will increase the estimate of the mean if integration is carried out over the range zero to infinity (Bowker and Stoll 1988). If the range of integration is truncated, the estimate of the mean will be sensitive to which point is chosen (Bateman *et al.* 1995). A graphical representation of the problem is given in Figure 7.3.

Boyle, Welsh and Bishop (1988) argue that if it is necessary to truncate the range of integration, there are problems with the cumulative distribution function. The original range and distribution of prices is inadequate to include what most people are actually prepared to pay. Obviously it is impossible and unreasonable to have offers to infinity, but ideally, the proportion of respondents prepared to pay the highest prices asked in the survey would be close to zero. Boyle, Welsh and Bishop have developed a sampling procedure, known as the method of 'complementary random numbers', which appears to minimise the potential for the estimated cumulative distribution functions having fat tails (Boyle, Welsh and Bishop 1988, p. 97).

In general, it is preferable to avoid truncation. Boyle, Welsh and Bishop (1988) and Hanemann (1984, 1989b) recommend that integration should be carried out over the range zero to infinity (where willingness to pay is non-negative) or minus infinity to infinity where negative responses are possible. Bateman *et al.* (1995, p. 177) also favour a 'truncation approach which eliminates the negative sums implied by the bid function and integrates beyond the upper accepted bid level to some logical limit' such as an income constraint or infinity.

If truncation is necessary to obtain meaningful estimates (Boyle and Bishop 1988) the estimated cumulative distribution functions must be normalised prior to computing the expected values, that is the area under the corresponding probability distribution function must be equal to one. The normalising procedure is described in Boyle, Welsh and Bishop (1988 p. 95). It is better to avoid the fat tails problem by careful pre-testing to establish an appropriate range of bids and design of the bid vector as any truncation is arbitrary.

ESTIMATION PROCEDURES

There are a number of estimation procedures to obtain estimates of mean and median willingness to pay from discrete choice data, both parametric and non-parametric. Other useful expositions of estimation procedures are found in Bateman and Willis (forthcoming), Johansson, Kriström and Mäler (1995), Kriström (1990a) and Li (1994). The first group of methods outlined below are parametric methods which differ in the model specification. Four approaches to model specification are discussed in this section.

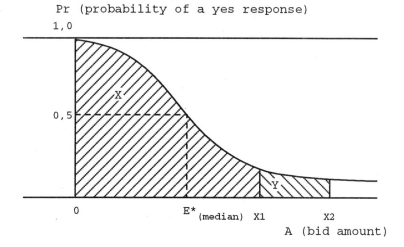

Pr (probability of a yes response)

Figure 7.3   *Effect on the estimate of the mean of truncating the range of integration. $E1^+$ (truncated mean) = area X if truncated at X1. $E2^+$ = areas X + Y if truncated at X2.*

Parametric Specifications

Initially, it must be decided which variables are to be included in the utility function. Then, an appropriate functional specification for these variables must be modelled.

Ad hoc specification - Bishop and Heberlein

Bishop and Heberlein specified a logit model of the form:

$$P_1 = F\eta(\Delta V)$$

(7.15)

where

$$\Delta V = \delta_0 + \delta_1 \ln A$$

(7.16)

This specification is not compatible with any explicit utility model, but can be treated as an approximation to a utility difference (Hanemann 1984). Other analysts have used similar specifications for estimating expected willingness to pay (Bowker and Stoll 1988 and Boyle and Bishop 1988). Equations for estimating mean willingness to pay using this specification are given by Hanemann (1984).

Specifications consistent with utility theory - Hanemann
Hanemann (1984) argues for the use of economic theory to guide specification, as opposed to *ad hoc* permutations and derives such specifications in detail in his 1984 paper. Equations for the willingness to pay situation (following Hanemann) are presented below.

For willingness to accept equations see Hanemann (1984). For the model given in (6), Hanemann defined two welfare functions consistent with utility theory, one linear and one log linear. The linear version is:

$$V(j,y;s)=\alpha_j+\beta_y \qquad (7.17)$$

where
$$\beta>0; \ j = 0,1 \text{ and } y \text{ is income.}$$
and

$$\Delta V=(\alpha_0-\alpha_1)-\beta A \qquad (7.18)$$

The logarithmic version is:

$$V(j,y;s)=\alpha_j+\beta \ln y \qquad (7.19)$$

where $\beta>0$; $j = 0,1$ and y is income and where,

$$\Delta V=(\alpha_1-\alpha_0)+\beta \ln(1-\frac{A}{y}) \qquad (7.20)$$

The welfare measures corresponding to these models are given by the equations below, where willingness to pay is unrestricted. In the case of the linear model, with no income effect, the compensating and equivalent measures are the same and the mean and median coincide, that is:
$$E^+ = E^* = C^+ = C^* \qquad (7.21)$$
The formula for calculation of these measures is:

$$E^+ = E^* = (\alpha_1 - \alpha_0)/\beta \text{ or } \alpha/\beta \text{ where } \alpha = (\alpha_1 - \alpha_0) \qquad (7.22)$$

This formulation can be interpreted as saying the 'average willingness to pay is obtained as the utility change, represented by α, converted into monetary terms by division with the marginal utility of money β'. (Kriström 1990a, p. 67)

For the logarithmic model, equivalent and compensating measures are different, as are the mean and median.

The median is given by:
$$E^* = y - ye^{\alpha/\beta} \tag{7.23}$$
where $\alpha = (\alpha_0 - \alpha_1)$ and the mean by:
$$E^+ = y - ye^{\alpha/\beta} E\{e^{\eta/\beta}\} \tag{7.24}$$

The parameters α and β are usually computed using logistic regression. In this process, $\ln(\Pi_i/(1-\Pi_i)$ is regressed on A_i where (Π_i) is the proportion of yes answers. (Kriström 1990a, p. 68). For the linear-in-income model, it can be shown that integration is unnecessary to obtain the expected willingness-to-pay (Kriström 1990a, pp 68-70 provides a proof).

Many studies have used the model specifications proposed by Hanemann (Bowker and Stoll 1988, Boyle 1985, Boyle and Bishop 1984, 1985, 1988 and Sellar, Chavas and Stoll 1986, among others). However, it has been observed that the utility-theoretic specifications of Hanemann do not perform as well in practice as some *ad hoc* specifications (Boyle and Bishop 1988).

Sellar, Chavas and Stoll (1986) found some specifications resulted in estimated coefficients which gave upwardly sloping demand functions. Boyle and Bishop (1988) also found that Hanemann's specifications did not give statistically significant coefficients and sometimes yielded coefficients with wrong signs. Using an *ad hoc* specification similar to that of Bishop, Heberlein and Kealy (1983), with only an index of scenic beauty and the natural logarithm of the offers as explanatory variables, Boyle and Bishop (1988) generated significant coefficients with signs meeting *a priori* expectations.

Bowker and Stoll (1988) also used Hanemann's specifications and an *ad hoc* model. The goodness-of-fit measures they used were similar for all models, although best for the *ad hoc* specification. Boyle and Bishop (1988) used the two Hanemann specifications and a third model and obtained nearly identical measures of goodness-of-fit for all three models, but markedly different expected values.

The logarithmic model yielded expected values in the order of three times greater than the linear model. Bowker and Stoll also achieved quite different measures of economic value from their different specifications, although when the highest offer amount was used as a truncation point, comparable values were obtained from the best of the utility-theoretic models and the *ad hoc* logarithmic model.

Distribution of willingness to pay - Cameron
A third approach has been developed by Cameron (1988). This approach focuses on the distribution of willingness-to-pay directly, without estimating a utility function. Willingness-to-pay is assumed to have a logistic distribution and estimates of G_{WTP} are derived via censored logistic regression (Kriström

1990b). Cameron (1988) argues that this approach is more flexible than the random utility method developed by Hanemann. By avoiding the utility function entirely, the parameters for inverse Hicksian demand functions can be estimated directly and simply. The approach is described in detail in Cameron (1988) and McConnell (1990).

In Hanemann's model, the response depends on the level of indirect utility in both states and the stochastic element is attached to the utility functions (McConnell 1990). Cameron's (1988) interpretation of responses is based on expenditure functions, with the individual calculating their willingness to pay and comparing it to the price asked in the survey. This gives rise to a variation (McConnell 1990) or valuation (Cameron 1988) function, specified as the sum of stochastic and deterministic parts. Thus, main distinction between the two models is in where the stochastic component is appended (McConnell 1990).

If marginal utility of income is assumed to be constant, that is, independent of income, constant across states of the experiment and constant across individuals in the sample, the two models will be the same. If the first two conditions hold, but marginal utility of income is not constant across individuals, the deterministic parts will be the same, but the stochastic components will differ (McConnell 1990).

Cameron's approach overcomes the limitation of Hanemann's method in handling complex utility functions. However, with Cameron's approach it is not known if the choice is consistent with economic theory. 'McConnell has shown that the two models are dual to each other and that neither model is clearly preferred' (Ready and Hu, undated, p. 2). The choice of method depends on the interpretation preferred by the analyst, as the methods seem to give similar results.

The approaches to estimation of willingness to pay described above are all parametric approaches. That is, an attempt is made to fit a functional form such as Weibull, exponential or log-normal to the data using maximum likelihood regression techniques. The advantage of parametric methods is that they enable regression of behavioural, attitudinal and demographic characteristics with the willingness to pay variable. The drawback to a parametric approach is that it is necessary to make an assumption about the shape of the distribution and hence the functional form of the willingness to pay curve. Different assumptions give different results, as discussed above.

Spike Models

The parametric models described above have the disadvantage that the distributional assumptions made do not allow for respondents to have zero willingness to pay, whereas in fact it is quite likely that this may occur (Kriström 1995).

Johansson, Kriström and Nyquist (1994) have developed a parametric 'spike' model which can deal with such zero responses. This method recognises distinct groups of possible answers - those who have a positive willingness to pay and those who have a zero willingness to pay. The model can also be extended to include people who have negative willingness to pay values. The method is clearly described in Kriström (1995) and Johansson, Kriström and Mäler (1995).

In the non-negative formulation of the spike model, it is assumed that the distribution function of the willingness to pay has the form shown below (following Kriström 1995, p. 4).

$$F_{wtp}(A) = 0 \qquad \text{if } A < 0$$
$$F_{wtp}(A) = p \qquad \text{if } A = 0$$
$$F_{wtp}(A) = G_{wtp}(A) \qquad \text{if } A > 0$$

Where $p \, \varepsilon \, (0,1)$ and $G_{wtp}(A)$ is a continuous and increasing function such that $G_{wtp}(0){=}p$ and $\lim_{A \to \infty} G_{wtp}(A){=}1$. The probability that a person is willing to pay a positive sum of money not exceeding A is therefore $G_{wtp}(A){-}p$. Thus, there is a jump discontinuity at zero.

Non-parametric Estimation - Kriström

Willingness to pay estimates can also be made using a non-parametric estimator, which removes the need to make any distributional assumptions. Two studies which have used non-parametric approaches in addition to parametric analysis are Imber, Stevenson and Wilks (1991) and Kriström (1990a and 1990b). The method developed by Kriström 'relates to utility theory via a first order approximation argument, as the probabilities (of a yes or no answer) will depend only on the size of the bid'. (Kriström 1990a, p. 87). Essentially the method uses the sequence of proportions of 'yes' responses for each bid, by convention beginning with the lowest bid. Thus;

> Ayer et al. (1955) show that if the sequence of proportions forms a monotonic non-increasing sequence of proportions, then this sequence provides a distribution free maximum likelihood estimator of the probability of acceptance. (Kriström 1990b, p. 137)

In a very large sample survey, the proportions of 'yes' bids would be expected to be strictly decreasing as the size of the bid increased. However, this is not likely to be so for a smaller sample. If the initial sequence is not monotonic, it can be transformed via an algorithm (Ayer *et al.* 1955) to a monotonic one. The transformed sequence of probabilities is graphed against the offer amounts to form a survivor curve. The mean is calculated as the area bounded by the survivor function and the median is the bid at which the probability of a 'yes' response is 0.5. In an application of this technique, Kriström (1990b) obtained similar expected values from the non-parametric estimator as from using the Bishop and Heberlein method.

Minimum Legal Willingness to Pay

Harrison and Kriström (1995) propose another method of estimation based on the interpretation of the tax price (bid) offered to each respondent as a 'minimal legal willingness to pay'. That is, if a respondent agrees to pay a price of $20 this can be regarded as a 'contract' between, for example, the government and the respondent and this is the amount that should be attributed to that respondent.

This interpretation enables a simple calculation of expected willingness to pay. The probability of asking a particular bid is multiplied by the probability of a 'yes' response multiplied by the bid amount and summed over all bid amounts.

ANALYSIS OF ZERO RESPONSES

One of the crucial issues in the analysis of contingent valuation studies is how to deal with those respondents who give a zero valuation of the good in question. There is a general belief that because of the unfamiliar and hypothetical nature of the surveys, some people who in fact have a positive value for the good in question will give a bid of zero for strategic reasons (Römer 1992). For example, if the respondent believes there will be a positive correlation between the survey results and an actual payment obligation they may have an incentive to understate their true valuation. Alternatively, some respondents may object to the idea of putting a monetary valuation on environmental commodities and bid zero as a protest, even though they may have a positive valuation.

Freeman (1986, pp 152-153) discusses the problem of protest bids in relation to strategic bias. For example, a respondent refusing 'to state a monetary value for a good on the grounds that it is unethical to do so or that he has an inherent right to the good' is not indicating their true valuation, which may be quite high. Hanley, Spash and Walker (1995) interpret these responses as evidence of lexicographic preferences, that is, people refuse to make trade offs with respect to some environmental goods.

Zero bids usually account for a substantial proportion of the total responses. Römer (1992) notes that 'the percentage of zero bids ranges even in elaborated surveys is between 15% and 30% ... Studies with less elaborated scenarios often exhibit a much higher share of zero bids.' Römer quotes a study by Holm-Müller *et al.* in 1991 with the proportion of zero bids for different scenarios ranging from 31 per cent in more detailed scenarios to 74 per cent in the less specific scenarios. Some other studies have also reported significant zero bids, including Bennett (1981) 30 per cent, Kirkland (1988) 73 per cent, Imber, Stevenson and Wilks (1991) 31 per cent and Johansson, Kriström and Nyquist (1994) 78 per cent.

Given the large proportion of zero bids in many contingent valuation studies, 'it is evident that the treatment of zero bids can have a major impact on the aggregate results of contingent valuation studies as well as on the attempts to assess the reliability and validity of the obtained bids' (Römer 1992, p. 3). There have been three responses to the problem of zero bids in the contingent valuation literature.

Firstly, all zero responses may be considered as the true valuation of the respondents and included in benefit estimations. For example, Imber, Stevenson and Wilks (1991) treat all 'no' responses as real 'no' responses. This results in conservative estimates of the public's willingness to pay (Carson 1991). The higher the number of strategic or protest responses the more conservative the benefit calculations will be, which may result in erroneous policy implications. Including strategic and protest zero bids may also cause difficulty in estimating the willingness to pay function correctly (Römer 1992).

A second strategy (rarely used) is to eliminate all zero bids (Römer 1992). This is also unsatisfactory as it may cause 'a sample selection bias, since the remaining bids no longer originate from a random sample of the basic population' (Römer 1992, p. 4). Again, this makes estimation of a reliable willingness to pay function difficult.

A third and more commonly used approach is to identify and exclude protest bids from estimates of willingness to pay (Mitchell and Carson 1989), although clear justifications for doing so are seldom given. To identify strategic and protest bids, zero bidders are questioned as to their motive for bidding zero. Those whose answers indicate strategic or protest behaviour are removed. This method may result in a sample selection bias since the remaining bids no longer originate from a random sample of the basic population. The selected sample should not be used for estimation of the willingness to pay function (Römer 1992).

More recently, some alternative procedures have been developed. The spike model developed by Johansson, Kriström and Nyquist (1994) treats all zeros as valid and includes them explicitly in the analysis.

Römer (1992) has applied a two-step procedure developed by Heckman which avoids the problems described above. 'At the first step a probit model based on the full sample is set up, in order to explain statistically what factors determine the probability that a randomly chosen bid will be selected. From the estimated parameters a corrective variable can be computed, which is included as an additional regressor in the OLS equation of the selected sample at the second step' (Römer 1992, pp 4-5).

At the second step, the willingness to pay function is estimated from non-zero bids only, using the corrective variable. Römer's application showed that in some cases the Heckman procedure resulted in significantly better fitting bid functions, with a significant increase in the explanatory power and the accuracy of the willingness to pay model.

CONCLUSION

In this chapter a simple discrete choice model has been developed which will enable an application to a practical valuation issue. Despite a range of shortcomings which have been identified, this method seems to offer robust prospects of analysis of the species valuation problem which will follow.

PART FOUR

The Survey Application to Species Conservation

8. A Contingent Valuation Survey of Endangered Species in Victoria

INTRODUCTION

This chapter outlines the structure and implementation of a contingent valuation survey of willingness to pay for conservation of endangered flora and fauna in Victoria. There were two basic questionnaires in the survey. The first group of questionnaires were concerned with people's willingness to pay for preserving all the endangered species of plants and animals in Victoria, while the second group of questionnaires were concerned with willingness to pay for the conservation of a single species.

The survey and the questionnaires are described in detail in this chapter, and they are related to hypotheses set to test a range of particular contingent valuation methodological issues. The choice of survey type and design are considered and justified. Each question and the responses to it are discussed and the possible implications for the estimation of willingness to pay values are considered. Estimation of the willingness to pay values is discussed in Chapter 9. Finally, the socioeconomic characteristics of the survey respondents are reported and compared with the socioeconomic characteristics of the population from which they were drawn.

THE QUESTIONNAIRES

In this study, the two main questionnaires, each with five variations, were designed to test a range of hypotheses relating to particular methodological issues identified through the literature review in Chapter 6. The ten questionnaires are described below, followed by the hypotheses and how the hypotheses are to be tested.

Flora and Fauna Questionnaires - A to E

In these questionnaires people were asked their annual willingness to pay for the conservation of all endangered species of flora and fauna in Victoria. Although it is hard to be precise about the number of species which may be considered endangered, an estimate of 700 was given in the questionnaire (Department of Conservation, Forests and Lands, undated). The introductory information is shown in Box 8.1 and the illustration used on the front page is shown in Figure 8.1.

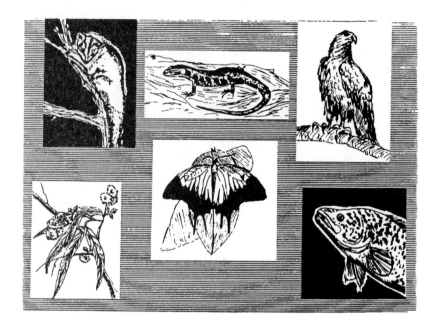

Figure 8.1 Illustration used on the flora and fauna questionnaire.

Box 8.1 Introduction to the flora and fauna questionnaires

INTRODUCTION

Thank you for your assistance in completing this questionnaire. If you do not understand a question or wish to expand on your answer, please write comments in the margin. When you have completed the questionnaire, please return it to; Research, La Trobe University, Bundoora 3083, in the postage paid, business reply envelope provided.

NATIVE PLANTS AND ANIMALS

There are about 4000 species of native plants and animals in Victoria, some of which occur only in this State.

It is estimated that about 700 (18%) of Victorian plant and animal species are endangered to the point where they may die out completely if no further action is taken to protect them.

The questionnaires varied in the form of payment question used and the information given. Questionnaires A, B, C and D used a discrete choice payment question followed by an open-ended (continuous) valuation question, whereas questionnaire E used a payment card. Questionnaires A, B and E were given information on the current (at the time) Government expenditure on conservation of flora and fauna, whereas C and D were not. Government expenditure was calculated as an average per adult Victorian using the Government budget figure of $9.8 million per year of direct expenditure on conservation and came to roughly $2.30 per Victorian adult per year.

Box 8.2 The flora and fauna questionnaires

Questionnaire A - discrete choice valuation question.
- payment through increased tax
- current expenditure information given
- closed question 2

Questionnaire B - discrete choice valuation question.
- payment through increased tax
- current expenditure information given
- open question 2

Questionnaire C - discrete choice valuation question.
- payment through increased tax
- no current expenditure information
- closed question 2

Questionnaire D - discrete choice valuation question.
- payment through increased tax
- no current expenditure information
- open question 2

Questionnaire E - payment card valuation question.
- payment through increased tax
- current expenditure information given
- open question 2

Question 2 in versions A to E took one of two forms (Boxes 8.9 and 8.10). In the closed-ended form (questionnaires A and C) respondents were asked how important each of a list of reasons for preserving species was to them. In questionnaires B, D and E respondents were simply asked why they felt preserving species was important.

The intention was to see whether respondents gave different reasons for conservation when not prompted and if prompting them to think in more detail (with the closed-ended form) about why species should be protected influenced the willingness to pay results.

Leadbeater's Possum Questionnaires - F to J.

In the Leadbeater's possum questionnaires respondents were asked for their willingness to pay to protect Leadbeater's possum only. A discrete choice question followed by an open-ended question was used in all questionnaires but they varied in the payment mechanism and the information given. The introduction to the questionnaire is shown in Box 8.3 and the illustration used is shown in Figure 8.2.

Box 8.3 Introduction to the Leadbeater's possum questionnaires

INTRODUCTION

Thank you for your assistance in completing this questionnaire. If you do not understand a question or wish to expand on your answer, please write comments in the margin. When you have completed the questionnaire, please return it to; Research, La Trobe University, Bundoora 3083, in the postage paid, business reply envelope provided.

LEADBEATER'S POSSUM

Leadbeater's possum is a small, shy nocturnal possum (above picture). It occurs only in the Central Highlands area of Victoria in mountain and alpine ash forests.

The present population of Leadbeater's possum is about 7000 - 8000, but numbers are declining and the possum may die out completely if no action is taken to protect and manage it.

Figure 8.2 Illustration used in the Leadbeater's possum questionnaire.

In questionnaires F and G it was stated that payment would be through an increase in taxes whereas in questionnaires H and I it was stated payment would be as a donation to an independent conservation organisation. Questionnaire J used a discrete choice question on willingness to accept compensation for the loss of Leadbeater's possum rather than willingness to pay. Questionnaires F, H and J had a picture of the possum but versions G and I did not. The questionnaire variations are summarised in Box 8.4.

Box 8.4 The Leadbeater's possum questionnaires

Questionnaire F - discrete choice valuation question
      - payment through increased tax
      - picture of possum included
Questionnaire G - discrete choice valuation question
      - payment through increased tax
      - no picture of possum
Questionnaire H - discrete choice valuation question
      - donation to conservation organisation
      - picture of possum
Questionnaire I - discrete choice valuation question
      - donation to conservation organisation
      - no picture of possum
Questionnaire J - willingness to accept compensation
      - discrete choice valuation question
      - picture of possum

THE SURVEY HYPOTHESES

The methodological issues investigated in the survey are listed below. The background to these issues is discussed in more depth in Chapter 6. The hypotheses set up to test the methodological issues and how the questionnaire versions relate to the hypotheses are described.

Scope Effects

The issues of scope and amenity mis-specification biases have provoked much debate about the contingent valuation method. In this survey, a split-sample approach was used to examine whether there is a significant difference in the mean willingness to pay values estimated for all endangered species valued collectively and for Leadbeater's possum individually. If the values are not significantly different it may be evidence that respondents are insensitive to scope (valuing one species the same as many species). It may also be interpreted as 'mental account' bias, that is people allocate most of their endangered species budget to the first species they are asked about without taking into account the other species.

In this survey, for example, if respondents are insensitive to scope, the respondents to the Leadbeater's possum questionnaire could be expected to allocate most or all of what they are willing to pay for all endangered species to Leadbeater's possum. Thus, the estimates of willingness to pay for Leadbeater's possum should be the same as a substantial proportion (say 90 per cent or more) of the estimate of willingness to pay for all endangered species.

The hypothesis that respondents are insensitive to scope will be accepted if the estimates of mean willingness to pay for all endangered species and for Leadbeater's possum are not significantly different.

The test of this hypothesis is to compare Leadbeater's possum willingness to pay values with willingness to pay values for all endangered flora and fauna in Victoria, that is, questionnaires F, G, H and I are compared with versions A, B, C, D and E.

The hypothesis (H1) is:

$$H1 = V_{LP} \text{ (Leadbeater's possum)} = V_{ES} \text{ (all species)}$$

Where V_{LP} is the mean willingness to pay for Leadbeater's possum and V_{ES} is the mean willingness to pay for all the endangered species collectively.

Willingness to Accept Compensation or Willingness to Pay Measures

Willingness to accept compensation questions are seldom used in contingent valuation studies because of perceived problems of validity and the far greater than expected differences from willingness to pay estimates. In early contingent valuation literature, it was expected that differences in willingness to pay and willingness to accept compensation valuations should be small and explainable by the different income effects of the two questions.

In practice in contingent valuation surveys, willingness to accept values have been found to be far greater than willingness to pay values for the same goods (Knetsch 1993). Hanemann (1984 p. 339) presents a result that 'dispels the notion that compensating and equivalent surpluses must somehow be close in value'.

This issue is investigated in this study by comparing the values obtained from questionnaires F, G, H and I (which used a willingness to pay question) with questionnaire J, which used a willingness to accept compensation question.

The hypothesis (H2) is:

$$H2 = V_{WTP} = V_{WTA} \text{ after adjusting for the income effect.}$$

That is, the values resulting from the willingness to pay question (V_{WTP}) will be equal to the values obtained from the willingness to accept question (V_{WTA}), unless there is an income effect resulting from making a payment as opposed to receiving compensation.

Different Types of Payment Question

Differences in estimates of mean value have been found when the same good is valued using different forms of payment question. To investigate this issue, three forms of willingness to pay question were used - a discrete choice question, an open-ended direct question and an open-ended payment card question. This allowed two comparisons; the discrete choice question with the open-ended (or continuous) question, which were in the same questionnaires (ABCD), and the two forms of open-ended question (between different versions of the questionnaire).

The issues of interest are whether the discrete and continuous questions give the same values and whether the discrete choice question preceding the open-ended question influences the answers to the open-ended question (anchoring bias).

The tests were to:

(a) compare the answer to the discrete valuation question (DVQ) with that to the continuous (open-ended) valuation question (CVQ) in questionnaires A,B,C and D; and
(b) compare the answer to the CVQ in AB with that to the CVQ in questionnaire E (current expenditure information is given in A, B and E but not C and D).

The hypothesis (H3a) is:

$$H3a = V_{DC} = V_{OE}$$

That is, the estimates of value for a particular good will be the same using either discrete choice (V_{DC}) or continuous valuation questions (V_{OE}).

The hypothesis (H3b) is:

$$H3b = V_{OE} = V_{PC}$$

That is, the estimates of value from continuous valuation questions which are preceded by a discrete choice question will be the same as the estimates derived from the open-ended payment card with no discrete choice question.

Different Payment Mechanisms

The issue here is whether a different payment mode will affect mean willingness to pay. In this survey, two payment mechanisms were used. These were paying for Leadbeater's possum conservation through additional taxes versus paying a donation to an independent conservation organisation.
The hypothesis (H4) is:

$$H4 = V_T = V_D$$

That is, the estimates of value for the conservation of Leadbeater's possum will be the same whether the payment is through increased taxation (V_T) - questionnaires F and G - or through a donation to a conservation organisation (V_D) - questionnaires H and I.

Different Amounts of Information

Values estimated from contingent valuation surveys have been found to vary with the information provided about the good being valued. This study looked at three tests of providing different information and tested the hypotheses that the differences in information had no effect on the estimates of value obtained.
The hypothesis (H5a) is:

$$H5a = V_E = V_{NE}$$

The test here is to compare values from flora and fauna questionnaires A and B (V_E) - with expenditure information - with C and D (V_{NE}) - without expenditure information.
The hypothesis (H5b) is:

$$H5b = V_P = V_{NP}$$

The test compares values from questionnaires F and H (V_P), with picture, to G and I (V_{NP}), without picture.
The hypothesis (H5c) is:

$$H5c = V_O = V_C$$

The test compares open-ended as against closed questions designed to make people think about the values of species. Flora and fauna questionnaires A and C are compared with questionnaires B and D.

CHOICE OF SURVEY TYPE, QUESTION TYPE AND PAYMENT MECHANISM

Survey Type

The survey was administered by mail, for several reasons. Firstly, the use of a mail survey allows respondents to take as much time as they wish to formulate their answers. Secondly, there is no interviewer presence which may lead to interviewer bias or yea-saying, where respondents may answer 'yes' to a discrete choice question to 'please' the interviewer rather than because they would really pay the suggested amount.

The mail survey also allowed the inclusion of a picture of Leadbeater's possum, which would not be possible in a telephone survey. In addition, a mail survey made best use of the limited financial resources available for the survey.

Measure of Value

It can be argued that Victorian residents currently hold the property rights to Victorian flora and fauna (including Leadbeater's possum) and that the theoretically correct benefit measure should be willingness to accept compensation for the loss of species. This would give a compensating surplus measure of benefit. However, willingness to accept compensation questions have proved to be difficult for respondents to answer for many environmental goods and may give results of doubtful validity.

Willingness to pay questions are used most frequently and, because they result in lower estimates than willingness to accept compensation questions, are considered to produce a conservative estimate of benefits. Nine of the questionnaires in this survey used willingness to pay questions, while the tenth questionnaire used willingness to accept compensation for the loss of Leadbeater's possum.

In this survey, respondents were asked their willingness to pay to avoid either a decline in the number of endangered species (the flora and fauna questionnaires) or the loss of Leadbeater's possum. These questions yield Hicksian equivalent surplus measures of benefit.

Question Type

Use of a mail survey limited the type of willingness to pay question that could be used. Iterative bid questions cannot be used in a mail survey and neither can anchored payment cards as they need to be related to the respondent's income level. This leaves open-ended questions, discrete choice questions or an unanchored payment card as possibilities. In this survey, the discrete choice question was chosen as the primary valuation question because it is more like a market decision than the other types of questions and should be easier for respondents to answer.

There was also a second stage to the discrete choice question, which in effect was an open-ended bid (or continuous valuation) question. Respondents who agreed to pay the given amount were then asked if they would pay more than this amount. If they agreed to pay more they were asked to specify how much in total they would pay. Respondents who refused to pay the given amount were asked if they would pay a smaller amount. If they agreed to pay a smaller amount again they were asked to specify how much.

Eight of the nine willingness to pay questionnaires (A to D, F to I) used the discrete choice question. The ninth questionnaire (E), used an unanchored payment card only, in effect an open-ended question. The tenth questionnaire (J) asked for willingness to accept compensation, also as a discrete choice question.

Payment Mechanism

The method of payment for most questionnaires was an increase in annual State taxes (the other two questionnaires used an annual donation to an independent conservation trust). The tax increase was chosen because conservation programmes and management of parks and natural areas are currently funded through State taxes. The compensation question stated that the forestry companies would pay compensation for the loss of Leadbeater's possum in order to have the right to continue logging.

Pre-testing and Choice of Bid Amounts

The questionnaires were pre-tested using an open-ended willingness to pay question on a group of about 50 university staff (including academic, administrative and technical staff) and postgraduate students in order to establish a range of values to use in the discrete choice questions and to determine if any questions were too difficult or complicated. The pre-test group had a higher average income than the general population, but this is an advantage as one of the main objectives of the pre-test was to establish an upper bid range that would cover most values that respondents are likely to hold and so avoid the 'fat tail' problem (Chapter 7).

Based on the pre-test results, a range of $1 to $500 per year was chosen for the flora and fauna questionnaires and a range of $1 to $150 per year for the Leadbeater's possum questionnaires. Within each range, twenty bid amounts were used. The flora and fauna questionnaire E used an unanchored payment card with values starting at $1 and ending at $2,000 (Box 8.15).

The Leadbeater's possum questionnaire J had a discrete choice willingness to accept compensation question rather than willingness to pay question. Compensation was to be paid as a once and for all lump sum payment so the bid amounts used are far higher than those used in the willingness to pay questions which were annual payments. Twenty compensation bid amounts were used, ranging from $1 to $10,000. This version was not pre-tested and was thus somewhat of an experiment.

ADMINISTRATION OF THE SURVEY

The questionnaires were sent to a random sample of 3,900 Victorians over the age of 18 drawn from the Victorian Electoral Roll. The different versions were evenly distributed across the sample of 3,900. Two hundred and sixty three unopened envelopes were returned because the intended recipient was no longer at the address listed on the Electoral Roll. This amounted to about 6.7 per cent of the original sample.

Preparation and mailing out of the questionnaires was based on a guidebook for mail questionnaire surveys developed by Dillman (1978). The questionnaire was four pages, with 13 or 14 questions depending on the version. It was photocopied onto white A3 paper and folded into an A4-sized booklet. The questionnaire was accompanied by a single page covering letter on La Trobe University letterhead paper and a postage-paid envelope for return of the completed questionnaire. The cover letter (Box 8.5) was designed to motivate respondents by explaining the policy relevance of the questions and the importance of representative participation in the survey. Each letter was addressed to the individual and personally signed by the project director.

The questionnaires were mailed out on the 28th and 29th November 1988. About 14 days later a follow-up letter (Box 8.6) was sent out to the whole sample of Victorians reminding them about the questionnaire and offering a replacement copy if necessary. Due to budget constraints this was the only follow-up letter. Dillman (1978) recommends three follow-ups, the original to be followed by a postcard reminder, a second letter and replacement questionnaire and a final registered letter with replacement questionnaire.

Box 8.5 The covering letter

Name   27/11/88
Address
Dear

Recently, environmental issues such as the protection of endangered species of native plants and animals have received much media and Government attention. Researchers at La Trobe University are conducting this study to establish the opinions and values Victorians hold concerning the protection of native plants and animals within their State. We believe that it is important that the Government should know the opinions of Victorians when deciding on policies for conservation.

You are one of a small number of people who have been selected (from the electoral roll) to give your opinions on these matters. Your participation in this study is entirely voluntary and you may refuse to answer any question. Because only a small number of people have been selected for the study, your participation is extremely important if the results are to truly represent the opinions and values of all Victorians.

The information you provide will be kept <u>strictly confidential</u> and will be used only for overall statistical results. Returned questionnaires cannot be identified with you.

The results of this research will be made publicly available. If you wish to receive a copy of the results (in a few months time), please print your name and address on the back of the return envelope. Please <u>do not</u> put this information on the questionnaire itself.

If you have any questions regarding the study, please write to the above address or telephone (03) 479-2165.

The questionnaire should take only about 5 to 10 minutes to complete. When you have completed the questionnaire, please return it in the postage paid, return addressed envelope provided. Thank you for your help.
Yours sincerely,

Kristin Jakobsson
Project Director

DESCRIPTION OF QUESTIONNAIRE RESPONSES

The following sections consist of a descriptive analysis of the data base generated from the questionnaire responses. The questions, reasons for their inclusion and the responses to each question are described. Socioeconomic data are compared both amongst the questionnaires and with the general population. The re-categorisation and combination of data for analysis of the willingness to pay functions is detailed. Opportunities occurred at several points in the questionnaires for respondents to add comments.

The overall return rate of the questionnaires was about 35 per cent, with about 2 per cent of the questionnaires lacking enough information to be useable. About 740 replies were received from the first mailing before the follow-up letter was posted out. A further 615 replies arrived after the follow-up letter, but it is not clear how many were due to the follow-up letter. A further 24 undelivered letters from the first mailing and 82 undelivered follow-up letters were received. Total response rate for all questionnaires are given in Table 8.1, while response rates by version are in Table 8.12 near the end of the chapter. Reasons for unusable replies and refusals are in Table 8.2.

The response rate in this study of 33 per cent is low, but falls within the range obtained in other mail contingent valuation surveys, usually around 30-60 per cent with lower response rates expected in surveys of the general population. Loomis (1987a) found the average to be around 40 per cent. For example, Walsh, Gillman and Loomis (1982) achieved 41 per cent, Kerr and Sharp (1987) achieved 37 per cent, Kirkland (1988) achieved 51 per cent, Sappideen (1992) achieved 31 per cent, Loomis and du Vair (1993) had responses of 43 per cent and 47 per cent with two follow ups and Kriström (1990a) achieved a 67 per cent response rate after three follow ups. The use of one follow-up letter in this survey may well have contributed to the low response rate. It was also close to school holidays and the Christmas break.

Box 8.6 Follow-up letter

Dear   9/12/88

A few days ago a questionnaire seeking your opinion about the protection of endangered species of plants and animals in Victoria was mailed to you. Your name was drawn in a random sample of people in Victoria.

If you have already completed and returned it, please accept our sincere thanks. If not, please do so today. Because the questionnaire has been sent to only a small, but representative, sample of Victorian residents it is extremely important that yours also be included in the study if the results are to accurately represent the opinions of Victorians.

If by some chance you did not receive the questionnaire, or it has been misplaced, please call me on (03) 479-2165 and I will send you a replacement.

Yours sincerely,

Kristin Jakobsson
Project Director

Table 8.1 Response to species contingent valuation survey, Victoria, 1988

Response	Number	Per cent
Total questionnaires posted	3,900	100.0
Undelivered	263	6.7
No reply	2282	58.5
Unusable reply or refusal	71	1.8
Usable reply	1284	32.9

Table 8.2 Reasons for unusable replies and refusals

Reason	Number
Deceased	6
Illness or age	21
Overseas	3
Didn't speak English	1
Illiterate	1
Answered by two people	2
Objection to questionnaire or some aspect	9
Refused - no reason given/not interested	18
Inadequate answer	4
Antagonistic/rude reply	5
Total	71

FREQUENCIES OF RESPONSES TO SELECTED QUESTIONS

The survey questions and the frequency of responses to each question are described in the sections below.

Responses to Question 1

Questions 1 and 2 were designed to ascertain respondents' attitudes to the importance of protecting endangered species. In question 1 respondents were asked how important protecting Victorian plants and animals (or Leadbeater's possum) was to them, on a scale of one to four. The two questions are listed in Boxes 8.7 and 8.8.

Question 1 had a missing value rate of 6.9 per cent on average for all samples (up to 14.4 per cent in questionnaire C). This is considerably higher than the rate for most other questions and may have been due to the questionnaire design. It was the only question on the front page. In questionnaire J it occurred with the other questions on the second page and had a missing rate of only 0.5 per cent, leading to the possibility that respondents simply missed the question on the first page in the other questionnaires.

Box 8.7 Importance of protection: Flora and fauna questionnaires (A-E)

1. How important is the protection of Victorian native plants and animals to you? (Please circle the number next to the answer of your choice, for example (5) DON'T KNOW).

1 VERY IMPORTANT
2 MODERATELY IMPORTANT —— GO TO QUESTION 2
3 SLIGHTLY IMPORTANT
4 NOT IMPORTANT AT ALL ——— GO TO QUESTION 3
5 DON'T KNOW ————————— GO TO QUESTION 2

Box 8.8 Importance of protection: Leadbeater's possum questionnaires (F-J)

1. How important do you think it is to protect animals like the Leadbeater's possum? (Please circle the number next to the answer of your choice, for example (5) DON'T KNOW).

1 VERY IMPORTANT
2 MODERATELY IMPORTANT —— GO TO QUESTION 2
3 SLIGHTLY IMPORTANT
4 NOT IMPORTANT AT ALL —— GO TO QUESTION 3
5 DON'T KNOW ————————— GO TO QUESTION 2

Overall, 66 per cent of all respondents (or 71 per cent of those answering question 1) felt protecting species is very important, with a further 20 per cent considering it moderately important. The high proportion of respondents indicating that species conservation is very important may be due to a number of reasons;

1. a large proportion of the population genuinely believes species conservation is important,
2. there is a bias towards people who favour conservation amongst those answering the survey or,
3. the question was not specific enough, that is, people agree with idealistic statements that conservation is important but these statements are not supported by their actions.

Certainly a significantly lower proportion of people were actually prepared to pay for conservation than stated it was very important, although respondents' answers to this question did have a significant influence on their preparedness to pay. Responses to question 1 are presented in Table 8.3.

Responses to Question 2

There were two versions of question 2 in the flora and fauna questionnaire, which were designed to establish why respondents felt protecting endangered species was important if they had stated this in question 1. One form was a closed-ended question asking how important each of several reasons for protecting species was (Box 8.9). The other form simply asked why they felt protecting species is important (Box 8.10). Question 2 in the Leadbeater's possum questionnaire attempted to establish the relative importance of option, existence and bequest values.

The results for questionnaires A and C (closed-ended question 2) are given in Table 8.4. These results indicate existence and bequest type values are considered more important than use values. There is an overwhelming belief (78 per cent) that species have a right to exist, closely followed by a belief that species should be preserved for future generations. About 44 per cent of respondents believed that consumptive uses were not important at all.

In questionnaires B, D, and E, respondents were allowed to specify their own reasons for species protection (Box 8.10), resulting in different responses from A and C. Part of the reason for the difference was that there was a larger range of reasons for B, D and E (Table 8.5). The responses were coded into the five reasons listed in A and C (future generations, species have a right to live, science and education, consumptive uses and non-consumptive uses).

Other commonly occurring reasons suggested by respondents were; the importance of preserving species to maintain the ecological balance; species are unique and part of our heritage; and species should be preserved to prevent extinction. 'Other' reasons included considerations such as 'too much has been lost already' and 'humans have a responsibility to take care of the environment' and a range of other reasons none of which occurred frequently.

The number of respondents listing use values (science and education, consumptive and nonconsumptive uses) is considerably lower than in questionnaires A and C, where answers were prompted. Another major difference is the 'maintenance of the ecological balance' reason which was not included in A and C. The 'species are unique and part of our heritage' reason could be considered as similar to 'future generations', which would give an overall figure of 80 per cent, closer to the results for A and C.

The motivation for people to 'preserve to prevent extinction' is not clear. Respondents may have had a variety of reasons such as preserving for future generations, the right of species to live and so on. The right of species to live (the most important reason in questionnaires A and C) was mentioned by only 9.5 per cent of respondents in questionnaires B, D and E. It seems that the closed-ended version of question 2 in questionnaires A and C did influence people's answers on why they felt species protection was important.

The second question in the Leadbeater's possum questionnaires F to J (Box 8.11) was included for the relative importance of existence, bequest and option values as motivations for preserving Leadbeater's possum (Table 8.6).

Table 8.3 Importance of protection (percentage of respondents for all questionnaires)

	Importance					
Questionnaire	Very	Moderately	Slightly	Not at all	Don't know	Missing
Flora & fauna						
A	58.1	20.9	6.1	1.4	1.4	12.2
B	72.9	18.1	2.1	0	0	6.3
C	64.0	16.8	3.2	0	1.6	14.4
D	67.3	21.2	2.9	2.9	2.9	2.9
E	64.6	24.3	3.2	1.1	1.1	5.8
Leadbeater's						
F	65.2	18.8	7.1	2.7	1.8	4.5
G	56.6	24.5	5.7	2.8	0.9	9.4
H	64.2	20.8	3.8	0.9	1.9	8.5
I	63.2	18.4	4.6	1.1	3.4	9.2
J	75.6	15.0	2.8	1.9	4.2	0.5
Total	65.7	19.8	4.0	1.5	2.0	6.9

Box 8.9 Question 2, flora and fauna questionnaires A and C

2. This question lists some reasons why people may believe protecting
native plants and animals is important. Please circle a number for each
reason to show how important (if at all) each of these reasons is to you as
a reason for protecting endangered species of native plants and animals.
(i) Species should be protected because future generations of people should
be able to see and enjoy native plants and animals.
    1 VERY IMPORTANT
    2 MODERATELY IMPORTANT
    3 SLIGHTLY IMPORTANT
    4 NOT IMPORTANT AT ALL
    5 DON'T KNOW
(ii) Native plants and animals have a right to live.
    1 VERY IMPORTANT
    2 MODERATELY IMPORTANT
    3 SLIGHTLY IMPORTANT
    4 NOT IMPORTANT AT ALL
    5 DON'T KNOW
(iii) Native plant and animal species should be protected because they have
scientific and educational values.
    1 VERY IMPORTANT
    2 MODERATELY IMPORTANT
    3 SLIGHTLY IMPORTANT
    4 NOT IMPORTANT AT ALL
    5 DON'T KNOW
(iv) Native plant and animal species should be protected because they
provide opportunities for hunting, fishing and plant collecting.
    1 VERY IMPORTANT
    2 MODERATELY IMPORTANT
    3 SLIGHTLY IMPORTANT
    4 NOT IMPORTANT AT ALL
    5 DON'T KNOW
(v) Native plant and animal species should be protected because they
provide opportunities for bird watching, photography and bush walking.
    1 VERY IMPORTANT
    2 MODERATELY IMPORTANT
    3 SLIGHTLY IMPORTANT
    4 NOT IMPORTANT AT ALL
    5 DON'T KNOW
(vi) Other? Please specify...

Box 8.10 Question 2, flora and fauna questionnaires B, D and E

2. Why do you consider that the protection of Victorian native plants and animals is important?

Table 8.4 Reasons given for protecting species (percentage of respondents, questionnaires A and C)[1]

Reason	Importance			
	Very	Moderately	Slightly	Not at all
Future generations	75.8	18.3	4.4	0.3
Species right to live	78.0	13.9	5.5	1.0
Science and education	60.0	26.4	9.5	1.8
Consumptive uses	19.0	15.8	17.6	44.0
Nonconsumptive uses	49.0	29.0	15.4	4.0

1. Respondents not included answered either 'don't know' or did not answer.

Table 8.5 Reasons given for protecting species (percentage of respondents, questionnaires B, D and E)[1]

Reason	Percentage of respondents
Future generations	39.6
Right of species to live	9.5
Science and education	5.7
Consumptive uses	0.2
Nonconsumptive uses	22.6
Ecological balance	32.0
Unique/part of heritage	41.1
To prevent extinction	9.3
Other	17.5

1. Multiple answers allowed.

Box 8.11 Reasons for protecting Leadbeater's possum

---

2. Why do you think it is important to protect Leadbeater's possum? Please circle a number for each reason to show how important (if at all) each reason is to you as a reason for protecting this possum.

(i) You would like to keep the option of being able to visit or see a Leadbeater's possum in the future.
   1 VERY IMPORTANT
   2 MODERATELY IMPORTANT
   3 SLIGHTLY IMPORTANT
   4 NOT IMPORTANT AT ALL
   5 DON'T KNOW

(ii) The value to you of knowing that Leadbeater's possum exists in its natural habitat even if you will never see one.
   1 VERY IMPORTANT
   2 MODERATELY IMPORTANT
   3 SLIGHTLY IMPORTANT
   4 NOT IMPORTANT AT ALL
   5 DON'T KNOW

(iii) The value to you of knowing that future generations will have the opportunity to see Leadbeater's possum.
   1 VERY IMPORTANT
   2 MODERATELY IMPORTANT
   3 SLIGHTLY IMPORTANT
   4 NOT IMPORTANT AT ALL
   5 DON'T KNOW

Table 8.6 Reasons given for protecting Leadbeater's possum (percentage of respondents, questionnaires F to J)

| Reason | Importance | | | |
	Very	Moderately	Slightly	Not at all
Option value	41.1	25.6	19.4	9.0
Existence value	64.5	20.5	7.4	3.8
Bequest value	65.0	18.9	9.3	3.5

Table 8.7 Respondents having seen or heard of Leadbeater's possum

Know of the possum	Percentage
Heard of Leadbeater's possum	53.8
Seen possum in the wild	4.8
Seen possum in captivity	18.2
Seen on TV	0.8

About 65 per cent of respondents felt existence and bequest values were very important reasons for preserving Leadbeater's possum and another 20 per cent felt these values were moderately important. The option of seeing a possum in the future was felt to be very important by only 41 per cent of respondents, indicating that existence and bequest values were more important than use values. This result would be expected given the inaccessibility of Leadbeater's possum. Most people are unlikely to ever see a Leadbeater's possum in the wild because they are nocturnal, extremely shy and usually remain high in the canopy.

In questions 3 and 4 in the Leadbeater's possum questionnaires respondents were asked if they had heard of Leadbeater's possum prior to the survey and if so, whether they had seen one and where they had seen it. Just under 5 per cent of respondents claimed to have seen a Leadbeater's possum in the wild (Table 8.7). It is unlikely that this many people would really have seen one in the wild because of the difficulty in locating them and correctly identifying them. They may be confused with other possum species or sugar gliders.

Captive specimens are fairly accessible, being kept at the Melbourne Zoo and at the Healesville Sanctuary near Melbourne and about 18 per cent of respondents reported having seen them in captivity. About 45 per cent of respondents had never heard of Leadbeater's possum prior to the survey and would have had to rely on the limited information given in the questionnaires.

As there are a range of species of possum in Australia, it is fairly certain that most respondents would have a general idea of a possum as a furry, tree dwelling marsupial. However, the common possums are considerably larger than the Leadbeater's possum and can cause domestic problems such as noise and fruit damage. Respondents thinking of these possums may express lower willingness to pay than if they had more information.

It might be expected that respondents who were already aware of Leadbeater's possum would be more prepared to pay for its conservation, either because they have more information than that provided in the questionnaires or because people who were aware of it were more interested in environmental issues to begin with. Crosstabulations of the binary variable 'willing to pay or not willing to pay' with 'having heard of the possum' were run and, as might be expected, those who knew of the possum already were more likely to say 'yes' to the willingness to pay question (Table 8.8).

Table 8.8 Crosstabulation of response to the discrete choice willingness to pay question and whether or not respondents had heard of Leadbeater's possum[1]

	Not willing to pay	Willing to pay	Total
Not heard	140	39	179 (44.9%)
Heard	131	89	220 (55.1%)
Total	271	128	399 (100%)
	(67.9%)	(32.1%)	(100%)

1. Chi square value is 15.78 with 1 df and significance level of 0.00007.

Box 8.12 Willingness to pay questions for questionnaires A, B, C, D

3. To ensure the protection and preservation of all 700 known endangered native plants and animals in Victoria, funds are needed.
Imagine the Victorian Government wishes to raise money specifically to protect endangered species of plants and animals and proposes to raise this money through an extra tax. Assume the money raised by this tax will be used exclusively for the protection of native plants and animals in Victoria.
    Would you be prepared to pay an extra tax of $_____ each year to ensure that Victoria's native plants and animals are fully protected. (Remember this is an imaginary situation - the money will not be collected and your answer cannot be identified with you.) Please circle the number next to the answer of your choice.
    1 YES _____ GO TO QUESTION 4
    2 NO _____ GO TO QUESTION 5

THE WILLINGNESS TO PAY QUESTION

In all questionnaires except E and J, the willingness to pay question was asked in two stages. Firstly, the respondent was asked to say 'yes' or 'no' to paying a specified amount (the discrete choice question). If the answer was 'yes', the respondent was asked if they would pay more than this amount and if so, what was the highest amount they would pay. If the respondent answered 'no' to the discrete choice question, they were asked why they said 'no'. One reason for saying 'no' was that the discrete choice question amount was too high, in which case they were asked what lower amount they would pay.

Box 8.13 Further willingness to pay questions for questionnaires A, B, C, D

4. Would you be prepared to pay <u>more</u> than the amount given above?

          1   YES

        2   NO ___ GO TO QUESTION 6 (next page)

How much would you be prepared to pay each year?

$_____ <u>each year</u> (WRITE IN THE HIGHEST DOLLAR AMOUNT THAT YOU ARE PREPARED TO PAY).

NOW GO TO QUESTION 6 (next page)

5. Why did you answer NO to question 3? Please circle the number of any of the reasons listed which apply to you (you may circle more than one).

1 THE AMOUNT GIVEN IS TOO HIGH, BUT I <u>WOULD</u> PAY $____ PER YEAR (WRITE IN THE HIGHEST DOLLAR AMOUNT YOU WOULD PAY).

2 I DID NOT WANT TO PUT A DOLLAR VALUE ON PROTECTING PLANTS AND ANIMALS.

3 SOCIETY HAS MORE IMPORTANT PROBLEMS THAN PROTECTING PLANTS AND ANIMALS.

4 PROTECTING PLANTS AND ANIMALS IS NOT WORTH ANYTHING TO ME.

5 THE GOVERNMENT SHOULD PROTECT PLANTS AND ANIMALS USING TAXES ALREADY PAID.

6 NOT ENOUGH INFORMATION IS GIVEN.

7 I OBJECT TO THE WAY THE QUESTION IS ASKED.

8 I CAN'T AFFORD TO PAY ANYTHING.

9 OTHER (Please specify) ....

   COMMENTS..

The willingness to pay questions for flora and fauna questionnaires ABCD are shown in Boxes 8.12 and 8.13. Questionnaires A and C had some additional information on current government expenditures on species conservation, which is shown in Box 8.14. Questionnaire E used an open ended willingness to pay question with a payment card, which is in Box 8.15.

The willingness to pay questions for the Leadbeater's possum questionnaires F and G (taxation payment mechanism) and H and I (donation payment mechanism) are shown in Boxes 8.16 and 8.17. Questionnaire J (willingness to accept compensation) is discussed later in the chapter.

Responses to the willingness to pay questions and analysis of these responses is presented in Chapter 9. Responses to question 3 (flora and fauna questionnaires ABCD) and question 5 (Leadbeater's possum questionnaires) result in a binary variable (WTP1) where 1 = willing to pay and 0 = not willing to pay the given amount. A binary variable (WTP2) is also constructed from the response to the second stage of the willingness to pay question, which establishes whether the respondent is willing to pay any positive amount. The percentages of 'yes' responses in WTP1 and WTP2 are given in Table 8.9. Of those willing to pay the amount specified (that is WTP1 = 1), about 40 per cent were willing to pay more than this amount.

Box 8.14 Information on government expenditure in questionnaires A and C

3. The Victorian Government spends about $9.5 million per year on activities related to protecting endangered native plants and animals (about $2.30 per Victorian). To ensure the protection and preservation of all 700 endangered native plants and animals in Victoria, more money is needed.

   Imagine the Victorian Government wishes to increase the amount spent on protecting endangered plants and animals and proposes to raise this additional money by asking all Victorians to pay an extra tax. Assume the money raised by this tax will be used exclusively for the protection of native plants and animals in Victoria.

   The rest of the question is the same as in Box 8.16.

Box 8.15 Willingness to pay question and payment card in questionnaire E

4. How much would you be prepared to pay? Using the table below as a guide only, please write in the amount you would be prepared to pay. The amount you write in does not have to be in the table.

AMOUNT I WOULD PAY $_____ PER YEAR

1	50	100	200	400	1000
5	55	110	220	450	1100
10	60	120	240	500	1200
15	65	130	260	550	1300
20	70	140	280	600	1400
25	75	150	300	650	1500
30	80	160	320	700	1600
35	85	170	340	750	1700
40	90	180	360	800	1800
45	95	190	380	850	2000

A further variable (OEPRICE) is the actual dollar amounts people stated they were willing to pay. OEPRICE is in effect the open-ended valuation question and consists of the answers to questions 3 and 4 or 3 and 5(1) in the flora and fauna questionnaires and the answers to questions 5 and 6 or 5 and 7(1) in the Leadbeater's possum questionnaires.

Box 8.16 Willingness to pay questions for questionnaires F and G

5. To ensure the full protection and long term survival of Leadbeater's possum, money is needed. Imagine the Victorian Government wishes to raise money to protect Leadbeater's possum, and proposes to raise this money by asking all Victorians to pay an extra tax. Assume the money raised by this tax will be used exclusively for the protection of Leadbeater's possum in Victoria.

Would you be prepared to pay an extra tax of $_____ each year to ensure that the Leadbeater's possum is fully protected and will not become extinct? (Remember this is an imaginary situation - the money will not be collected and your answer cannot be identified with you.) Please circle the number next to the answer of your choice.

1 YES _____ GO TO QUESTION 6 (next page)
2 NO _____ GO TO QUESTION 7 (next page)

Questions 6 and 7 are the same as questions 4 and 5 in Box 8.12, with 'Leadbeater's possum' substituted for 'plants and animals'.

Box 8.17 Willingness to pay question for questionnaires H and I

5. To ensure the full protection and long term survival of Leadbeater's possum, money is needed. Imagine that an independent conservation trust will be set up to protect and manage Leadbeater's possum. This conservation trust would raise money by donations from the public. Would you be prepared to pay a donation of $_____ each year to an independent conservation organisation to ensure that the Leadbeater's possum is fully protected and will not become extinct?

The rest of the question is the same as in Box 8.16.

SOCIOECONOMIC VARIABLES

The socioeconomic information asked for in this section of the questionnaires included sex, age, education, occupation, number of dependents, individual income and household income (Boxes 8.18 and 8.19).

The socioeconomic information was used to determine whether the respondents for each questionnaire came from the same population and whether this was the same as the population from which the respondents were drawn, in this case the Victorian Electoral Roll which represents all Victorians over the age of 18. Given the low rate of response to the questionnaires it is of interest to see if any particular characteristics distinguish respondents and non-respondents.

Table 8.9 Responses to willingness to pay questions

Questionnaire		Respondents willing to pay (%)	
		Amount specified WTP1	Any positive amount WTP2
Flora	A	45.8	51.4
and	B	48.4	58.9
Fauna	C	41.0	49.6
	D	57.4	70.3
	E	N.A	65.1
Leadbeater's	F	39.6	51.4
Possum	G	35.0	50.5
	H	30.5	46.7
	I	18.6	39.5
J (WTA)		11.0	N.A

The following comparisons were made:
1. Comparison of the socioeconomic profiles of the respondents to the ten questionnaires to see if the people who answered different questionnaires were significantly different from one another.
2. Comparison of the respondents with census data to determine if respondents were significantly different from the general population.

Socioeconomic Comparison of Respondents by Questionnaire

Crosstabulations of questionnaire by each socioeconomic variable were carried out and tested using chi-squared analysis to establish if there were any differences among respondents to the ten questionnaire versions. Results of the analyses are summarised in Table 8.10.

There were no significant differences between the responses to the ten questionnaires except in education and occupation. In the original coding of the questionnaires education and occupation had several categories, some of which covered very few people. This led to a large number of cells with very low expected cell counts in the chi-square analysis which meant the analysis might not be valid. To overcome this problem, the analyses for education and occupation were redone with some of the categories combined.

Education was recategorised into three groups (secondary or less, tertiary and trade and other) and occupation into four groups. With the combined categories, questionnaire version by occupation showed no significant differences and questionnaire version by education remained significantly different at the 5 per cent level for chi-square. It was concluded that the questionnaire versions were not significantly different from one another with respect to socioeconomic characteristics.

Box 8.18 Socioeconomic questions

The next few questions ask you for some information about yourself. This information will help us to analyze the survey results by allowing us to compare the answers different people give.

6. What sex are you?
   1 FEMALE
   2 MALE

7. What age are you? Please circle the number that applies to you.
   1 18 - 24
   2 25 - 34
   3 35 - 44
   4 45 - 59
   5 60 and over

8. If you have obtained a trade or educational qualification since leaving school, please write in the name of your highest qualification.

9. What is your present occupation? (If you are not in the paid workforce, please write RETIRED, UNEMPLOYED, HOME DUTIES or whatever is applicable to you). ....

10. Do you have any dependents?
   1 YES....How many?_____
   2 NO

Box 8.19 Income questions

---

11. What is your weekly or annual income from all sources, before tax? Please circle the number next to the range that best describes your income.

   1 less than $77 a week OR less than $4000 a year
   2 $77 - 154 a week OR $4000 - 7999 a year
   3 $155 - 231 a week OR $8000 - 11999 a year
   4 $232 - 307 a week OR $12000 - 15999 a year
   5 $308 - 384 a week OR $16000 - 19999 a year
   6 $385 - 481 a week OR $20000 - 24999 a year
   7 $482 - 577 a week OR $25000 - 29999 a year
   8 $578 - 769 a week OR $30000 - 39999 a year
   9 $770 - 961 a week OR $40000 - 49999 a year
   10 $962 - 1153 a week OR $50000 - 59999 a year
   11 $1154 or more a week OR $60000 or more a year

12. If you are married or live with a partner, please write down the number from the list given in question 11 that best describes your joint weekly or annual income from all sources before tax.

   NUMBER _____

Table 8.10 Chi-square analysis by socioeconomic variables (all versions)

Variable	Degrees of freedom	Chi-square	Probability	Effective sample size	Frequency missing
Sex	9	4.21	0.897	1247	20
Age group	18	21.58	0.972	1249	18
Occupation (original)	81	102.33	0.055	1230	37
Occupation (recoded)	27	32.18	0.226	1230	37
Education (original)	54	88.39	0.002	1218	49
Education (recoded)	18	31.43	0.026	1218	49
Dependents	36	45.35	0.137	1231	36
Own Income	45	46.17	0.423	1045	222
Joint Income	45	50.62	0.261	1103	164

Socioeconomic Comparison of the Sample with the General Population

The socioeconomic characteristics of the survey respondents were compared to relevant information from census data for Victoria. The sample characteristics of sex, age, education, employment status and joint income were compared with these characteristics in the 1986 census data using a chi-squared analysis. The relevant statistics are given below in Table 8.11.

None of the sample characteristics is significantly different from the census data except joint (household) income, which is significantly different at the 1 per cent level. The survey respondents are concentrated more in the lower to middle income groups than in the census data. It is not clear why this has occurred. There were many respondents who objected to reporting their income category. The income questions had the highest non-response rate (11 to 12 per cent as opposed to 1 to 2 per cent for most of the other questions), which may have contributed to the downward bias.

There is a positive relationship between income and willingness to pay in this study, so the concentration of respondents in lower to middle income groups will cause a downward bias in value estimates when aggregating from the sample to the general Victorian population. Given that the sample population is not significantly different from the population from which it was drawn except in income characteristics which will cause a downward bias, it is considered acceptable to aggregate estimates of willingness to pay from the samples to the general Victorian population.

Table 8.11 Comparison of the sample and population socioeconomic variables

Sex	Survey %	Census %
Female	52.6	51.0
Male	47.4	49.0
Chi-squared value: 0.102	95% value: 3.80	

Age	Survey %	Census %
18 - 24	13.0	15.3
25 - 34	25.4	21.0
35 - 44	24.0	18.4
45 - 59	20.4	19.1
60 +	17.2	19.3
Chi-squared value: 3.31	95 % value: 9.50	

Education	Survey %	Census %
Secondary or less	68.9	75.9
Technical/trade	15.3	15.9
Graduate	13.9	8.5
Postgraduate	2.0	0.6
Chi-squared value: 7.37	95 % value: 7.80	

Employment	Survey %	Census %
Employed	59.0	55.44
Not employed	40.4	44.55
Chi-squared value: 0.616	95 % value: 3.80	

Joint income A C J	Survey %	Census %
< $12 000	15.8	16.0
$12 - 20 000	19.5	11.0
$20 - 30 000	20.9	15.2
$30 - 50 000	29.8	40.6
$50 000 +	14.0	17.2
Chi-squared value: 12.18	95 % value: 7.80 99 % value:11.30	

Joint income B D E F G H I J	Survey %	Census %
< $15 000	27.1	20.5
$15 - 20 000	10.8	6.5
$20 - 25 000	11.1	6.3
$25 - 30 000	10.9	8.9
$30 - 40 000	14.3	29.9
$40 - 50 000	9.7	10.7
$50 000 +	16.1	17.2
Chi-squared value: 17.28	95 % value: 12.60	99 % value: 16.80

CONSISTENCY CHECKS AND MISSING DATA

After the analysis described above, a few further cases were removed from the data base because they had too many missing observations (that is, unanswered questions) or because the data was inconsistent and could be considered unreliable. Thirty cases were removed because of missing observations and nine were removed because of inconsistent data. Cases failing to meet any of the consistency checks, listed in Box 8.20, were deleted on the grounds that the information given is likely to be unreliable. Mitchell and Carson (1989) note that in most contingent valuation studies, certain data are outliers or unreliable and consistency removals are needed.

Outliers deleted through consistency edits are typically from 'very low income respondents who gave willingness to pay amounts representing an implausibly large percentage of their income, or from upper income respondents giving zero or very low willingness to pay amounts even though their other answers indicate a strong demand for the good' (Mitchell and Carson, 1989, p. 268).

Box 8.20 Consistency checks

Check 1 - if income >$50,000 per year and age <24. Unlikely high income for age (no cases).

Check 2 - if joint income < $4,000 and open-ended willingness to pay = or> $100. Unlikely high payment given declared income (3 cases).

Check 3 - if joint income < $12,000 and open-ended willingness to pay = or >$200. Unlikely high payment given declared income (5 cases).

Check 4 - if Q1 equals 3 or 4 and open-ended willingness to pay = $150 plus (no cases).

Inconsistent answer - conservation of species is not important but respondent is prepared to pay a large sum to help conservation (one case).

It was difficult to distinguish the latter group in this study because of the large proportion of respondents who felt conservation of endangered species was 'very important'. However, removal of protest zero bids (Chapter 9) is likely to remove outliers in this category. The nine cases removed, through failing to meet consistency checks, is low compared with some other studies. For example, Carson (1991 p. 55) notes that 'the 9.5 per cent of cases dropped through consistency checks is fairly typical of public opinion survey and is on the low side for many CV studies'.

However, few obvious outliers were evident in this study. Removal of the unreliable cases, will have the effect of reducing the estimated willingness to pay. Following the removal of 39 cases, the number of cases for each questionnaire are given in Table 8.12. All analysis was done on the adjusted data sets. Analysis of the willingness to pay results is described in Chapter 9.

Table 8.12 Number of cases for each questionnaire

Questionnaire	Initial response rate (%)	Initial number of respondents	Adjusted number of respondents
A	42.0	147	144
B	32.0	96	95
C	35.1	123	117
D	34.7	104	101
E	29.0	189	186
F	32.3	113	111
G	35.6	107	101
H	30.8	108	105
I	29.0	87	86
J	34.9	213	202

9. Estimation of Willingness to Pay

INTRODUCTION

The focus of this chapter is on estimating the mean and median willingness to pay values from the data derived from both the discrete choice and the continuous valuation questions. The implications of the results for the survey hypotheses are discussed in the following chapter.

In the first section of this chapter, the identification and treatment of true zero willingness to pay responses and 'protest' zero responses are considered. Subsequently, the distributions of the responses to the discrete choice question were compared across questionnaires in order to determine whether responses to some questionnaire versions could be combined to overcome the problem of small sample size due to the low response rate. This comparison is also an initial test of the hypotheses described in Chapter 8.

The remainder of the chapter is concerned with the estimation of willingness to pay values and the comparison of estimates from the discrete choice and continuous valuation questions. Logistic regression models are developed for the discrete data and multiple regression models are generated for the continuous valuation data. All estimates of willingness to pay were made from models which included and excluded responses identified as protest bids. Three methods of estimating mean and median willingness to pay values are used for the discrete choice data.

In the final part of the chapter, the estimates of mean willingness to pay are aggregated over both Victorian households and individual adult Victorians. Best estimates of aggregate value for the conservation of flora and fauna and the conservation of Leadbeater's possum are presented and justified.

REFUSALS AND ZERO RESPONSES

The issue of dealing with zero responses is discussed in Chapter 7. In this study, the proportion of responses which are zero ranges from 30 to 60 per cent across all questionnaires for those not willing to pay any positive amount (Table 9.1). A further 8 to 21 per cent of respondents were unwilling to pay the initial discrete choice amount suggested because it was too high, but they were willing to pay a lower amount.

Possible reasons for the high number of refusals and zero responses may be that the respondents were unfamiliar with this kind of survey, the survey might have been too hypothetical or the scenarios and questions could have been too simplistic and unspecific. Some individuals may not have been prepared to value species existence in monetary terms. It may also have been that the respondents genuinely had a zero valuation for the good described. As might be expected, a greater proportion of people were found to have a zero willingness to pay for Leadbeater's possum than for flora and fauna generally. Fifty five per cent of respondents to the Leadbeater's possum questionnaire were unwilling to pay any positive amount as against 42 per cent of the respondents to the flora and fauna questionnaires.

Respondents who were not willing to pay the amount specified in the questionnaire were asked why they had responded 'no'. Multiple answers from a given list of reasons were allowed (Box 9.1). The overall frequencies for response to each reason are given in Table 9.2.

Table 9.1 Percentages of respondents refusing the discrete choice amount or refusing to pay any amount for species preservation

Questionnaires A to E - flora and fauna	% of refusals to the initial discrete choice question	% of refusals to make any positive payment
A	54	49
B	52	41
C	59	50
D	43	30
E	N.A.	35
ABCD	52	44
ABCDE	N.A.	42
Questionnaires F to I - Leadbeater's	% of refusals to the initial discrete choice question	% of refusals to make any positive payment
F	60	49
G	65	49
H	69	53
I	81	60
FGHI	68	55

Box 9.1 Reasons for not being willing to pay for species protection

1 = The amount given is too high, but I would pay $_ per year.

2 = I did not want to put a dollar value on protecting plants and animals (or Leadbeater's possum).

3 = Society has more important problems than protecting plants and animals (or Leadbeater's possum).

4 = Protecting plants and animals (or Leadbeater's possum) is not worth anything to me.

5 = The government should protect plants and animals (or Leadbeater's possum) using taxes already paid.

6 = Not enough information is given.

7 = I object to the way the question is asked.

8 = I can't afford to pay anything.

9 = Other.

Table 9.2 Percentage of respondents giving reasons for refusing to pay the given discrete choice amount (multiple responses)

Reason[1]	Flora and fauna Questionnaires ABCD	Flora and fauna Questionnaire E (open ended question)	Leadbeater's possum Questionnaires FGHI
1	7.4	0.0	13.9
2	11.2	3.7	10.0
3	6.3	0.0	16.3
4	0.4	4.8	1.9
5	37.2	26.5	36.3
6	6.3	3.2	7.3
7	3.2	1.6	3.9
8	8.7	8.5	15.1
9	11.6	7.4	14.1

1. See reasons in Box 9.1.

Considering the multiple responses, about 35 to 40 per cent of respondents felt existing taxes should be reallocated to species conservation from other areas of government spending (reason 5). This comment was also often made by people who were prepared to pay something, although these responses are not included in Table 9.2.

Suggestions as to the form of payment were frequently made and most respondents who commented seemed to be clearly aware that spending money on species conservation would result in less government spending in other areas. There was also a strong feeling that the government could not be trusted to spend special purpose taxes on the activity for which they were to be collected. The example of petrol taxes and roads was most commonly mentioned.

Overall, 8 to 10 per cent of the respondents felt they did not want to put a dollar value on species, which could be interpreted as an indication of lexicographic preferences. About 9 per cent of those answering the flora and fauna questionnaires and 15 per cent of those answering the Leadbeater's possum questionnaires said they couldn't afford anything and about 3 per cent objected to the question. The response that the good was not worth anything to them was given by 0.4 per cent of the respondents to the discrete choice flora and fauna questions, 5 per cent of those answering questionnaire E and 2 per cent of those answering the Leadbeater's possum questionnaire.

Reclassification of Multiple Responses to Single Responses

In order to discriminate between valid and 'protest' zero bids, the multiple answers were recoded into single responses. Overall, about 73 per cent of respondents gave single answers with the remaining 27 per cent giving two or more responses. The multiple answers were recoded into single responses according to a hierarchy of reasons. The recoding is of necessity somewhat arbitrary.

However, although the single answer after recoding may not have been the predominant one, there are very few cases where a protest vote would be coded as a true zero or vice versa. The recoding process is described in detail below.

Any respondent listing 1 (would pay a lower amount) was counted as a genuine bid as far as the discrete choice format was concerned whether or not other reasons were given. The respondent has clearly indicated they would pay a positive amount, but not the amount initially asked of them. Reason 9 (other) was generally disregarded if any of reasons 1 to 8 were also given because of the unacceptable cost of going through each individual case. Reason 5 (government should pay) was also disregarded if other reasons were given because it was given so commonly, both by respondents who were and who were not willing to pay.

The most common multiple response was 2 with 5, which was recoded to 2. However, both are considered as protest bids, so recoding to 5 would have given the same end result. Other multiple protest responses were: 2 and 6; 2 and 7; 2, 5 and 6; 2, 5 and 7; 5 and 6; 5 and 7; and 5, 6 and 7.

There were some answers with both protest and valid reasons but with the exception of 5 and 8 (29 cases in total) there were only two or three cases of each. The 5 and 8 combination was recoded to 8. Other combinations were 3 and 5 (recoded to 3), 4 and 5 (recoded to 4), 2, 4 and 6 (recoded to 4), 5, 6 and 8 (recoded to 8), 3, 4 and 7 (recoded to 4). Ten individuals gave four or more reasons.

In these cases a subjective assessment of what the respondents' intentions seemed to be was made when there were conflicting protest and valid reasons. In general recoding was on the conservative side, that is, accepting as a genuine zero bid rather than excluding as a protest bid.

The recoded responses were classified into valid and protest bids. Those who stated that species in general or Leadbeater's possum in particular had no worth to them (category 4), those who regarded other problems as more important (category 3) and those who couldn't afford to pay anything (category 8) are regarded as valid zero bids.

Respondents in category 1, those who refused to pay the amount requested in the questionnaire but were willing to pay a smaller amount, are also regarded as valid no bidders for the purposes of analysing the discrete choice data. The remaining categories - 0, 2, 5, 6, 7 and 9 - are regarded as protest bids. The percentages of respondents in the protest bid, valid no and positive bid categories are shown in Table 9.3.

Table 9.3 Protest bid, valid no and positive bids as a percentage of all bids

Questionnaire (1)	Protest zero bids (2)	Valid zero bids (3)	WTP less bids (4)	Willing to pay discrete choice amount (WTP1) (5)	Total stating they are willing to pay some positive amount (WTP2) (6) = 100-(2)-(3)
ABCD	31.3	12.4	12.5	43.8	56.3
E	22.0	12.9	N.A.	N.A.	65.1
FGHI	28.0	24.8	15.3	31.9	47.2

Effect of Excluding Protest Bids on Estimates of Willingness to Pay

People answering with reason 2 (not wanting to put a dollar value on species conservation), which accounted for about 20 per cent of the responses identified as protest bids, could possibly value species conservation highly, but do not wish to express this value in economic terms. If this is so, then there will be a self selection process resulting in a downward bias in mean values estimated when these bids are excluded. Other protest bidders may have any range of values.

The models with the protest bids removed will result in higher estimates of willingness to pay than those which include all zero bids as true zero bids. Using data with all bids and with protest bids excluded gives a range of estimates of mean willingness to pay, with the all bids case giving a lower bound to the estimates.

Proportion of Protest Bids

The proportion of protest bids in this survey is substantial. Protest bids in the flora and fauna questionnaires averaged 31 per cent of all responses. In the Leadbeater's possum questionnaires the average was 28 per cent of all responses. Although it is difficult to find guidelines in the literature on what is an acceptable level of protest bids (and why this level is acceptable), around 30 per cent would seem to be excessive. Walsh, Gillman and Loomis (1982) quote a US Water Resources Department guideline for protest bids of 10 per cent of total responses. Moser and Dunning (1986) state that excessive numbers of protest bidders indicates that some questions may have been misunderstood and should be rewritten but do not define what they mean by excessive.

Other Australian and New Zealand studies have also had substantial proportions of protest bids. Bennett (1981) had a similar proportion of protest responses to that in this study, although he did not distinguish between valid and protest votes in his analysis. Kirkland (1988) identified 18 per cent of responses as protest bids in a general population mail survey on wetland valuation and Sappideen (1992) identified 24 per cent, also in a general population mail survey.

It may be that the level of protest bids reflects a feeling that generally the public has little influence on specific government policies. It is also possible that the proportion of protest bids indicates that respondents had difficulty in understanding the survey scenario and/or were not convinced of its realism. It is particularly difficult with general population surveys to present material in a completely unambiguous and detailed manner that everyone will interpret as the researcher intended. It is even more difficult in a short mail survey. However, the questionnaires were pre-tested and the pre-test respondents did not indicate any difficulty with understanding the questionnaire.

Around 8.5 per cent of protest bidders felt that not enough information was provided and a further 4 per cent of protest bidders objected to the willingness to pay question. Twenty per cent of the protest bidders (about 8-10 per cent of all respondents) did not want to put a dollar value on species conservation.

The predominant reason for refusing to pay was reason 5; that government should provide for conservation out of taxes already paid. This reason accounted for 17 per cent of all respondents and about 60 per cent of those identified as protest bidders. It is possible that some people do not realize that more taxes spent in one area means less spent in another, or they do not relate government spending ability to taxes collected. There were a few comments such as 'the government should pay but not out of taxes' which indicated that some respondents had not thought through where the money should come from. On the other hand, there were many comments indicating that some respondents did understand the trade off situation. There did seem to be some antagonism to the idea of special taxes, which are not common in Australia, although there was no difference in the proportion of protest bids between the tax and donation questionnaires.

WILLINGNESS TO PAY DISTRIBUTIONS AND DATA SETS

A preliminary comparison of the discrete choice willingness to pay responses was made in order to establish whether there were any questionnaire versions (Boxes 8.2 and 8.4) for which response distributions were sufficiently similar to allow combination of the data sets. This became necessary because some of the data sets were too small for any meaningful analysis due to the low response rate. For example, questionnaire I had 86 respondents. These comparisons are also an initial test of the hypotheses formulated in Chapter 8 and discussed in depth in Chapter 10. The Kruskal-Wallis test, based on a chi-squared distribution, was used to compare the discrete choice responses (Norusis 1985). Results are presented in Table 9.4.

Based on the results in Table 9.4, it appears that the distribution of responses to paying to preserve Leadbeater's possum through increased taxes is different from the distribution of responses to paying though a private donation at the 7 per cent level for F and H and the 1 per cent level for G and I when protest bids are excluded. For FG combined compared with HI combined the difference is significant at the 1 per cent level for both the all bids case and with no protest bids. No difference in response distributions is apparent at the 10 per cent level between the flora and fauna questionnaires when information on current expenditure is given, in A and B, or not given, in C and D.

There is also no difference at the 10 per cent level for the Leadbeater's possum questionnaires whether a picture of the possum in included, in F and H, or not included, in G and I. The use of a closed question 2 (in A and C) compared with the use of an open ended question 2 (in B and D) results in a significant difference at the 1 per cent level for C compared with D, but there is no significant difference in distribution of responses at the 10 per cent level for A compared with B or for AC combined compared with BD combined.

On the basis of these tests, the data from some questionnaires were combined for further analysis, because the low response rate to the survey had resulted in small sample sizes in some of the data sets. Questionnaire data sets were combined where the Kruskal-Wallis test showed that there were no significant differences in distribution of responses at the 10 per cent level. Questionnaire A was combined with C, B with D, F with G and H with I. Further analysis was also done on the combined data set of A, B, C and D. Questionnaire E is analysed separately because of the different payment question used in this version.

Table 9.4 Comparison of discrete choice responses, all bids and no protest bids

Questionnaires compared	Hypothesis1	Sample size (all bids)		p value - (probability the distributions from same population)	
		n_1	n_2	all bids	no protest bids
A with C	H5a	A 144	C 117	0.37	0.96
B with D	H5a	B 95	D 101	0.33	0.55
A with B	H5c	A 144	B 95	0.63	0.19
C with D	H5c	C 117	D 101	0.01	0.48
F with G	H5b	F 111	G 101	0.41	0.68
H with I	H5b	H 105	I 86	0.07	0.15
F with H	H4	F 111	H 105	0.22	0.07
G with I	H4	G 101	I 86	0.16	0.01
AB with CD	H5a	AB 239	CD 218	0.89	0.84
AC with BD	H5c	AC 261	BD 196	0.05	0.16
FG with HI	H4	FG 210	HI 190	0.01	0.00
FH with GI	H5b	FH 216	GI 187	0.10	0.29
ABCD with FGHI	H1	ABCD 447	FGHI 400	0.00	0.00

1. The hypotheses are described in Chapter 8.

The four Leadbeater's possum questionnaires are also analysed together (FGHI), with a dummy variable TD indicating whether payment is through tax (TD = 0) or donation (TD = 1). Questionnaire J was analysed separately because this version had a willingness to accept compensation rather than a willingness to pay question.

The combined data sets resulting from the analysis described above are used for all further analysis. The data sets, their sample sizes and the notation used to refer to them throughout the rest of the book are listed in Table 9.5. Definitions of variables which appear in the logistic and multiple regression models used for analysis are given in Table 9.6 for reference throughout the rest of the analysis.

Table 9.5 Combined questionnaire versions for analysis

	Notation	No. of cases
Flora and fauna questionnaires:		
A and C (closed question 2) with all cases	AC all	261
A and C excluding protest bids	AC npb	172
B and D (open-ended question 2) with all cases	BD all	196
B and D excluding protest bids	BD npb	142
A, B, C and D including all cases	ABCD all	447
A, B, C and D excluding protest bids	ABCD npb	308
E (payment card) including all cases	E all	186
E excluding protest bids	E npb	145
Leadbeater's possum questionnaires:		
F and G (tax payment) including all cases	FG all	210
F and G excluding protest bids	FG npb	149
H and I (donation payment) including all cases	HI all	190
H and I excluding protest bids	HI npb	138
F, G, H and I including all cases	FGHI all	400
F, G, H and I excluding protest bids	FGHI npb	287

Table 9.6 Definitions of variables

	Questionnaire	Definition and coding
Dependent Variables		
WTP1	All except E	Binary variable indicating whether respondent will or will not pay the discrete choice amount posed in the survey. Dependent variable for logistic regression.
OEPRICE	All	Maximum amount respondent willing to pay. Dependent variable for multiple regression.
Explanatory variables		
DA	All except E	Dollar amount posed to each respondent in discrete choice question.
LDA	ABCDE	Log of DA
AGE	All	Age group. 18-24, 25-34, 35-44, 45-59, 60 plus.
EDUC	All	Education level (0=secondary or less, 1=trade or other, 2=tertiary)
DEPNT	All	Dependents. Actual number=0,1,2,3. 4 or more =4.
OWN	All	Own income. 6 categories (questionnaires A,C,J). 11 categories (questionnaires B,D,E,F,G,H,I).
JNT	All	Joint (household) income. As for OWN.
OPT	FGHI	Importance of having option to see species in future (3=very, 2=moderately, 1=slightly, 0=not).
Dummy variables		
RR	All	Results requested (1=yes, 0=no)
IMP	All	Importance of species protection (1=important, 0=not important)
OCC	All	Occupation (1=paid employment, 0=otherwise)
ECOBAL	BDE	Reason for protecting species - ecological balance (1=mentioned, 0=otherwise)
RTLIVE	BDE	Reason for protecting species - species have right to live (1=mentioned, 0=otherwise)
UNIHERIT	BDE	Reason for protecting species - unique/part of heritage (1=mentioned, 0=otherwise)
HD	FGHI	Heard of Leadbeater's possum (1=yes, 0=no)
SN	FGHI	Seen Leadbeater's possum (1=yes, 0=no)
TD	FGHI	Tax or donation payment (1=donation, 0=tax)

REGRESSION ANALYSIS OF DISCRETE CHOICE DATA

Equation Fitting

The discrete choice data was analysed using logistic regression, the most commonly used approach in analysis of binary response data. The model is:

$$Pr(''yes'') = \frac{1}{1+e^{-z}} \qquad (9.1)$$

Here Z is given by the linear combination,

$$(9.2)$$
$$Z = \beta_0 + \beta_1 X_1 + \beta_2 X_2 + ... + \beta_p X_p$$

and X_1 ...... X_p are explanatory variables.

Computation was done using SPSSPC (SPSS Inc. 1983). Forward stepwise logistic regression was used to select the most appropriate model. The forward stepwise process involves entering one variable after another and checking the effect on the goodness of fit of the model. The criteria for entry of a variable is the significance level of the score statistic. At each step, the variable with the smallest significance level of the score statistic is entered into the model. Variables with significance levels greater than 0.05 are not entered. All variables in the model are also examined to see if they meet the removal criteria. Variables with significance levels for the Wald statistic exceeding the cutoff value of 0.1 are removed. The Wald statistic, which has a chi-squared distribution, is used to test that a coefficient is 0.

Outliers and influential observations were identified. Although examination of the responses indicated no reason for deleting these cases, models were run both with and without them. Deleting these cases made little or no difference to the outcome, so they were included in all subsequent analyses. The correlation coefficients did not indicate any problems with multicollinearity.

Logistic regression models were run using both the dollar amount posed to respondents in the discrete choice question (DA) and the log of this variable (LDA). For 9 of the 12 questionnaire samples, the regression models with DA as the regressor are better fitting. For the remaining three samples the LDA models are very slightly better fitting models, using the percentage of correctly predicted responses, but are not consistent with utility theory. The DA models are preferred and have been used in all further analysis because they are compatible with the utility-maximisation hypothesis (Chapter 7).

Goodness of fit statistics from the SPSSPC logistic regression routine are given in Table 9.7. The goodness of fit measures indicate how well the model explains the actual data. The first measure presented in Table 9.7 is a goodness of fit statistic based on the comparison of the observed probabilities with the predicted probabilities. This statistic has a chi-squared distribution. The hypothesis that the model fits is not rejected if the observed significance level of the goodness of fit statistic is large. The smallest significance level for this measure is 0.37.

The second evaluative measure is how well the model classifies the data, that is, the proportion of predicted 0 responses that actually are 0 and the proportion of predicted 1 responses that actually are 1. This gives an idea of the predictive power of the equation. The percentage of correctly predicted responses ranges from about 70 to 85 per cent which indicates the models perform well in predicting whether or not a respondent will pay a particular dollar amount. In general, the two goodness of fit measures presented in Table 9.7 indicate that the models fit the data fairly well.

Table 9.7 Goodness of fit measures from logistic regression analysis[1]

Questionnaire	Goodness of fit[2]	Per cent correct
AC all	202.11 (0.445)	69.27
AC npb	138.24 (0.407)	76.43
BD all	172.09 (0.548)	72.07
BD npb	101.88 (0.666)	82.93
ABCD all	354.23 (0.561)	69.15
ABCD npb	260.17 (0.365)	78.60
FG all	169.78 (0.469)	74.71
FG npb	121.45 (0.446)	77.60
HI all	160.59 (0.807)	78.69
HI npb	101.27 (0.797)	78.81
FGHI all	326.42 (0.802)	72.03
FGHI npb	230.48 (0.708)	77.11

1. Significance levels are given in brackets
2. Defined as $Z^2 = $ (Sum of the residual i^2) $/$ $(P_i(1-P_i))$ where the residual is the difference between the observed value Y_i and the predicted value, P_i.

Contingent Valuation and Endangered Species

Interpretation of the Regression Coefficients

The explanatory variables included in the models as a result of the stepwise regression process and their coefficients are listed in Tables 9.8 and 9.9. The significance levels of the coefficients and standard errors for the coefficients are also given in Tables 9.8 and 9.9.

One indication of the validity of the results of a contingent valuation survey is whether willingness to pay is affected by the variables suggested as important by economic theory (for example, income, education, views on preserving species) and whether the signs of the coefficients of the variables are in line with *a priori* expectations.

For example, according to economic theory, income and willingness to pay are positively related (Imber, Stevenson and Wilks 1991). The explanatory variables in this study include variables measuring income, attitudes to species conservation and prior knowledge of the Leadbeater's possum, as well as age, employment status and number of dependents in some of the models.

The signs of the coefficients of the variables included in the models are all in the expected direction. The probability of a yes response decreases as the dollar amount (DA) the respondents are asked to pay increases in all questionnaire versions. Respondents who believe conservation of species is important (IMP) are more likely to pay a positive amount than those who do not believe it is important in all models except BD all and HI all. In BD all, mentioning 'maintaining an ecological balance' as a reason for protecting species (ECOBAL) increased the probability of paying.

In HI all, the importance of maintaining the option to see Leadbeater's possum at some time in the future (OPT) was positively related to the probability of paying. Although it would be expected that people who believed option value was important (OPT) would be more willing to pay than those who did not, it is not immediately obvious why option value should be more influential than preserving species for future generations or than existence value.

Preparedness to pay increases as household income (JNT) increases for all the flora and fauna models and for the FG Leadbeater's possum questionnaires. In the HI and FGHI models employment status (OCC) was included as an explanatory variable. Although a question on age was included in all questionnaires, it was significant only in the AC models, where preparedness to pay decreased with older age groups. This is consistent with other studies (Bennett 1981).

The variables SN (seen) was included in the Leadbeater's possum FG models and HD (heard) was included in the FGHI model with no protest bids. It would seem reasonable that prior knowledge of the species (SN and HD) should be positively related to willingness to pay. Perhaps those with prior knowledge are more interested in 'nature' to begin with. Number of dependents was included in the Leadbeater's possum HI model with no protest bids. It would also seem reasonable for respondents with more dependents (DEPNT) to be less able to pay and hence to be less willing to pay.

The variable TD is a dummy variable used only in the combined FGHI models to distinguish the tax payment mechanism (used in F and G) from donation to a private conservation trust (used in H and I). The negative sign on the coefficient indicates that respondents are more likely to say yes to paying a dollar amount if payment is through a tax increase than if payment is through a donation to a private conservation trust.

Table 9.8 Logistic regression coefficients of the explanatory variables for the AC, BD and ABCD flora and fauna questionnaires[1]

Questionnaires	Constant	DA	IMP	JNT	AGE	ECOBAL
AC all	-0.9200	-0.0060	0.856	0.358	-0.2200	
	(0.200)	(0.000)	(0.015)	(0.003)	(0.074)	
	{0.717}	{0.001}	{0.352}	{0.121}	{0.123}	
AC npb	-0.9400	-0.0064	1.320	0.592	-0.2940	
	(0.317)	(0.000)	(0.004)	(0.000)	(0.078)	
	{0.930}	{0.002}	{0.458}	{0.162}	{0.167}	
BD all	-1.0100	-0.0068		0.239		1.272
	(0.027)	(0.000)		(0.000)		(0.002)
	{0.457}	{0.002}		{0.065}		{0.402}
BD npb	-0.6100	-0.0104	1.075	0.312		1.082
	(0.415)	(0.000)	(0.069)	(0.001)		(0.082)
	{0.751}	{0.002}	{0.590}	{0.097}		{0.623}
ABCD all	-1.7100	-0.0061	0.707	0.466		
	(0.000)	(0.000)	(0.008)	(0.000)		
	{0.451}	{0.001}	{0.268}	{0.090}		
ABCD npb	-1.7300	-0.0075	1.254	0.676		
	(0.003)	(0.000)	(0.001)	(0.000)		
	{0.585}	{0.001}	{0.365}	{0.126}		

1. Significance levels given in () brackets; Standard errors given in {} brackets.

Table 9.9 Logistic regression coefficients of the explanatory variables for the FG, HI and FGHI Leadbeater's possum questionnaires[1]

Questionnaires	Constant	DA	IMP	JNT	SN	
FG all	-1.1500	-0.0220	1.367	0.103	0.832	
	(0.040)	(0.000)	(0.001)	(0.094)	(0.041)	
	{0.561}	{0.005}	{0.422}	{0.061}	{0.408}	
FG npb	-1.4300	-0.0243	1.854	0.238	1.303	
	(0.035)	(0.000)	(0.000)	(0.004)	(0.033)	
	{0.677}	{0.006}	{0.520}	{0.083}	{0.613}	
	Constant	DA	IMP	OPT	OCC	DEPNT
HI all	-2.5300	-0.0284		1.095	0.508	
	(0.000)	(0.000)		(0.000)	(0.205)	
	{0.630}	{0.007}		{0.237}	{0.400}	
HI npb	-0.9400	-0.0332	2.874			-0.4220
	(0.158)	(0.000)	(0.000)			(0.019)
	{0.664}	{0.008}	{0.735}			{0.180}
	Constant	DA	IMP	TD	OCC	HD
FGHI all	-1.0000	-0.0223	1.713	- 0.773	0.528	
	(0.008)	(0.000)	(0.000)	(0.003)	(0.048)	
	{0.375}	{0.004}	{0.334}	{0.259}	{0.266}	
FGHI npb	-0.7900	-0.0265	1.953	- 1.296	0.938	0.962
	(0.077)	(0.000)	(0.000)	(0.000)	(0.005)	(0.005)
	{0.450}	{0.005}	{0.400}	{0.340}	{0.333}	{0.338}

1. Significance levels given in () brackets; Standard errors given in { } brackets.

The coefficients in Tables 9.8 and 9.9 were used in the estimation of mean and median willingness to pay for the questionnaire versions detailed in Table 9.5. The estimation methods are described in the following sections.

Mean and median values were not estimated for the FGHI sample because the different payment mechanisms in the FG and HI versions resulted in significantly different willingness to pay distributions.

ESTIMATION OF WILLINGNESS TO PAY FROM DISCRETE CHOICE DATA

Estimates of mean and median willingness to pay were made in three different ways. The theory of these methods is described in Chapter 7. Application of the first two methods makes use of the equations in Tables 9.8 and 9.9. The first method was to estimate the mean and median values using the formulae developed by Hanemann (1984, 1989b). The second method was to integrate the cumulative distribution function of the probability of saying 'yes' to the given discrete choice amount. The first and second methods are mathematically equivalent and give the same results provided the upper and lower integration limits are not truncated. The third method of estimating willingness to pay used was the non-parametric method developed by Kriström (1990a, 1990b).

Method 1 - The Hanemann Formulae

The basis of this method is discussed in more detail in Chapter 7. The equations developed in Tables 9.8 and 9.9 are of the general form:

$$\log(\frac{Pr("yes")}{1-Pr("yes")})=\alpha+\beta_1X_1+\beta_2X_2+...+\beta_pX_p+\beta_nA \qquad (9.3)$$

Here X_1 ... X_p are explanatory variables and A is either the dollar bid or the log of the dollar bid. The utility difference is specified as $\Delta V = \alpha - \beta DA$, the linear functional form specified by Hanemann (Hanemann 1984, 1987 and 1989b). In these models, the mean and median can be calculated as mean or median = α/β (Chapter 7).

Table 9.10 Equations and willingness to pay estimates from the discrete choice questions

Model	Equation	Mean and median (\$ per year)
AC all	0.4920 - 0.0060 DA	82.00
AC npb	1.5460 - 0.0064 DA	241.56
BD all	1.0076 - 0.0068 DA	148.18
BD npb	2.7695 - 0.0104 DA	266.30
ABCD all	0.7189 - 0.0061 DA	117.85
ABCD npb	2.0040 - 0.0075 DA	267.20
FG all	0.6421 - 0.0220 DA	29.19
FG npb	1.6620 - 0.0243 DA	68.40
HI all	-0.0800 - 0.0284 DA	-2.80
HI npb	0.7816 - 0.0332 DA	23.54

The equations in Table 9.10 were obtained from those in Tables 9.8 and 9.9 by calculating the grand coefficient alpha (α) which is composed of the constant plus the coefficients of the other variables multiplied by the mean value of the appropriate variable. Beta (β) is the coefficient on the dollar amount variable. The estimated willingness to pay values are also given in Table 9.10.

Method 2 - Cumulative Distribution Function

The second method of estimating mean willingness to pay uses the area under the cumulative distribution function of the probability of saying 'yes' to given bid amounts. The theory of this method was also developed by Hanemann (1984 and 1987) and is discussed in Chapter 7.

The integration function is:

$$E(WTP)=\int_0^\infty (1-(1+e^{-\Delta v})^{-1})dDA - \int_{-\infty}^0 (1+e^{-\Delta v})^{-1}dDA \qquad (9.4)$$

Here

$$\Delta V = \alpha - \beta DA \qquad (9.5)$$

Integration was carried out over both untruncated and truncated integration ranges. Integration limits for the untruncated distribution were set at minus 10,000 and 10,000 as a satisfactory practical approximation to $-\infty$ and $+\infty$. Ranges truncated at both the left and right tails were used to investigate whether there is a problem with 'fat tails'.

The truncated ranges for the flora and fauna questionnaires were minus 200 to 500 and minus 10,000 to 1,000. The maximum discrete choice bid was $500. The ranges for the Leadbeater's possum questionnaire versions were minus 200 to 150 (the maximum bid) and minus 10,000 to 250. Less sensitivity analysis was done for the left hand tail because it approached the axis more closely than the right hand tail. The results are given in Tables 9.11 and 9.12.

The estimated cumulative distribution functions for all the questionnaires with all bids and without protest bids are illustrated in Figures 9.1 to 9.10.

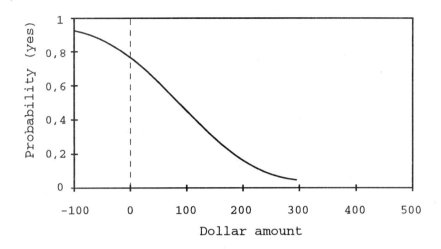

Figure 9.1   *Cumulative distribution function for flora and fauna questionnaires AC, all bids.*

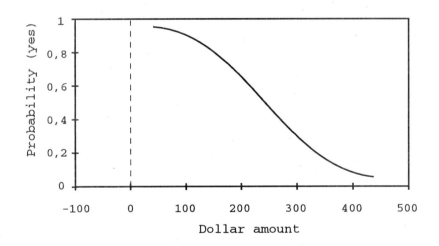

Figure 9.2   *Cumulative distribution function for flora and fauna questionnaires AC, protest bids excluded.*

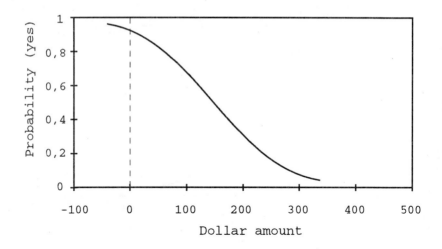

Figure 9.3   Cumulative distribution function for flora and fauna
                      questionnaires BD, all bids.

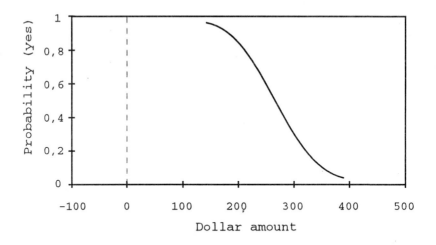

Figure 9.4   Cumulative distribution function for flora and fauna
                      questionnaires BD, protest bids excluded.

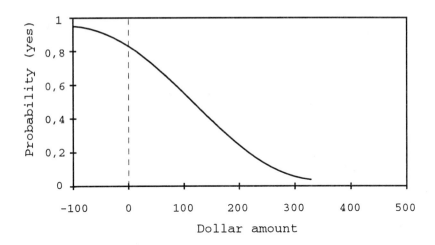

Figure 9.5   *Cumulative distribution function for flora and fauna questionnaires ABCD, all bids.*

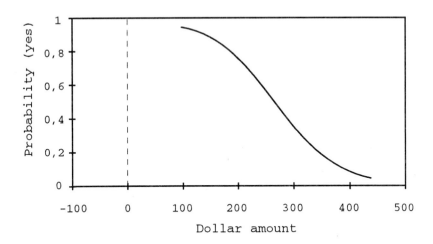

Figure 9.6   *Cumulative distribution function for flora and fauna questionnaires ABCD, protest bids excluded.*

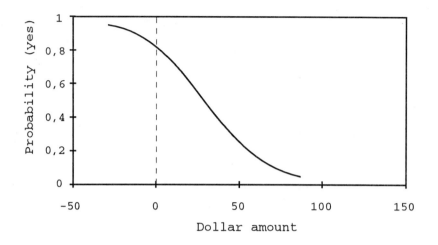

Figure 9.7   *Cumulative distribution function for Leadbeater's possum questionnaires FG, all bids.*

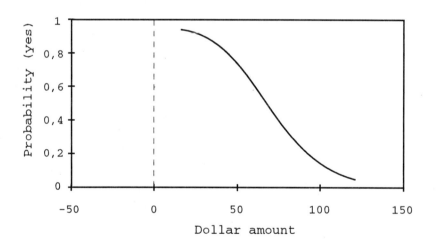

Figure 9.8   *Cumulative distribution function for Leadbeater's possum questionnaires FG, protest bids excluded.*

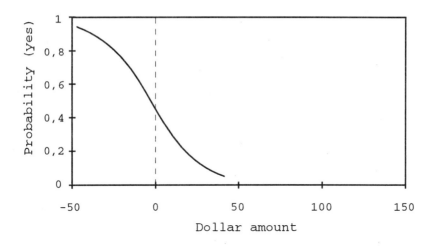

Figure 9.9   *Cumulative distribution function for Leadbeater's possum questionnaires HI, all bids.*

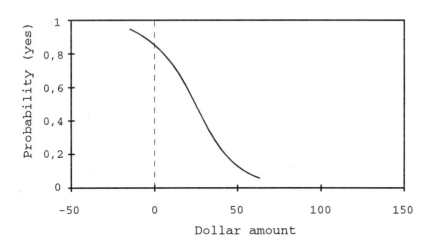

Figure 9.10   *Cumulative distribution function for Leadbeater's possum questionnaires HI, protest bids excluded.*

Table 9.11 Estimated mean willingness to pay ($ per year) flora and fauna questionnaires ABCD

Questionnaires	Utility difference	Integration limits	Mean WTP
AC all	0.4920 - 0.0060 DA	- 200 to 500	74.88
		- 10,000 to 1,000	81.32
		Untruncated	82.00
AC npb	1.5460 - 0.0064 DA	- 200 to 500	223.21
		- 10,000 to 1,000	240.34
		Untruncated	241.55
BD all	1.0076 - 0.0068 DA	- 200 to 500	138.48
		- 10,000 to 1,000	147.72
		Untruncated	148.17
BD npb	2.7695 - 0.0104 DA	- 200 to 500	258.94
		- 10,000 to 1,000	266.24
		Untruncated	266.30
ABCD all	0.7189 - 0.0061 DA	- 200 to 500	102.63
		- 10,000 to 1,000	117.08
		Untruncated	117.84
ABCD npb	2.0040 - 0.0075 DA	- 200 to 500	249.71
		- 10,000 to 1,000	266.64
		Untruncated	267.19

The sensitivity analysis of integration limits shows that there is no problem with fat tails. The values estimated when the upper range is truncated at the maximum dollar amount offered in the questionnaires is in the order of 90 to 95 per cent of the untruncated values for both the flora and fauna data and the Leadbeater's possum data.

The mean and median estimates of willingness to pay from method 1 and method 2 when no truncation occurs are shown to be the same (Tables 9.10, 9.11 and 9.12). All the estimates are positive except those for conservation of Leadbeater's possum with payment through donations when all bids are included (HI all). Here the estimates are negative but not significantly different from zero. There are a large number of zero responses to these questionnaires, which contributed to this result. Questionnaires HI had around 74 per cent zero bids for the discrete choice question and around 56 per cent for any positive amount, compared with 62 per cent and 49 per cent for the payment through taxation (FG) questionnaires. There were many comments that showed respondents considered their other donations in answering this question, for example, 'prefer to donate to other causes'. Others commented that it was Government's responsibility. This issue is discussed in the following chapter.

Method 3 - Non-parametric Estimation of Willingness to Pay

Non-parametric estimates of mean and median willingness to pay were derived using the approach developed by Kriström (1990a, 1990b) which is explained in Chapter 7. The steps taken are described below.

Initially, the actual (observed) proportions of yes responses for each bid level were calculated. Because the observed yes proportions do not follow a consistent decline as the bid amount increases it was necessary to 'smooth' the estimates using the method developed by Ayer *et al.* (1955) to get a monotonic sequence. The absence of a monotonic decline may be partly due to small sample size. There also seem to be problems with particular values; for example, $55 was rejected most of the time and $250 was accepted often. The survival functions of observed and smoothed (grouped) proportions for the all bids versions of all models using the conservative upper limit are shown in Figures 9.11 to 9.15.

Table 9.12 Estimated mean willingness to pay ($ per year) Leadbeater's possum questionnaires FGHI

Questionnaires	Utility difference	Integration limits	Mean WTP
FG all	0.6421 - 0.0220 DA	- 200 to 150	26.39
		- 10,000 to 250	28.83
		Untruncated	29.18
FG npb	1.6620 - 0.0243 DA	- 200 to 150	63.15
		- 10,000 to 250	67.90
		Untruncated	68.40
HI all	- 0.08 - 0.0284 DA	- 200 to 150	-3.09
		- 10,000 to 250	-2.88
		Untruncated	-2.80
HI npb	0.7810 - 0.0332 DA	- 200 to 150	22.74
		- 10,000 to 250	23.23
		Untruncated	23.54

Median willingness to pay is at the point where the probability of a yes response (Π) is 0.5. The mean willingness to pay estimate, using the non-parametric procedure, is the area bounded by the empirical distribution. To estimate the mean, it is necessary to make some simplifying assumptions;

1. linear interpolation is a suitable approximation of behaviour between known points,
2. $\Pi = 1$ when the bid amount (DA) = 0. This constrains willingness to pay to be 0 or positive,
3. $\Pi = 0$ at an assumed maximum value of DA. Two maximum values of DA are assumed, a conservative estimate and an extended estimate, based on extending the slopes of segments of the distributions by eye to meet the axis. In the case of HI npb $\Pi = 0$ at an actual value of 125.

Mean values are sensitive to which value of maximum A is used. The minimum value of A is constrained to be zero because of the difficulty of extrapolating below zero. The non-parametric estimates of mean and median of willingness to pay are given in Table 9.13.

Median values are given as the mid point of a range, because with the smoothing of the curve, there were a range of values for which the probability of acceptance was 0.5.

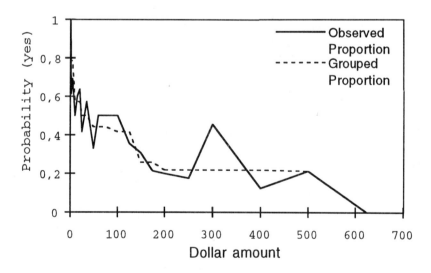

Figure 9.11   *Proportions of `yes' responses at different bid levels for questionnaires AC, all bids*

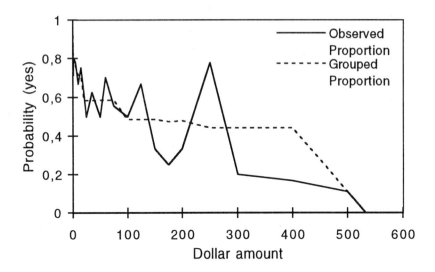

Figure 9.12   *Proportions of `yes' responses at different bid levels for questionnaires BD, all bids.*

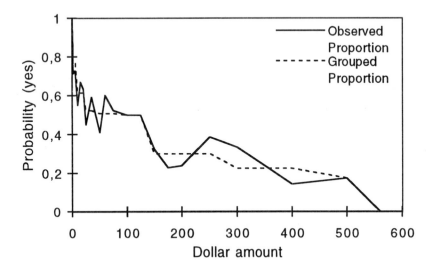

Figure 9.13   *Proportions of `yes' responses at different bid levels for questionnaires ABCD, all bids.*

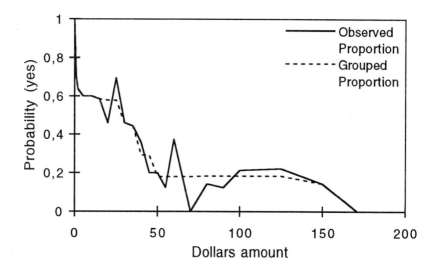

Figure 9.14   *Proportions of `yes' responses at different bid levels for questionnaires FG, all bids.*

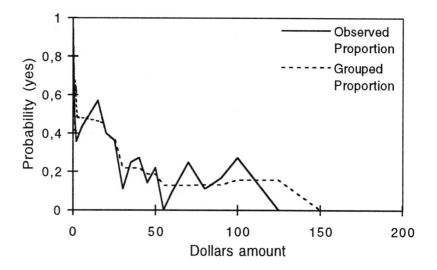

Figure 9.15   *Proportions of `yes' responses at different bid levels for questionnaires HI, all bids.*

Comparison of the Methods

Results from the parametric and non-parametric methods of estimating willingness to pay are compared in Table 9.14. The non-parametric method results in higher estimates than the estimates from the parametric methods. This occurs partly because the non-parametric distribution is constrained to zero or positive willingness to pay values by the assumption that $\Pi = 1$ at DA $= 0$ (Kriström 1990a, 1990b), whereas the parametric models can take negative willingness to pay values.

To obtain parametric estimates which are comparable with the non-parametric approach, values were re-estimated using method 2 conditional on willingness to pay being greater than or equal to zero, that is, truncated at zero for the left tail and untruncated at the right tail (Kriström 1990a). These results are also presented in Table 9.14.

The integration expression when willingness to pay is greater than or equal to zero is given by:

$$E(WTP) = \int_0^{\infty} (1 - (1 + e^{-\Delta v})^{-1}) dDA \qquad (9.6)$$

Here

$$\Delta V = \alpha - \beta DA \qquad (9.7)$$

Method 1 and the untruncated method 2 are equivalent and give the same results. The non-parametric estimate and the method-2 estimate which is truncated at zero are similar to each other. They result in higher estimates than the untruncated estimate because the possibility of negative willingness to pay responses is excluded. The non-parametric estimates range from 81 to 127 per cent of the truncated method 2 estimates with a mean of 101 per cent.

The untruncated method 2 results range from 51 to 98 per cent of the truncated results (if the HI all figures are not included) with a mean of 77 per cent. Assumptions about whether or not individuals' willingness to pay values can be negative, and hence what integration range is appropriate, clearly affects the estimates of willingness to pay that are made. Serious consideration must be given to whether large negative values are likely, or whether there is only a large proportion of zero responses.

For goods where it is unlikely that willingness to pay responses could take negative values, the non-parametric method offers a computationally simple method of estimating mean willingness to pay which avoids distributional assumptions. However, sample sizes must be adequate to obtain a monotonic decline in the proportion of respondents paying as the bid amount increases.

Table 9.13 Non-parametric estimates of mean and median willingness to pay ($ per year)

Questionnaire	Conservative upper limit on maximum DA		Extended upper limit on maximum DA		Median (mid point)
	Mean	Upper limit	Mean	Upper limit	
AC all	159.90	625	203.88	1035	30.00
AC npb	291.84	757	351.86	1077	137.50
BD all	226.25	533	230.91	618	87.50
BD npb	254.07	530	261.07	600	262.50
ABCD all	167.85	560	207.92	1021	112.50
ABCD npb	276.49	673	328.89	1013	262.50
FG all	43.77	171	49.00	244	27.50
FG npb	61.41	168	68.40	240	37.50
HI all	28.91	150	28.91	150	0.50
HI npb	36.45	125	36.45	125	22.50

Table 9.14 Comparison of the methods of estimating mean willingness to pay ($ per year)

Questionnaire	Method 1 and Untruncated method 2	Method 2 Truncated at 0	Non-parametric conservative
AC all	82.00	161.52	159.90
AC npb	241.55	271.74	291.84
BD all	148.17	193.94	226.25
BD npb	266.30	272.15	254.07
ABCD all	117.84	182.93	167.85
ABCD npb	267.19	284.06	276.49
FG all	29.18	48.40	43.77
FG npb	68.40	75.55	61.41
HI all	- 2.80	22.71	28.91
HI npb	23.54	35.96	36.45

ESTIMATION OF WILLINGNESS TO PAY FROM CONTINUOUS VALUATION DATA

There is some evidence in the literature that estimates of willingness to pay derived from discrete choice questions and estimates derived from open-ended questions (also known as continuous valuation) for the same good will differ (Chapter 6). In general, surveys using discrete choice questions appear to result in higher estimates of willingness to pay (Kriström 1990a, 1993 and Walsh, Johnson and McKean 1989 and 1992).

To investigate this issue, questionnaires on the conservation of flora and fauna using discrete choice and open-ended willingness to pay questions were sent to separate samples, ABCD for the discrete choice question and E for the open-ended question.

In addition to the initial discrete choice question, the questionnaires had a follow up open-ended question which was included to examine the issue of starting point bias or anchoring bias (Chapter 6). The hypothesis is that the respondent will use the value given in the discrete choice question as an implied value cue which will influence their answer to the open-ended question (Kahneman, Slovic and Tversky 1982, Kriström 1990a and 1993, Mitchell and Carson 1989).

The first step in the analysis was to estimate willingness to pay from the continuous valuation data. Secondly, the responses to both questions from questionnaires ABCD were compared and thirdly, the results of the continuous valuation question in ABCD were compared with the responses from questionnaire E. Much of the analysis follows Kriström (1990a and 1993), who undertook a similar survey in 1987.

Equation Fitting

Responses to the open-ended willingness to pay questions were analysed using ordinary least squares regression (Moser and Dunning 1986). Several models were run using a stepwise process of both inclusion and exclusion of the explanatory variables. Variables are included in the equation if the probability associated with the F test for the hypothesis that the coefficient of the entered variable is 0 is less than or equal to 0.05. Variables are removed if the maximum probability of the F statistic is 0.10 (Norusis 1983). The correlation coefficients did not indicate the presence of multicollinearity. This was confirmed by the high tolerance levels of the variables (generally in the range 0.7 to 0.98). The tolerance is the proportion of the variability in an independent variable not explained by the other independent variables (Norusis 1983). Deleting or retaining possible outliers made almost no difference to the models so these cases were retained.

The adjusted R^2 results for all models are given in Tables 9.15 and 9.16. The adjusted R^2 are very low for all the models, with the lowest being 0.029 for questionnaire E and the highest being 0.342 for questionnaires ABCD. The low adjusted R^2 indicates that there is not a good linear relationship between willingness to pay and the independent variables and the regression equations are not useful for predicting a respondent's willingness to pay. The regression for questionnaire E is particularly poor.

Low adjusted R^2 values are common in general population surveys (Kriström 1990a and Stone 1992). For example, Stone reported R^2 values of 0.16 and 0.17 in a contingent valuation study of a wetland and Bennett (1981) obtained a value of 0.20 in a study of an Australian nature reserve. Some researchers attribute this to the presence of hypothetical bias which may work in either direction (Bennett 1981). Hageman (1985) attributes the low explanatory power to the fact that utility functions which determine values for public goods tend to be highly individualised.

Interpretation of the Regression Coefficients

The signs of the coefficients of the variables which were included as explanatory variables in the multiple regression models are all in line with *a priori* expectations. For example, joint income and stating that conservation of species is important are positively related to willingness to pay. Bennett (1981), in another Australian study, also found that age, household income and conservation attitudes were important in determining willingness to pay.

The regression results for the flora and fauna questionnaires (ABCD) show that the dollar amount given in the discrete choice question (DA), joint income (JNT) and the importance of protecting endangered species (IMP) are linearly related to willingness to pay.

Age (AGE) is included as an explanatory variable in the models AC npb and ABCD npb. Education (EDUC) is included in all the BD and ABCD models. The results for questionnaire E showed that the only variable for which the *t*-statistic is significant (at the 10 per cent level) is UNIHERIT, and only when protest bids are removed.

Willingness to pay for Leadbeater's possum is linearly related to joint income and the importance of protecting species, in all models. Whether or not the respondent believed they had seen (SN) the possum (including on television or at the zoo) was included as an explanatory variable in the FG models. Whether or not the respondent was in paid employment (OCC) and whether or not they felt retaining the option of seeing the possum (OPT) was an important reason for conservation were in the HI models.

It is evident that the dollar amount given in the discrete choice question (DA) had a positive influence on the responses to the continuous valuation question. In most cases, the significance level of the t-statistic for DA is in the range of 0 to 0.005 (Tables 9.15 and 9.16).

The exception to this is in the results from questionnaires HI in which respondents were asked to pay for Leadbeater's possum through donation to an independent conservation organisation. The significance level of the t-statistic for DA in HI all is 0.5797 and is 0.4998 for HI npb. A possible explanation may be that the response to the payment mechanism outweighed the response to the dollar amount.

The positive influence of the bid amount given to respondents (DA) would seem to support the hypothesis of anchoring bias. This occurs if respondents use the dollar amount given in the discrete choice question as a value cue in determining their response to the open-ended question. Boyle (1985) included both discrete choice and open-ended valuation questions in the same questionnaire and also found evidence of anchoring bias. He did not use the results of the continuous valuation question because of starting point bias (Boyle *pers. comm.* 1992).

Given the poor performance of the multiple regressions, further models using various transformations of some of the variables were tried, without any marked improvement in performance or difference in estimates of willingness to pay. The most successful of these resulted from taking the logs of both the dependent willingness to pay variable (OEPRICE) and the dollar bids given to the respondents (DA).

These transformations resulted in higher adjusted R^2 values ranging from 0.27 for the Leadbeater's possum HI versions to 0.65 for versions BD of the flora and fauna questionnaires. Most of the adjusted R^2 values were around 0.3 to 0.4, indicating there is still a large amount of unexplained variation, particularly in the Leadbeater's possum models.

No transformations improved the performance of the results from questionnaire E. The willingness to pay values given by respondents to questionnaire E were quite markedly clustered around such 'round' numbers as \$10, \$50, \$100, \$200 and \$500 which may account for the lack of a clear relationship between the explanatory variables and payment amounts. This clustering could be expected in the valuation of an unfamiliar good (Kirkland 1988 and Stone 1992). Even for more familiar goods people are more likely to answer a willingness to pay type question with a round number rather than a figure in between.

The regression equations in Tables 9.15 and 9.16 were used to estimate mean willingness to pay. However, the poor model performance means that little confidence can be placed in these estimates. The mean willingness to pay estimates from the continuous valuation data are presented in Table 9.17. The mean bid results from the discrete choice data are also shown in Table 9.17 for comparison with the continuous valuation results.

Table 9.15 Regression coefficients and adjusted R^2 results for the flora and fauna questionnaires[1]

Questionnaire	Const	DA	JNT	IMP	AGE	EDUC	Adj R^2
AC all	-77.12 (0.006) {27.72}	0.186 (0.000) {0.05}	18.95 (0.001) {5.44}	33.13 (0.036) {15.66}			0.13
AC npb	-57.74 (0.154) {40.24}	0.407 (0.000) {0.07}	23.94 (0.000) {6.56}	49.17 (0.013) {19.39}	-16.22 (0.021) {6.93}		0.33

	Const	DA	JNT	IMP	ECOBAL	EDUC	
BD all	-116.24 (NS) {27.99}	0.285 (0.000) {0.06}	6.69 (0.032) {3.10}	38.45 (0.041) {18.71}	50.79 (0.004) {17.49}	31.62 (0.006) {11.24}	0.26
BD npb	-143.49 (0.000) {33.94}	0.472 (0.000) {0.08}	7.27 (0.046) {3.60}	52.74 (0.018) {22.02}	53.70 (0.009) {20.06}	37.29 (0.005) {13.00}	0.39

	Const	DA	JNT	IMP	AGE	EDUC	Adj R^2
ABCD all	-107.34 (0.000) {21.76}	0.223 (0.000) {0.04}	17.77 (0.000) {4.31}	36.43 (0.004) {12.55}		21.24 (0.008) {7.92}	0.18
ABCD npb	-102.52 (0.002) {31.84}	0.429 (0.000) {0.05}	20.94 (0.000) {5.11}	53.55 (0.000) {14.99}	-10.58 (0.049) {5.34}	22.90 (0.014) {9.22}	0.34

	Const		JNT	IMP	UNIHERIT		Adj R^2
E all	1.56 (0.925) {16.44}		2.916 (0.167) {2.10}	14.99 (0.209) {11.89}	18.12 (0.103) 11.05}		0.03
E npb	4.50 (0.818) {19.48}		2.917 (0.229) {2.41}	20.25 (0.147) {13.87}	22.47 (0.085) {13.00}		0.04

1. Two-sided significance levels of the *t*-statistic given in (). Standard errors given in { }.

COMPARISON OF WILLINGNESS TO PAY FROM DISCRETE AND CONTINUOUS DATA

The results from the discrete and continuous valuation questions are compared to determine if they have come from significantly different distributions. The mean estimated from the discrete choice question varies with the estimation technique and distributional assumptions made (Tables 9.14 and 9.17). This raises the question of which discrete choice estimates should be compared with the continuous valuation estimates. To overcome the problem of which mean should be compared with the continuous valuation mean, a test developed by Kriström (1990a and 1993) which compares the distributions directly has been used.

Table 9.16 Regression coefficients and adjusted R^2 results for Leadbeater's possum questionnaires[1]

Questionnaire	CONST	DA	JNT	IMP	SN	OPT	OCC	Adj R^2
FG all	-24.01	0.211	2.67	19.78	18.72			0.13
	(0.015)	(0.005)	(0.016)	(0.006)	(0.015)			
	{9.80}	{0.07}	{1.09}	{7.10}	{7.62}			
FG npb	-38.87	0.357	4.42	23.37	29.65			0.24
	(0.002)	(0.000)	(0.001)	(0.010)	(0.002)			
	{11.81}	{0.09}	{1.35}	{8.98}	{9.46}			
HI all	-11.32	0.026	0.46	6.19		6.64	5.61	0.12
	(0.065)	(0.580)	(0.494)	(0.193)		(0.002)	(0.211)	
	{6.08}	{0.05}	{0.68}	{4.73}		{2.08}	{4.23}	
HI npb	-11.89	0.041	1.12	8.76		5.81	5.26	0.12
	(0.138)	(0.500)	(0.230)	(0.202)		(0.056)	(0.353)	
	{7.95}	{0.06}	{0.92}	{6.82}		{3.01}	{5.63}	

1. Two-sided significance levels of the *t*-statistic given in (); Standard errors are given in {}.

The survival function from the discrete choice data was compared with the survival function from the continuous valuation data. The continuous survival function is the proportion of people willing to pay at least A_i dollars at each A_i dollar amount. The survival functions are shown graphically in Figures 9.16 and 9.17 for the all bids case and for the no protest bids case, respectively. For all values of A_i, the proportion of respondents willing to pay at least A_i is greater in the discrete choice function than in the continuous valuation function.

184   *Contingent Valuation and Endangered Species*

To test the hypothesis that the replies to both valuation questions are generated by the same distribution, Kriström (1990a and 1993) used a chi-squared test, computing the difference between the expected and observed number of no answers at each bid. The proportion of respondents rejecting each bid A_i in the discrete choice case (D_i) is compared with the observed proportion of rejectors in the continuous case (C_i).

The chi-squared statistic is:

$$\sum_i ((C_i - D_i)^2 / D_i) \qquad (9.8)$$

Complete figures for each A_i are given in Tables 9.18 and 9.19. The summed chi-squared value for the 'all-bids' case is 160.43 and for the case with protest bids removed the value is 606.76. The critical value at the 95 per cent level for a chi square distribution with 12 degrees of freedom is 21.03, much less than either of the calculated values. The hypothesis that the discrete choice and continuous valuation responses are generated from the same distribution must be rejected, a finding consistent with Kriström's results (Kriström 1990a and 1993).

Table 9.17 Mean willingness to pay values ($ per year) estimated from the discrete choice valuation data (DVQ) and continuous valuation data (CVQ), all bids cases

	DVQ			CVQ	
Questionnaire	Method 2 Untruncated	Method 2 when WTP≥0	Method 3 Non-parametric	Mean (Std error)	95% Confidence Interval
AC all	82.00	161.52	159.90	49.66 (13.84)	22.3 - 77.1
BD all	148.18	193.94	226.25	63.35 (19.30)	25.1 - 101.6
ABCD all	117.85	182.93	167.85	55.02 (12.00)	31.3 - 78.8
E all				39.01 (10.71)	17.8 - 60.2
FG all	29.19	48.40	43.77	21.53 (7.04)	7.6 - 35.5
HI all	- 2.80	22.71	28.91	13.43 (4.57)	4.4 - 22.5

Table 9.18 Comparison of discrete choice and continuous valuation responses in samples ABCD all bids - chi square calculations

Bid	% No responses DVQ (D_i)	% No responses CVQ (C_i)	$\sum((C_i - D_i)^2/D_i)$
1	22.5	44.4	21.32
5	22.5	49.5	32.40
10	38.6	52.5	5.00
15	38.6	58.2	9.95
20	38.6	60.2	12.09
25	47.6	65.0	6.36
35	47.6	67.6	8.40
50	49.2	68.2	7.34
60	49.2	76.2	14.82
75	49.2	77.5	16.28
100	50.0	79.0	16.28
200	70.0	91.9	6.85
500	82.6	97.8	2.80
		Sum	159.90

Table 9.19 Comparison of discrete choice and continuous valuation responses in samples ABCD with no protest bids - chi square calculations

Bid	% No responses DVQ (D_i)	% No responses CVQ (C_i)	$\sum((C_i - D_i)^2/D_i)$
1	3.1	20	92
5	3.1	23.4	132.93
10	14.6	31.8	20.26
15	14.6	40	44.19
20	14.6	42.8	54.47
25	21.4	49.7	37.42
35	21.4	53.5	48.15
50	31.9	54.4	15.87
60	31.9	65.7	35.81
75	31.9	67.6	39.95
100	32.4	69.8	43.17
200	49.1	88.4	31.46
500	69.2	96.9	11.08
		Sum	606.76

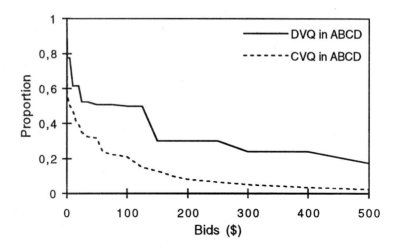

Figure 9.16   *Survival functions for all bids DVQ in ABCD compared with CVQ in ABCD.*

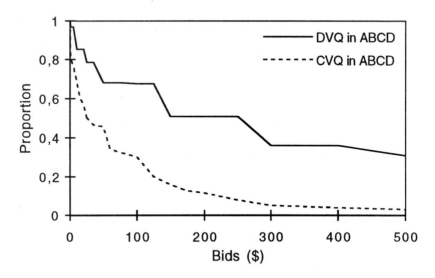

Figure 9.17   *Survival functions for all bids DVQ in ABCD compared with CVQ in ABCD.*

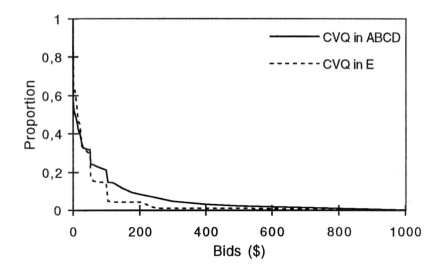

Figure 9.18   *Survival functions for all bids, CVQ in ABCD compared with CVQ in E.*

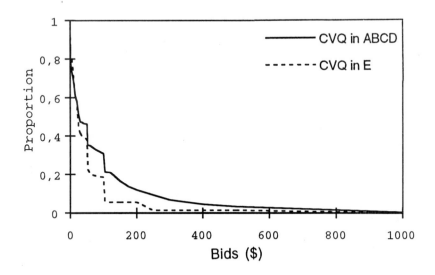

Figure 9.19   *Survival functions with no protest bids, CVQ in ABCD compared with CVQ in E.*

COMPARISON OF CONTINUOUS VALUATION RESPONSES BETWEEN QUESTIONNAIRES

The responses to the continuous valuation questions from questionnaires ABCD, which included a prior discrete choice question, are compared with the responses to the continuous valuation question from questionnaire E, which had no prior discrete choice question. Given the influence of the discrete choice question illustrated in the previous sections it is plausible that the responses from the two samples might be different.

Following the methodology of Kriström (1993), two comparisons have been made to test the hypothesis that the willingness to pay distributions from the two samples (ABCD and E) are the same. Firstly, a non-parametric test of medians was made. Secondly, a Kolmogorov-Smirnov test of the maximum distance between the two empirical survival functions (Figures 9.18 and 9.19) was performed.

Test of Medians

The medians of the distributions of responses to the continuous valuation questions in the combined questionnaires ABCD and questionnaire E were compared using the Wilcoxon statistic (Table 9.20).

Table 9.20 Comparison of the medians of the continuous valuation responses

Questionnaires	Sample size		Wilcoxon statistic	
	ABCD	E	Z	Z probability
ABCD all and E all	447	186	0.644	0.52
ABCD npb and E npb	308	145	-1.476	0.14

The Z probability gives the probability that the two medians are not significantly different. Neither probability is less than the 10 per cent level so it is likely the medians are the same. However, even if the medians are the same it is possible that the samples have different distributions of willingness to pay responses.

Kolmogorov-Smirnov Test

The maximum distance between the empirical functions using the Kolmogorov-Smirnov test is 0.120 (at $4) in the all bids case and 0.157 (at $104) with protest bids excluded, with most distances being much less (Tables 9.21 and 9.22).

Table 9.21 Comparison of continuous valuation responses (all bids) between ABCD and E

Bid $	Survival function CVQ in ABCD	Survival function[1] CVQ in E	Difference CVQA - CVQE
0	1.000	1.000	0.000
1	0.554	0.645	-0.091
2	0.536	0.629	-0.093
4	0.509	0.629	-0.120
5	0.507	0.629	-0.082
10	0.476	0.564	-0.088
15	0.418	0.462	-0.044
20	0.398	0.451	-0.053
25	0.351	0.338	0.013
30	0.326	0.322	0.004
35	0.324	0.322	0.002
40	0.320	0.311	0.009
50	0.318	0.295	0.023
52	0.242	0.177	0.065
60	0.240	0.155	0.085
75	0.227	0.150	0.077
100	0.211	0.145	0.066
104	0.151	0.048	0.103
105	0.147	0.048	0.099
120	0.145	0.043	0.102
125	0.141	0.043	0.098
150	0.114	0.043	0.071
175	0.094	0.043	0.051
200	0.083	0.043	0.040
250	0.065	0.011	0.054
300	0.047	0.011	0.036
400	0.031	0.011	0.020
500	0.022	0.011	0.011
1000	0.002	0.000	0.002

1. Survival functions are the proportion of 'yes' responses at the given bid level.

Table 9.22 Comparison of continuous valuation responses (no protest bids) between ABCD and E

Bids $	Survival function[1] CVQ in ABCD	Survival function CVQ in E	Difference CVQA - CVQE
0	1.000	1.000	0.000
1	0.804	0.830	-0.026
2	0.778	0.809	-0.031
4	0.739	0.809	-0.070
5	0.736	0.809	-0.073
10	0.691	0.726	-0.035
15	0.607	0.595	0.012
20	0.578	0.581	-0.003
25	0.510	0.436	0.074
30	0.474	0.415	0.059
35	0.471	0.401	0.070
40	0.465	0.401	0.064
50	0.462	0.380	0.082
52	0.352	0.228	0.124
60	0.349	0.200	0.149
75	0.330	0.193	0.137
100	0.307	0.186	0.121
104	0.219	0.062	0.157
105	0.213	0.062	0.151
120	0.210	0.055	0.155
125	0.204	0.055	0.149
150	0.165	0.055	0.110
175	0.136	0.055	0.081
200	0.120	0.055	0.065
250	0.094	0.014	0.080
300	0.068	0.014	0.054
400	0.045	0.014	0.031
500	0.032	0.014	0.018
1000	0.003	0.000	0.003

1. Survival functions are the proportion of 'yes' responses at the given bid level.

The critical levels in the all bids case are 0.119 at the 95 per cent level and 0.142 at the 99 per cent level, calculated from formula in Lindgren (1962 p. 401). The respective values for the case with protest bids excluded are 0.137 and 0.164. In both cases, the values fall between the critical levels at the 95 per cent and 99 per cent levels.

Therefore, there appears to be some evidence that the distribution of willingness to pay responses from the discrete and continuous valuation questions are different but this evidence is not very strong.

The main differences occur because of clustering of bids in version E around particular values, whereas in ABCD with the discrete choice question there were more 'in between' values, probably because the discrete choice bids included more values in between which prompted people to think of them.

Overall, the results for this study confirm those of Kriström. He concluded that the 'analysis provides some evidence that people interpret discrete and continuous valuation questions differently' (Kriström 1990a, p. 107). It also appears that the discrete choice amount posed does affect the subsequent continuous valuation response when both are asked which supports the hypothesis of anchoring. However, the results are not conclusive as the continuous responses are similar whether or not the discrete choice question is present.

ANALYSIS OF THE WILLINGNESS TO ACCEPT COMPENSATION RESPONSES

In questionnaire J respondents were asked their willingness to accept compensation for the loss of Leadbeater's possum, rather than their willingness to pay to protect it. The willingness to accept compensation question was expressed as a once only lump sum rather than an annual payment as in the other questionnaires because compensation payments are usually expressed as a lump sum and this seems more plausible.

Questionnaire J was sent to 650 people, of whom 213, or 32 per cent, replied. The responses to the general and socioeconomic questions are given in Chapter 8. Most respondents felt that conservation of species is very important (76 per cent) and few were prepared to accept compensation for the loss of Leadbeater's possum. The initial willingness to accept compensation question and the follow up question are in Box 9.2.

Twenty four of the 213 respondents were prepared to accept the initial amount of compensation suggested. This is 11.3 per cent of those who replied to the questionnaire and 3 per cent of all the questionnaires sent out. A further three people were prepared to accept compensation, but required a higher amount than was initially offered. One specified an amount of $1 million, another specified $5,000 (which was in the range of compensation amounts offered) and the third did not specify an amount.

Nine of the respondents were prepared to accept the initial compensation offer and would have accepted a lower amount than this (38 per cent of those accepting the initial compensation). Frequencies of the responses to each compensation amount are given in Tables 9.23 and 9.24.

No regression analysis of the willingness to accept compensation results was carried out because of the very small proportion of positive responses. The respective means calculated directly from the actual distributions of accepted compensation amounts are $311.55 from the initial discrete choice question and $5440.97 from the continuous valuation question. This second mean was greatly influenced by one very high compensation amount of $1 million. Deleting this response gave a mean value of $276.65, less than the discrete choice value. Medians in both cases are $0.00 because more than 50 per cent of respondents were not willing to accept any compensation.

The willingness to accept responses and the willingness to pay results must be expressed in equivalent terms for a comparison to be made. Because there is no definitive interest rate to use to express the lump sum in annual terms, interest rates of 10 per cent and four per cent have been used to give a range of values. Assuming an interest rate of 10 per cent and expressing the compensation amounts in annual terms gives means of about $31.40 for the discrete choice question and $550.00 (including the $1 million bid) or $28.00 (excluding the $1 million bid), for the continuous question, for the willingness to accept compensation values.

The respective annual values at an interest rate of 4 per cent are $14.50, $253 and $12.90. These amounts are well within the range of annual mean willingness to pay values (about $6 to $75) if the $1 million bid is not used. However, given the very low proportion of respondents who would accept compensation, it is difficult to place much faith in the validity of the results.

With the large proportion of respondents who were not willing to accept any compensation, it is of interest to consider the reasons people gave for their decision. Question 7 in the questionnaire gave a list of reasons for a 'no' response (Box 9.3). The reasons and responses are summarised in Table 9.25. Respondents could choose more than one response.

Fairly clearly, the two main reasons for people not being willing to accept compensation were that they 'did not wish to put a dollar value on protecting Leadbeater's possum', given by 47 per cent of respondents and that 'Leadbeater's possum has a right to exist and no amount could compensate me', given by 60 per cent of respondents. In general, respondents seemed very uncomfortable with the idea that they should be compensated in monetary terms for the loss of a species and some were offended by the suggestion, saying they felt it was 'obscene'.

Table 9.23 Responses to the initial discrete choice question on willingness to accept compensation

WTA Amount	Frequency	Percent
0[1.]	189	88.7
10	1	0.5
50	1	0.5
75	2	0.9
150	1	0.5
200	2	0.9
300	2	0.9
500	1	0.5
1000	3	1.4
2000	2	0.9
3000	1	0.5
4000	3	1.4
5000	1	0.5
7500	1	0.5
10000	3	1.4
Total	213	100
Mean	311.55	
Median	0	
Minimum	0	
Maximum	10,000	
Standard deviation	1422.73	

1. 0 indicates compensation was not accepted.

Table 9.24 Responses to the continuous valuation willingness to accept compensation question

WTA Amount	Frequency	Percent
0[1.]	189	88.7
1	1	0.5
50	1	0.5
75	1	0.5
150	1	0.5
200	3	1.4
500	1	0.5
1000	6	2.8
2000	1	0.5
4000	3	1.4
5000	2	1.0
7500	1	0.5
10000	2	1.0
1000000	1	0.5
Total	213	100
Mean	5440.97	
Median	0	
Minimum	0	
Maximum	1,000,000	
Standard deviation	68,512.68	

1. 0 indicates compensation was not accepted.

AGGREGATION OF WILLINGNESS TO PAY ESTIMATES

Once individual estimates of mean or median willingness to pay have been made, the next step is to estimate aggregate benefits. At a general level there is the theoretical problem of aggregating any individual measures into aggregate functions (Boadway and Bruce 1984). For example, 'one of the problems that arises in the aggregation of individual compensating or equivalent variations is that they may not be a sign-preserving measure of the underlying utility change' (Kriström 1990a).

Box 9.2 Willingness to accept compensation Leadbeater's possum questionnaire J

5. Preserving animals like the Leadbeater's possum often means choices must be made between protecting the animal and economic development. To ensure that the Leadbeater's possum does not become extinct, some forestry activity in the area where the possum lives will have to be stopped. If forestry operations continue in this area, it is highly probable that Leadbeater's possum will die out completely.

Imagine that the Government will allow forestry to continue in this area only if the forestry companies were to pay sufficient compensation for each Victorian to agree to the loss of Leadbeater's possum. If the total amount of compensation is more than the profit from forestry, no forestry will take place and no compensation will be paid.

What is the minimum compensation that you personally would accept for the loss of Leadbeater's possum? Would you be prepared to accept a lump sum payment of $_____ ?

1 YES _____ GO TO QUESTION 6
2 NO _____ GO TO QUESTION 7

6. Would you be prepared to accept less than the amount in question 5?

       1   YES

       2   NO _____ GO TO QUESTION 8

How much would you be prepared to accept?
$_____ (WRITE IN THE LOWEST DOLLAR AMOUNT THAT YOU ARE PREPARED TO ACCEPT).

Box 9.3 Reasons for not being willing to accept compensation for the loss of Leadbeater's possum

7. Why did you answer NO to question 5? Please circle any of the reasons listed below which apply to you (you may circle more than one).

1 THE AMOUNT GIVEN IS TOO LOW, BUT I WOULD ACCEPT $___ (WRITE IN THE LOWEST DOLLAR AMOUNT YOU WOULD ACCEPT).
2 I DID NOT WANT TO PUT A DOLLAR VALUE ON PROTECTING LEADBEATER'S POSSUM.
3 LEADBEATER'S POSSUM HAS A RIGHT TO EXIST AND NO AMOUNT COULD COMPENSATE ME.
4 NOT ENOUGH INFORMATION IS GIVEN TO ANSWER THE QUESTION.
5 I OBJECT TO THE WAY THE QUESTION IS ASKED.
6 OTHER (Please specify) ....

Table 9.25 Reasons for not being willing to accept compensation for the loss of Leadbeater's possum (multiple responses)

Reason for a no response	Number	Respondents %	Answers %
Amount offered too low	3	1.4	1.0
Did not wish to put a $ value on possum	99	46.5	32.7
Possum has a right to live	127	59.6	41.9
Not enough information given to answer	15	7.0	5.0
Object to the question	26	12.2	8.6
Other	33	15.5	10.9

Another issue is the extent of the market, or what population the estimates should be aggregated over. In this study, estimates of value were aggregated over the population of Victoria. This may result in an underestimate of value because people outside Victoria may also hold values for Victorian species.

There are several problems involved in extending the information gathered from a particular sample to the population from which it came. Firstly, there is the question of whether the mean or median estimate should be used. This is discussed in Chapter 7. Another issue is how to deal with respondents who give a zero willingness to pay, that is, should those zero bidders who are identified as being 'protest' bidders be included or excluded. This has been discussed extensively in Chapter 7. This study uses both approaches to provide lower and upper bounds to the estimates.

A third issue, which becomes particularly important in surveys with low response rates, is how to deal with the non-respondents. In this survey, the response rate is 35 per cent. There are two approaches which may be taken. All non-respondents can be treated as zero (Boyle and Bishop 1985) which gives a conservative aggregate estimate. Alternatively, assuming that respondents reflect the general population from which they were drawn, the non-respondents can be treated as missing values and assigned the mean or median willingness to pay estimated from those who did respond (Kriström 1990a). The second approach was followed in this study as there is no strong reason to assume all non-respondents have a zero value. There were no significant differences between the socioeconomic characteristics of the respondents and those of the population from which the sample was drawn.

Another question is whether values should be aggregated over individuals or over households (Chapter 6). The willingness to pay question in this survey asked for individual willingness to pay but the significance of joint income in determining willingness to pay shows that at least some people treated household income as their budget constraint. This was supported in some cases by individuals' comments. As a consequence, aggregate estimates have been made over both households and individuals.

At the time of the survey, there were about 2.89 million individuals and 1.36 million households in Victoria (1986 census). Aggregate estimates have been calculated for minimum and maximum estimates of the mean using the results from the discrete choice analysis (Table 9.14). The minimum estimates are also the median estimates.

For flora and fauna, the minimum estimate is ABCD all (method 1) and the maximum estimate is ABCD npb (method 2, truncated at zero). The Leadbeater's possum figures are based on questionnaires FG (taxation payment mechanism) only, as the tax payment mechanism is believed to be the more appropriate one for conservation of endangered species in Victoria (Chapter 10). The minimum is FG all (method 1) and the maximum is FG npb (method 2, truncated at zero). The aggregate results are shown in Tables 9.26 and 9.27.

Table 9.26 Aggregate mean estimates for protection of flora and fauna using discrete choice valuation data from ABCD versions ($ per year)

Household aggregation		Individuals aggregation	
Minimum	Maximum	Minimum	Maximum
$160 million	$386 million	$340 million	$821 million
($118/household)	($284/household)	($118/individual)	($284/household)

The estimate from questionnaire E, with the continuous valuation question only, is $54 million. However, in view of the poor performance of the models for the continuous valuation data, the discrete choice estimates are regarded as the more reliable estimate of willingness to pay.

After considering the range of figures and erring on the conservative side, as recommended by Arrow *et al.* (1993), 'best' aggregate estimates of $40 million per year ($29 per household) for the conservation of Leadbeater's possum and $160 million per year ($118 per household) for all endangered flora and fauna have been made using mean values. The estimates have been aggregated over the number of households in Victoria to give a conservative estimate of values. They are based on the all bids models, which produce more conservative estimates than the no protest bids cases.

Table 9.27 Aggregate mean estimates for protection of Leadbeater's possum using discrete choice valuation data from FG versions ($ per year)

Household aggregation		Individuals aggregation	
Minimum	Maximum	Minimum	Maximum
$39.7 million	$103 million	$84.4 million	$218 million
($29.2/household)	($75.6/household)	($29.19/individual)	($75.6/individual)

CONCLUSIONS

This chapter has focussed on the estimation of the mean and median willingness to pay values from the survey responses. Estimates were made both including zero bids identified as protest bids and excluding them. The logistic regression models used fit the data reasonably well. The bid vector selected appeared to cover the range of willingness to pay distribution adequately.

The estimates of mean willingness to pay were made using three different methods resulting in significantly different values. The differences occurred largely because the untruncated parametric bid functions and the Hanemann formulae allow for negative values of willingness to pay, whereas the parametric bid function truncated at zero and the non-parametric estimation methods do not. The truncated parametric function and the non-parametric method resulted in similar estimates.

The continuous valuation responses gave lower estimates of willingness to pay than the discrete choice responses. Estimates could not be made from the willingness to accept compensation responses because so few respondents agreed to accept compensation.

The validity of the estimates which have been made and the implications of the results for the hypotheses are discussed in the following chapter.

PART FIVE

Conclusions

10. Conservation Value: Estimation and Methodological Inference

INTRODUCTION

In this chapter, an overview of the survey results and tests of the hypotheses is presented and discussed. The methodological consequences of the hypotheses tests are outlined and appraised in terms of both the theoretical principles underlying contingent valuation and the actual results derived from the analysis.

Subsequently, the implications of the results are considered for conducting future contingent valuation studies in Australia and elsewhere. Some suggestions for further research are made.

The validity of the estimated values and the existence of any biases or survey characteristics which would cause an over or under estimation of the willingness to pay values are discussed.

REVIEW OF SURVEY RESULTS

The results of the five principal hypotheses tested in the survey are reviewed here. The main hypotheses related to the insensitivity of respondents to the scope of the good, willingness to pay versus willingness to accept questions, open ended and discrete choice questions, use of different payment mechanisms and the effects of varying information and they are considered in this order. The background to the hypotheses and the hypotheses themselves are presented in Chapter 8.

Insensitivity to Scope

The hypothesis tested in relation to insensitivity to scope was whether valuing a species individually will give a similar estimate of mean willingness to pay as valuing all species collectively. The test of this hypothesis is to compare the willingness to pay for conservation of Leadbeater's possum with the willingness to pay for all species (about 700) of endangered flora and fauna in Victoria.

The values for conservation of Leadbeater's possum are significantly less than values for conservation of all endangered flora and fauna. This clearly indicates respondents are sensitive to scope and value one individual endangered species significantly less than a collection of endangered species. The values for Leadbeater's possum are in the order of 25 per cent of the estimates for all endangered flora and fauna (Table 10.1).

Table 10.1 Leadbeater's possum estimates as a percentage of the equivalent flora and fauna estimates

	Methods 1 and 2 mean	Non-parametric mean
ABCD and FG all	24.8%	26.0%
ABCD and FG no protest bids	25.6%	22.2%

An extension of this study would have been to include willingness to pay questions for both flora and fauna and Leadbeater's possum in the same questionnaire and to compare the values from this questionnaire to those from a questionnaire in which Leadbeater's possum alone was valued. This value could be less than the 25 per cent of the total species value for a number of reasons.

Respondents may have tried to estimate what proportion of the total budget Leadbeater's possum should get, but in the absence of any information underestimated the impact and importance of other species. It is also possible that the Leadbeater's possum value may include some other components. For example, some respondents may have included some or all of their valuation for the habitat of the possum and for the fact that improving conditions for Leadbeater's possum may also benefit other species.

If each of the 700 endangered species in Victoria were valued equally, the value for Leadbeater's possum should be 1/700th of the total valuation for endangered species conservation. However, it could be expected that a species such as Leadbeater's possum would be valued at more than this proportion because it is 'cute and furry' and more attractive to most people than various little known plants, reptiles or insects which are included in the total. Leadbeater's possum also has some significance as one of the two faunal emblems of Victoria. However, whether 25 per cent of total valuation is the true proportion is open to speculation.

It is possible that had the respondents to the Leadbeater's possum questionnaire been given information on how many other endangered species need conservation in Victoria their valuation for the possum may have been lower. It is also possible that the mean estimates of willingness to pay for Leadbeater's possum are close to the 'true' value. The estimates for Leadbeater's possum are close to the current expenditure on species conservation in Victoria as Leadbeater's possum is one of three species which together account for more expenditure than all the other species combined.

The comments offered by many respondents showed that they were aware of other species, other environmental issues and other social problems that also require expenditure. About half the respondents made comments such as 'all species should be protected, not just one' and 'concerned with conservation as a whole so it is difficult to value species individually'. No information was given in the Leadbeater's possum questionnaires of any other species or environmental problems so the initiative for these statements came entirely from the respondents.

The results from the survey indicate that respondents do consider other species and environmental issues even when given no reminders of them. They do not allocate most or all of their endangered species budget if asked to value one species. The hypothesis of insensitivity to scope can be clearly rejected.

Willingness to Accept Compensation Versus Willingness to Pay

The issue of whether willingness to accept compensation questions give similar results to willingness to pay questions for the same good was tested by including a questionnaire which used a willingness to accept question and by comparing the results with the willingness to pay questions.

However, there were not enough responses to the willingness to accept compensation question in this survey to have any confidence in the resulting values. When the willingness to accept compensation values are expressed as annual payments, using discount rates of 4 per cent and 10 per cent, they are in the same range as the willingness to pay results, but with only 11 per cent of respondents (26 people) indicating they would accept compensation it is not possible to draw any conclusions. The small number of respondents accepting compensation and the high proportion of protest bids obtained in this survey are common to many willingness to accept compensation surveys (Mitchell and Carson 1989).

The willingness to accept format appears to give acceptable estimates for some use values in situations where respondents are familiar with the use and the allocation of access to that use (Bishop and Heberlein 1979). However, at this stage the use of willingness to accept compensation questions for species (or any environmental good) with mostly non-use values is not recommended because respondents have such difficulty formulating a value.

Respondents' comments on the willingness to accept questionnaire indicated that they had a great deal of difficulty in accepting the concept of being compensated in monetary terms for the loss of a species they considered had a right to exist.

Open-ended and Discrete Choice Questions

Three forms of willingness to pay question were asked; a discrete choice question, an open-ended direct question and an open-ended payment card question. This allowed two comparisons;

(i) the discrete choice question with the open-ended (or continuous) question, which were in the same questionnaires (ABCD) and
(ii) the two forms of open-ended question (between different versions of the questionnaire).

The issues of interest are whether the discrete and continuous questions give similar estimates of mean values and whether the discrete choice question preceding the open-ended question influences the answers to the open-ended question (anchoring bias).

Comparison of discrete and continuous valuation responses

The continuous valuation questions resulted in lower values than the discrete choice format in all the flora and fauna questionnaires (Table 10.2). The estimates from the continuous responses in the flora and fauna questionnaires range from 44 per cent to 60 per cent of the estimates from the discrete choice format.

The divergence between the continuous and discrete estimates is greater when the cumulative distribution function for discrete choice estimation is truncated at zero, which is probably the most appropriate estimate to compare with the continuous valuation estimate. Kriström (1990a) argues that a continuous valuation question may not allow for negative willingness to pay because it may not occur to a respondent to report a negative willingness to pay. Respondents who really have a negative value are more likely to give a zero willingness to pay or not answer at all.

In the Leadbeater's possum questionnaires the results differed. For the tax mechanism versions (FG) the continuous valuation question also resulted in estimates less than those from the discrete choice question with all estimation methods. With the private donation payment mechanism (HI), the continuous valuation estimate ($13.43) is less than the truncated discrete choice estimate ($22.71). However, the continuous valuation estimate is more than the untruncated discrete choice estimate, which was not significantly different from zero, largely due to the high proportion of zero bids (74 per cent).

Table 10.2 Comparison of discrete choice and continuous estimates ($)

Questionnaires (all bids)	Mean DVQ Untruncated	Mean DVQ Truncated at 0	Mean CVQ[1]
ABCD all	117.85	182.93	55.02
FG all	29.19	48.40	21.53
HI all	- 2.80	22.71	13.43

1. Standard errors and confidence intervals given in Table 9.17.

The estimates from the discrete choice and continuous valuation formats are different in all cases and the hypothesis that estimates of willingness to pay from discrete choice questions are the same as those from continuous valuation questions must be rejected. In all cases but the untruncated discrete choice estimate from donations for Leadbeater's possum, the continuous valuation estimates are lower than the discrete choice estimates.

This result is consistent with the results of other studies, for example, Sellar, Stoll and Chavas (1985) and Kriström (1990a). Walsh, Johnson and McKean (1989 and 1992) investigated the results of a large number of contingent valuation studies and their findings suggest higher estimates from discrete choice questions than from continuous valuation questions. They also found that discrete choice formats generally gave results closer to travel cost methods than continuous valuation questions.

The effect of a prior discrete choice question on continuous responses
The results of testing the differences between the two continuous valuation questions are inconclusive. The test of medians using Wilcoxon scores showed no significant differences in the medians at the 5 per cent level, while the Kolmogorov-Smirnov tests of maximum distance between the distributions were significant at the 95 per cent level.

The analysis is complicated by the fact that a straightforward 'how much would you pay' question was used in questionnaires ABCD, whereas in questionnaire E a payment card was used. The range and choice of amounts shown on the payment card may have some influence on respondents answers. Mitchell and Carson (1989) identify three possibilities; the maximum amount on the card may be less than the respondent's willingness to pay and thus constrain their response; the maximum amount may be taken to imply a reasonable upper bound and so pressure the respondent to give a higher amount than they would otherwise; and the amounts on the card may not include the respondent's preferred answer, causing them to choose an amount higher or lower.

Respondents are instructed that they may choose an amount not on the card, but in practice it has been found that people almost always choose an amount that is on the card (Mitchell and Carson 1989). The payment card used in questionnaire E had a wide range based on the pre-test results and had 60 amounts in total, so the possibilities discussed by Mitchell and Carson would not be expected to result in much bias. However, the dissimilar formats may account for some of the difference in the two distributions of continuous valuation responses in ABCD and E.

The results for comparison of continuous valuation questions with and without a preceding discrete choice question are inconclusive, but they do not disprove Kriström's (1990a) conclusion that anchoring bias does not necessarily occur. The hypothesis that the estimates of value from the two continuous valuation questions are different can be neither accepted nor rejected. There is some evidence of difference, but it is not strong.

Different Payment Mechanisms

It has been found in many contingent valuation studies that the specified method of payment may affect if, and how much, respondents will pay. In this study, paying for species conservation through additional taxes was compared to paying a donation to an independent conservation organisation. The hypothesis tested was that the different payment mechanisms should result in the same mean estimates of value. Leadbeater's possum questionnaires FG (taxation) were compared with questionnaires HI (donation).

The estimated mean willingness to pay values are higher when payment is through taxation than through donation, leading to a rejection of the hypothesis. The difference is greater in the discrete choice question (Table 10.3) than in the continuous valuation question. When all the Leadbeater's possum questionnaires were run in the same regression model with a dummy variable for tax (0) or donation (1) the coefficient of the dummy variable was negative and significant at the 1 per cent level, indicating that payment through donation resulted in lower willingness to pay.

Leadbeater's possum questionnaires HI had a very high proportion of zero responses, 74 per cent for the discrete choice question and 56 per cent for any positive amount, compared with 62 per cent and 49 per cent for the Leadbeater's possum questionnaires FG indicating that fewer people were prepared to pay through the donation mechanism.

It is concluded that the payment mechanism does significantly affect the estimates of mean willingness to pay in this survey and the hypothesis that payment mechanism will not cause a difference must be rejected.

Table 10.3 Comparison of mean estimates ($ per year) from payment through tax and payment through donation

Questionnaires	Discrete choice	Continuous[1]
FG all (tax)	29.19	21.53
HI all (donation)	-2.80	13.43
FG npb (tax)	68.40	30.19
HI npb (donation)	24.27	18.17

1. Standard errors and confidence intervals given in Table 9.17.

The nature of existing institutional arrangements in Australia may be one explanation for the effect of varying the payment mechanism. Two characteristics of a 'good' contingent valuation scenario described by Rowe and Chestnut (1983, p. 70) are that it must be 'realistic by relying upon established patterns of behaviour and legal institutions; and have uniform application to all respondents'. The donation payment mechanism meets neither of these criteria for this type of good in Australia.

Management of public land and species conservation in Australia is, and always has been, the responsibility of state governments with some input from the Federal Government. There is very little experience of private organisations undertaking these tasks in Australia, in contrast to the experience in some states in the US where there are more and higher profile independent organisations that own and/or manage large areas of land for conservation purposes (Stevens *et al.* 1991).

Conservation organisations in Australia have, in general, focussed on education, research and political lobbying and have no track record in managing large conservation areas. Hence, environmental conservation is generally seen as being the responsibility of government and the community as a whole rather than something private individuals should provide. There may be considerable scepticism that a conservation organisation is capable of providing the level of species conservation described in this survey. Doubts about the provision of a good may result in respondents understating their value (Mitchell and Carson 1989). The conclusion here is that taxation is a more appropriate payment vehicle in the Australian institutional environment.

Different Information

Respondents in contingent valuation surveys involving non-use values are trying to place a value on an unfamiliar good and so they are reliant to a large extent on the information provided in the described scenario. It could be expected that differences in the information provided might result in different valuations. Three variations on the information provided were used in this study; providing information on current expenditure on species conservation versus not providing it; including and not including a picture of Leadbeater's possum; and suggesting reasons for protecting species versus not suggesting reasons.

No effects on estimates of willingness to pay of varying information were found in this study. However, there are some qualifications to extending this result to a general conclusion that information has little effect. Firstly, the differences in information in this survey were all minor, although at the time of designing the survey it was not known what the estimate of mean willingness to pay would be in relation to the current expenditure.

A prior expectation was that either respondents would subtract their given current expenditure from their expressed willingness to pay, or that the information may act as a 'starting point' and respondents may, for example, double it or specify a figure in the same order of magnitude. In retrospect, the estimate of mean willingness to pay for endangered species conservation is in the order of $120 to $280 per household and would have been unlikely to be affected a great deal by informing respondents that expenditure on species conservation was actually $2.30 per adult ($5 per household). If a household is prepared to pay, for example, $200 per year in total, their additional expenditure is $195. The information certainly did not appear to be used as a starting point.

Secondly, the statistical test used is not a rigorous means of testing the differences in the distributions. However, given the small differences in information and the small sample sizes resulting from the low response rate, further statistical analysis was not warranted. Larger variations in information will almost certainly cause differences in estimates of willingness to pay as has been found in many other studies (Chapter 6).

VALIDITY OF THE SURVEY RESULTS

In this section, the validity of the estimates of willingness to pay obtained in this study is considered. The validation issue is one of 'determining if the questionnaire measures what it purports to measure' (Eberle and Hayden 1991). The validity of the estimated values depends on two assumptions; firstly, that the data are the unbiased responses of those that answered the questionnaire and secondly, that the values obtained represent those of an average Victorian adult (Stone 1992).

Estimating willingness to pay functions has been one of the principal means of assessing the validity of responses in contingent valuation studies (Mitchell and Carson 1989 and Bateman *et al.* 1993). As discussed in Chapter 6, validating contingent valuation studies which measure non-use values is particularly difficult because there is no market based measure the results can be compared with. If market based values existed, contingent valuation would not be required. Thus, although estimating bid functions is not a particularly convincing method of validation, it is the only practical approach in many cases.

In this study, the bid functions include the variables which might be expected from economic theory, such as household income, believing species conservation is important, having heard of Leadbeater's possum and so on (Chapter 9). The regression coefficients all have the expected signs (Tables 9.8, 9.9, 9.15 and 9.16 for the significance of the coefficients) and the willingness to pay functions predict around 70 to 80 per cent of the responses correctly. Very few (nine) of the responses had to be deleted because of inconsistent responses.

The comparison of the socioeconomic characteristics of the respondents with the socioeconomic characteristics of all adult Victorians (Chapter 8) indicated that the respondents were essentially the same as the population from which they were drawn. The observable characteristics which influence willingness to pay, such as age and household income, did not differ between respondents and non-respondents.

The significantly different values obtained for the two goods (all endangered species in Victoria and a single species) can also be regarded as evidence of the validity of the study (Carson and Mitchell 1995).

These characteristics all support the validity of the results and the contention that the values represent those of the average Victorian. However, it is also necessary to consider the possibility and effect of any biases on the estimated results.

POSSIBLE BIASES

In this section, the possibility of any biases and other factors which may have resulted in the systematic under or over valuation of willingness to pay for species conservation are considered in relation to the 'best estimates' (Chapter 9) of $29 per household per year for Leadbeater's possum and $118 per household per year for all endangered flora and fauna. These values are the means and medians from the untruncated discrete choice questions.

The best aggregate estimates are $40 million per year for Leadbeater's possum and $160 million per year for all endangered flora and fauna, calculated by multiplying the best mean estimates by the number of households in Victoria. The effect of any biases is not of concern for the comparisons across questionnaires but the effect on the absolute dollar values is clearly important.

Strategic Bias and Free Riding

Strategic bias occurs when respondents believe their answers will influence policy decisions (Chapter 6). Respondents may over or understate their willingness to pay to influence the end result. There is no *a priori* expectation about the direction of the bias. For example, a committed conservationist may overstate their value, but someone who believes conservation programmes reduce employment opportunities may understate their value.

In this survey the covering letter (Box 8.5) stressed the policy relevance of the questions in order to motivate respondents to answer. It is not clear how successful this was, but if some respondents did believe their answers would influence policy they may have answered strategically. However, the study by Imber, Stevenson and Wilks (1991) found that 73 per cent of Australians felt their input would have no influence on government policy. Comments made by respondents in the survey conducted for this study also indicated that many were sceptical of the Government's intentions. If respondents do not believe the good as described will be provided they may understate their value (Mitchell and Carson 1989).

It is difficult to test for strategic bias unless a survey is specifically designed to do so. However, if the estimated bid functions explain the data reasonably well, as in this study, then strategic bias is generally not considered to be a problem (Chapter 6).

Free riding behaviour occurs if people value the good, but rely on others to pay for it. Respondents who replied 'no' to the willingness to pay question and gave as their reason that someone else should pay could be interpreted as being free riders (Bateman *et al.* 1993). Alternatively, this response could be taken as an indication that they are dissatisfied with the current government expenditure priorities as many respondents stated that the government should pay out of taxes already paid.

The net result of either explanation is that willingness to pay would be understated. Bateman *et al.* (1993 p. 21) note that recent reviews 'have indicated that free riding behaviour may result in a reduction of stated willingness to pay to (very approximately) between 60 to 95 per cent of true willingness to pay'. Given the proportion of respondents who felt government or someone else should pay (about 16 to 18 per cent) it is possible that there has been some understatement of willingness to pay. However, Bateman *et al.* (1993) also point out that the taxation mechanism for payment reduces the possibility of free riding because if the policy is implemented it is not possible for most people to avoid paying the additional tax. Free riding is possible under the donation mechanism, which is another possible explanation of the lower willingness to pay estimates from the private donation mechanism.

Hypothetical Bias

This survey was completely hypothetical and so may have been subject to hypothetical bias. The statement that 'remember this is imaginary and the money will not be collected' may have 'set up both an overstatement of willingness to pay and signalled to respondents that they did not have to answer carefully' (Loomis *pers. comm.* 1993).

The only definitive way of testing whether hypothetical bias has occurred is to compare the hypothetical study results with actual payments, which has been done in several experiments designed to test for hypothetical bias (Chapter 6). However, comparison with actual markets is not possible in many studies, including this one. This study could have been validated by comparison with the results of a referendum, had the resources and appropriate institutional structure been available, but this was not a practical option.

Lack of Substitutes

If respondents are not reminded of substitutes for the good being valued the willingness to pay estimates are likely to be too high (Bishop and Welsh 1992). No substitutes were presented in this survey. There are no close substitutes for the endangered flora and fauna in Victoria. They are unique as an aggregate of species. There is some overlap with species in other Australian states, in particular New South Wales, but generally the states have quite different collections of flora and fauna as a function of diversity in climate, soils and so on.

In the case of Leadbeater's possum there are other possum species and species of arboreal marsupials that could be considered as substitutes, as well as other endangered species, although none are close substitutes.

Use of Willingness to Pay Estimates

The use of willingness to pay estimates of value instead of the correct measure of willingness to accept compensation will result in systematic and possibly large underestimates of value (Knetsch 1993). Thus, the use of willingness to pay questions rather than willingness to accept compensation for the loss of something Victorians already have (a given complement of species) will result in an underestimate, possibly a considerable one.

However, there are some major practical difficulties in using willingness to accept compensation measures to value non-use benefits (Chapter 6). The willingness to accept compensation questionnaire in this survey failed to elicit any meaningful responses because of a lack of responses and a high proportion of protest bids (Chapter 9). Thus, use of willingness to accept measures to estimate non-use values remains impractical at present.

There is also room for debate as to whether willingness to accept compensation is the theoretically correct measure (Chapter 6) because the allocation of property rights to natural resources in Australia is not clear. Mitchell and Carson (1989) have argued that in situations where a public good is maintained by annual payments through taxation, willingness to pay may be the appropriate measure. This is an issue which is yet to be resolved.

Uncertainty and Information

One of the aspects of the value of protecting endangered species which was not investigated in the surveys undertaken for this study was the effect of uncertainty on estimates of value. There were several reasons for this, including lack of resources, space constraints in the questionnaires and the absence of adequate information to enable assessments of the probabilities of survival or extinction under different circumstances.

No specific allowance for uncertainty was made in either the Leadbeater's possum questionnaire or the questionnaire on all endangered flora and fauna. The value requested in the willingness to pay question was willingness to pay for full preservation of either all endangered flora and fauna or Leadbeater's possum. Limited information was given on how the programmes might be carried out and what the consequences of conservation strategies might be.

Respondents were told that further money was required to ensure full conservation of species, but it was not made explicit what full conservation means in terms of survival of the endangered species. That is, would all species be guaranteed survival or would some still become extinct from natural causes or because the funding raised proved to be inadequate. It was left to respondents to make their own subjective assessment of the outcome and the probability of that outcome. It is possible that the implied full conservation of species has resulted in an overestimation of value, but it depends how the respondents interpreted the question.

In the case of Leadbeater's possum it was stated extinction would not occur if a conservation programme was implemented. In reality, no conservation programme can guarantee survival of a species. It is only possible to increase the probability of survival. If respondents accepted the guarantee of survival, the mean willingness to pay estimate will probably overestimate the benefits of a conservation programme for Leadbeater's possum. This overestimate could be accounted for in the policy process by reducing the valuation in line with the expected change in probability of survival from the conservation programme. This would require further information on whether changes in value are linear with respect to changes in survival probability and, if not, how the relationship varies.

Estimation Procedures

The general approach throughout the survey and the analysis has been to err on the side of a conservative technique or result. Thus, various characteristics of this survey result in the 'best' estimates being conservative estimates of value. Treating protest bids as zero bids will give a conservative estimate as it is likely that many of the protest zero bidders actually have a positive valuation for species conservation.

The lowest of the discrete choice estimates, from the untruncated parametric method, were chosen as the best estimates which may well result in an underestimate as these bid functions allowed for negative willingness to pay values which would be unlikely to be large for the goods valued in this survey.

The survey respondents were concentrated in the lower to middle income classes compared with the population from which they were drawn (Chapter 8) which will result in an underestimate as willingness to pay is positively related to income. Consequently, the values estimated here can be regarded as a lower bound to the possibilities.

Aggregation

The 'best' value estimates were aggregated over the number of households in Victoria (Chapter 9) which probably gives an underestimate since it is likely that some respondents replied on an individual basis. The willingness to pay question was intended to be answered on an individual basis, but the household was chosen as the unit over which to aggregate for the best estimate because there is a statistically significant relationship between willingness to pay and joint income but there is no statistically significant relationship between willingness to pay and individual income. Also, Arrow *et al.* (1993) and Mitchell and Carson (1989) strongly recommend taking the conservative option when there is any ambiguity over which choice to make and, given the sensitivity in the policy situation, this was the attitude here.

Imber, Stevenson and Wilks (1991) elicited individual willingness to pay values and attempted at several points in the survey to emphasis that answers should be made on an individual basis. They concluded that in general respondents did answer on this basis, but the evidence was not completely convincing. Imber, Stevenson and Wilks argue that respondents reported their individual income truthfully and so were likely to answer the willingness to pay question truthfully. However, the fact that a respondent knows and reports their individual income does not imply that budgeting and spending decisions are made in relation to individual income.

The survey asked only Victorian residents for their willingness to pay for the conservation of endangered species in Victoria. Other Australians and some people from other countries also derive value from the conservation of Victorian species. There is, for example, some eco-tourism activity which includes the Central Highlands region and Leadbeater's possum, along with other Victorian species (Lindenmayer *pers. comm.* 1993). Not including people outside Victoria will result in a further underestimate of the value of protecting endangered species in Victoria because other people may also derive benefit from the existence of Leadbeater's possum and other Victorian species.

Table 10.4 Sources of under or over valuation

Source of bias	Possible sign[a]
Strategic bias and free riding	?
Hypothetical	?
Uncertainty	+
No substitutes specified	+
WTP rather than WTA	−
Including all zero bids	−
Lower average income than general population	−
Aggregated over household rather than individuals	−
Victorian population only	−

a. Symbols
+ = overestimate of mean willingness to pay
? = effect unknown
- = underestimate of mean willingness to pay

Summary of Under and Over Valuations

The characteristics of this survey which possibly cause over or under valuations and their likely effects are summarised in Table 10.4. The net effect is unclear because it is not possible to estimate the size of each effect or, in some cases, to be sure of the direction of bias.

FURTHER RESEARCH

The contingent valuation technique of non-market valuation is potentially very useful for government level policy making, but there are still many issues to resolve. In this section, areas of further research arising directly from the study carried out in this book are identified and discussed. These suggestions also have relevance to contingent valuation research in general. Some of these issues were not covered in this study because of resource constraints and some became apparent from the results of the study.

Interpretation of the Survey Information

A difficulty with all contingent valuation surveys is communicating to survey respondents the exact nature of the good being valued and ensuring their interpretation of the question is that which is intended. Ideally, surveys should be exhaustively pre-tested using focus groups to reduce communication difficulties. Where this has not been done, follow up personal interviews of a group of respondents or a sample drawn from the population surveyed to ascertain what they believed was being valued would assist in the interpretation of the results. Arrow *et al.* (1993) recommend pre-testing and a follow up to ensure the interpretation has been as intended.

Pre-testing in this study did not reveal any difficulties with understanding the questionnaire. However, the information given was limited. For example, little information was provided on how the conservation programmes would be carried out and exactly what full conservation of species (or Leadbeater's possum) implies. Follow up interviews would have been useful to establish how respondents did interpret the information.

Motivation for Being Willing to Pay

Most contingent valuation questionnaires routinely contain questions on why people are *not* prepared to pay for a good. A few now include questions on why people *are* prepared to pay (Stevens *et al.* 1991, Bateman *et al.* 1993). This would be a useful adjunct to contingent valuation surveys in terms of shedding further light on what people included in the good they were valuing and also in determining what values (for example, use or non-use, bequest and existence) are most important in motivating people to pay. This would assist in the design of future questionnaires. In this study, respondents were asked directly why they felt the conservation of species is important, but these responses were not necessarily what motivated them to pay.

A related issue is whether people respond to contingent valuation surveys as 'consumers' or 'citizens' (Chapter 6). Respondent comments in this study support the possibility of 'citizen' responses. The comments indicated that some of respondents considered that conservation of species was a responsibility of society as a whole and the benefits accrued to all society rather than to themselves as individuals. It was not possible to determine how this affected their willingness to pay responses in this survey as the comments were volunteered rather than elicited and thus nothing could be concluded about those who made no comments.

Questioning people as to their motivation for being willing to pay would help to clarify this issue and may shed some light on the controversy over whether contingent valuation estimates are economic values which are directly comparable to monetary values or whether they reflect moral attitudes.

The Effect of Uncertainty

There has not been a great deal of research into the inclusion of uncertainty in contingent valuation surveys. Allowing for risk and uncertainty in contingent valuation surveys is problematic for a number of reasons (Chapter 6). It appears respondents have difficulty in comprehending changes in risk and there is also some evidence that the way in which the change in risk is presented may result in different valuations of the same change in risk (Loomis and du Vair 1993).

This raises the question of how the changes in risk should be presented. The cause of the change in probability may also affect the valuation. People may suffer a greater loss from a reduction in the number of a species if it is caused by human activity than if the same reduction is caused by a natural event (Knetsch 1993).

Many contingent valuation studies on species conservation have asked respondents to value outcomes which would occur with certainty. However, a predominant issue in respect to species conservation is uncertainty, so further research into how people perceive and respond to risk in contingent valuation scenarios is warranted. For example, is the value of increasing the probability of survival of a species from 40 per cent to 60 per cent the same as the value for increasing it from 60 per cent to 80 per cent? How is a change in probability of survival viewed when the likelihood of extinction is very high or very low?

Maguire (1986) suggests the relationship between changes in survival probability and changes in utility is not linear, with small changes in utility when the probability of extinction is near 1 or near 0, but with relatively large increases in utility for increasing probability of survival in the middle ranges. It would be useful to undertake a contingent valuation survey which attempted to ascertain values for a range of changes in survival probabilities of, for example, Leadbeater's possum, to gain some idea of how the estimates of value vary with changing probability.

A further question of interest, which has been partly addressed by Whitehead (1993), is the interrelationship between uncertainty on the supply and demand side and how this interaction affects valuation of species conservation programmes. Whitehead uses both subjective and objective probabilities, raising the issue of which probabilities should be used and in what circumstances.

Willingness to pay response will depend on the individual's assessment of their demand uncertainty as well as the supply uncertainty. Whitehead investigated the effect of changes in both supply uncertainty (which was given) and demand uncertainty (which was subjectively assessed by the respondents) on willingness to pay for a wildlife conservation programme. He found 'the larger the wildlife supply probability weighted by the demand probability the larger the potential effect of the proposed management programme and the higher the probability of a yes response' (Whitehead 1993, p. 129).

Aggregation on a per Household or a per Individual Basis

Willingness to pay questions in this survey were intended to be answered on an individual basis, but the significance of the joint (household) income variable and respondents' comments seemed to indicate that a proportion of respondents answered on a household basis (Chapter 10). There was no significant relationship between individual income and willingness to pay.

The aggregation of willingness to pay estimates was done per household and per individual to give a range of benefit estimates. The value estimated on a per household basis gives a lower bound to the aggregate estimates. Aggregating over households also follows the recommendation of Arrow *et al.* (1993) that where results are ambiguous the conservative result should be preferred.

A survey containing specific questions on what budget constraint (household or individual) respondents *do* relate to would be of benefit to future contingent valuation surveys as it is better to use the appropriate units for aggregation rather than simply to err on the safe side. Clear instructions as to whether individual or household responses are required should also be given.

Payment Mechanism - Tax or Donation

A variety of payment mechanisms have been used in Australian contingent valuation surveys (Tables 11.1 to 11.6). In cases where there is no appropriate mechanism such as an entrance fee, the payment method most commonly used is an increase in taxation or reduction in take-home pay. Two studies (Rogers

1992a,1992b and Stone 1992) use a donation to independent conservation organisations for the specific purpose described in the survey and two (Tracey 1992 and Lockwood, Loomis and DeLacy 1993) use a donation to an Australian Heritage Commission trust fund. Some other studies have used both mechanisms, as in this study, or have given respondents a choice of either tax or donation mechanisms (Bennett 1981).

Stone (1992) justifies the use of a donation to an independent organisation as 'neutral', but this is not the case in Australia. Very few natural areas are managed by independent or private organisations in Australia. Most general land management and conservation areas in Australia are funded and run by some form of government agency, whether federal, state or local, funded from tax revenue. It is true that some respondents may prefer to make a voluntary donation than be forced to pay higher taxes, but there are also many people who believe such activities are the responsibility of government and should be paid for by everyone through taxation.

There is also likely to be considerable scepticism that an independent organisation would be able to guarantee the survival of Leadbeater's possum. In this survey, there were significant differences in willingness to pay estimates from the tax and donation payment mechanisms. The donation payment vehicle provided considerably lower estimates of value.

A survey which offered a choice of payment mechanisms and also included questions on why people preferred particular mechanisms would provide some useful insights into which mechanisms may be best. This may need to be done for a number of environmental goods as the same mechanism may not be appropriate in all situations. Bennett (1981) found that about 10 per cent of respondents to his survey on preserving a nature reserve preferred to pay a donation rather than additional tax, but did not ascertain reasons for this preference.

Comparisons with Related Surveys

Reviewing related contingent valuation studies could be useful in two contexts; firstly, in the context of Australian contingent valuation studies and secondly, in the context of contingent valuation studies of wildlife. Reviewing Australian studies may provide some information on the type of survey administration that has achieved the best results in terms of response rates and validity of value estimates, as well as effects of different payment mechanisms and the range of values estimated for different resources. As more studies are completed it is useful to compare studies for the same type of resource.

An example of a comparative study is the 'meta-analysis' undertaken by Walsh, Johnson and McKean (1989 and 1992) of 281 US non-market studies of recreation values. The study results were compared to see if the findings are similar or not, and if not, what variables cause the differences. Arrow *et al.* (1993) recommend that further studies of this nature should be undertaken and that 'reference' values for particular types of non-market goods be established.

It will be some time before there are sufficient Australian studies to undertake this kind of analysis. The study by Dumsday, Jakobsson and Ransome (1992) used the results of 80 studies from the US, Australia and New Zealand to establish typical ranges of value for the benefits of protecting rivers and catchments. This technique is sometimes known as benefit transfer.

Reviewing other wildlife and species studies is of interest to gain an overview of what kind of values have been estimated and in what situations, although caution must be exercised in comparing values between countries as the estimates of benefit have been obtained within different institutional settings (Bateman *et al.* 1993). Some studies have estimated only use values, others have estimated total value and others have attempted to estimate the components of total value, such as use, option, bequest and existence value. The comparison of studies may provide some insight into what factors affect the proportional contribution of each component to total value. As there is considerable scepticism that respondents can distinguish the components of non-use value (Cummings and Harrison 1995), this is of most interest to determine the allocation of total value between use and non-use values.

With estimates of value for many individual species, it would be of interest to see if, in general, more obscure and less interesting or attractive species are valued less than the more interesting species. If so, this would provide some support for the validity of the contingent valuation method. Reviewing studies that value a group of species and a single species from that group would shed further light on the issue of sensitivity to scope. However, to date, few such studies have been done.

External Validation

A major barrier to more widespread acceptance of the contingent valuation method is the difficulty of external validation of the results. Because markets do not exist for most amenities valued with the contingent valuation method it is not possible to validate results by comparing them with what actually occurs in a market. There have been numerous studies comparing contingent valuation results with those from other non-market valuation techniques, notably hedonic pricing and the travel cost method, but the validity of these techniques is also open to question (Chapter 6).

There are two avenues of further research in this setting which may assist. Firstly, contingent valuation studies can be carried out for goods which are valued in a market, and the results compared with what actually happens in the market. There have been some experiments along these lines, but the evidence is insufficient to draw firm conclusions. However, although this kind of study may validate the use of contingent valuation for estimating use values, it is not certain that this conclusion can be extended to non-use values.

Secondly, discrete choice referendum-style contingent valuation surveys could be conducted, followed by an actual referendum on provision of the same amenity. It is unlikely that this kind of study can be done in Australia because referendums of any kind are rare, and they do not cover issues such as the provision of public goods. Such studies possible in parts of the US, where referenda are held on tax increases for particular purposes (Carson, Hanemann and Mitchell (1986).

11. From Contingent Valuation to Species Conservation Policy

INTRODUCTION

This study is the first major application of the contingent valuation method to the problem of species conservation in Australasia and it is also amongst the first of such applications internationally. Initially, the analysis in this book was focused on the strengths and weaknesses of the contingent valuation methodology in the setting of the continuing social problem of species conservation. On establishing the general robustness of the methodology in terms of providing estimates of value consistent with alternative valuations and the price information emanating from existing markets, the focus then turns to the actual estimation of species conservation values in a particular biological and institutional situation.

Substantially, such analysis has been completely general in inference in that the focus has been the consideration of the methodology and the value estimation process. Thus, this study has provided a benchmark and framework for the consideration of species conservation generally in a range of jurisdictions.

Now actual values for species conservation have been derived for a specific jurisdiction and the need is to consider the importance of the information obtained here for the species conservation management programme for Leadbeater's possum in particular and endangered species in Victoria in general. This consideration of the policy setting is useful for the issue of species conservation in Victoria, but also has relevance nationally and internationally in terms of both the comparison of contingent valuation estimates and the acceptance of the methodology generally. Thus, there will be a review of the major contingent valuation studies in Australasia and a discussion of their policy relevance, especially in comparison with international studies.

Finally, the focus in this chapter turns from the specific consideration of the contingent valuation methodology to individual species in Victoria to the fundamental and difficult questions of biological conservation at the international level, to conclude with a discussion of the methodological insights of contingent valuation and welfare economics generally for biological conservation. In this setting, there will be a review of international contingent valuation studies which have dealt with species conservation and finally a summary of the relevance of welfare economics and contingent valuation information to the international biological setting.

USING THE RESULTS OF THE VICTORIAN CONTINGENT VALUATION SURVEY

Estimates of the aggregate values of Victorians for the conservation of all endangered flora and fauna in the State and for the conservation of a single species (Leadbeater's possum) were obtained from the survey. The question now is how these values might be used in the Flora and Fauna Guarantee process and the species conservation policy setting generally.

The results of the survey could contribute directly in two ways under the Flora and Fauna Guarantee process. Firstly, the estimate of value for all endangered species relates to the third role of economic analysis identified in Chapter 2, that of ascertaining the total amount of funding which should be allocated to the conservation of endangered flora and fauna each year. The estimate does not provide information on the cost of conservation programmes each year, but it does demonstrate how much Victorians value species conservation and what priority should be given to expenditure on species conservation. The value obtained in the study is at least an order of magnitude larger than the current direct expenditures on flora and fauna conservation, $160 to 340 million per year as opposed to about $10 million per year. These figures indicate strong interest in the conservation of endangered species and support for an increase in expenditure of up to $340 million per year (with a 'best' estimate of $160 million per year) if this is required to ensure the survival of endangered species in Victoria.

The value derived from the contingent valuation survey can be regarded as the upper limit to expenditure on species conservation, as the actual cost may be considerably less. Chisholm and Moran (1993) favour the use of the contingent valuation methodology in this context. They have suggested that contingent valuation surveys be used to determine the upper limit for total expenditure on species conservation, with allocation within the budget made by wildlife managers. However, once the total budget was set, the contingent valuation method could also be used to determine public preferences for conservation of individual species within the budget total. Rogers (1992a) used this kind of approach to value conservation of old growth forest as part of willingness to pay for environmental conservation issues generally.

The second way in which the values estimated in this study could contribute to the Flora and Fauna Guarantee process is in evaluating the social and economic impacts of particular conservation programmes. As discussed in Chapter 2, techniques such as contingent valuation are likely to be used at the management plan stage and only in cases where the opportunity costs of the conservation programmes are large. This is because the expense of a well prepared and well executed survey is probably justified only in such cases.

Conservation of Leadbeater's possum may become an issue where there is disagreement over management alternatives, for example, if a management plan is adopted for Leadbeater's possum that entails the reduction or cessation of forestry activities in the main possum habitat of the Central Highlands area. This is quite likely for at least some of the area, as the possums require trees of 200 years and older for nesting, but rotations which maximise the net present value of timber production are in the order of 40 to 50 years (Chapter 2). According to the State Timber Industry Strategy (State Government of Victoria 1986) rotation length should be around 80 years, but at current cutting rates it appears to be considerably less (Lindenmayer *pers. comm.* 1993).

In an evaluation of the social and economic impacts of conservation, the benefits of conservation should be compared with the opportunity cost of conservation, that is, the lost benefits of forestry. It is beyond the scope of this book to undertake such an evaluation as considerable further research is required to estimate accurately many of the costs and benefits involved. However, it is useful to illuminate some of the issues which would need to be considered in a cost benefit analysis.

The classes of costs and benefits which would need to be considered in such a comparison are varied and complex and controversy surrounds their evaluation. An example of this controversy is the major cost benefit study of the Thompson River catchment (which is part of the Central Highlands region) carried out for Melbourne Water and the Department of Conservation and Environment (Read Sturgess and Associates 1992). This study has been revised because of contention over the values of some of the alternatives under consideration (Read Sturgess and Associates and Tasman Economic Research Pty Ltd. 1994)

The Central Highlands area has many uses. The region is easily accessible from the Melbourne metropolitan area and is an important camping, bushwalking and outdoor recreation venue, with some cross country skiing in the highest parts. The region is also important as a water catchment for the Melbourne metropolitan region. The Central Highlands region features some of the finest stands of mountain ash (*Eucalyptus regnans*) in Australia, which are highly valued by loggers as a source of timber and pulp. These forests are also highly regarded as natural forests and may have quite high conservation values in themselves.

With the exception of forestry, most uses of the region have little impact on the value of the area as Leadbeater's possum habitat and in some cases the coexistence of uses is beneficial. For example, management of the area for species conservation, which means that the area is largely undisturbed, is also valuable for obtaining high yields of clean water for urban users in Melbourne. Few attempts have been made to estimate monetary values for any of the recreation benefits mentioned above, although there have been some attempts to assess the value of the water output (Galapitage 1992 and Kennedy, Read and Sturgess 1993).

On the cost side, the management expenditures for most activities other than forestry are relatively minor. Expenditure for management of Leadbeater's possum, which also assists other species, recreation and water harvesting, was in the order of $106,000 in the 1992/93 financial year (Department of Conservation and Resources 1993). This figure compares with the annual benefits for Leadbeater's possum conservation estimated from this survey of around $40 million.

The social costs and benefits of the forestry activities are far from clear. Private logging on public land has been encouraged in the past by various governments for many reasons other than financial returns. In the early days of white settlement when the native *Eucalypt* forests appeared to be most plentiful, logging activities enabled the clearing of land for agriculture as well as providing the materials for the development of new settlements and infrastructure. At other times objectives have been to maintain relatively low costs of housing, to promote regional development, to provide local employment, to counterbalance the high rate of timber imports into the country and, more recently, to promote export earnings.

State agencies have traditionally undertaken some of the management aspects of forestry (for example, roading) and the State receives royalty payments on the timber harvested in return. For a variety of reasons, the costs of providing the logging base have rarely been compared with the revenues obtained. Recent attempts to do so indicate that royalty payments may fall short of the State expenditures. The Auditor-General's Report on logging in Victoria (1993) found Department of Conservation and Natural Resources management costs attributable to forestry exceeded the royalty payments from forestry to the State. This result is reinforced by studies by Clarke and Dragun (1989) and Dragun (1994), which came to the same conclusion.

In addition to the poor accounting of costs and benefits by State agencies, little is published on the economics of the private logging sector in Victoria. There are considerable uncertainties about the private costs and benefits incurred by companies logging on public lands. There are widely varying estimates of the costs and success of regeneration, both for the second and successive cycles, but there seems to be no agreement as to which estimates are correct. Attempts to get regrowth in areas where regeneration has initially failed may be very difficult and expensive with a high likelihood of failure, or may result in trees of little value for timber in subsequent rotations.

From society's viewpoint, timber prices are distorted by the State royalty structure. As well, recent estimates of market returns to forestry in the general region have not been particularly favourable (Streeting and Hamilton 1991, Auditor-General 1993). The timber prices also do not include any accommodation for a wide range of off-site and non-point pollution and degradation ranging from salinity in agricultural lands, land erosion and reduction in soil fertility generally, siltation, water quality reduction, weed infestation, increased greenhouse gas emission, road degradation and so on.

There are secondary effects associated with both the forestry and conservation options. Employment is a major concern at the political level and loss of forestry jobs is a contentious issue. However, employment may also be created through the conservation option in the recreation and tourism sectors. A small amount of eco-tourism related in part to Leadbeater's possum already exists. New technology and use of forests for pulpwood rather than logs is already reducing employment opportunities in forestry (Christoff and Blakers 1986). Increasing plantation forestry is an alternative.

There have been some attempts to value timber production and the net benefits of logging. The results vary with the assumptions made concerning management costs, regeneration costs and success rates, the appropriate timber prices and so on (Read Sturgess and Associates 1992). Chisholm and Moran (1993) place an annual value on lost income from timber production from precluding forestry in valuable Leadbeater's possum habitat areas at $11 million, which can be compared with the estimate of $40 million per year for preserving Leadbeater's possum. Lockwood, Loomis and DeLacy (1993) conducted a cost benefit study of logging in similar old growth native forests in the equally productive region of East Gippsland (although there are no Leadbeater's possums in the area). They compared contingent valuation estimates of willingness to pay to preserve old growth forests with the benefits from logging and calculated a positive net present value for preserving the forests.

The estimate of the value of preserving Leadbeater's possum would clearly be a useful input into a comprehensive cost-benefit analysis of the possible uses and management of the Central Highlands forest. Although a range of values for Leadbeater's possum was obtained, with a best estimate of $40 million per year, estimates of the other costs and benefits are also subject to considerable uncertainty. Sensitivity analysis of the key parameters would be a useful addition to any such study because of the range of possibilities.

Kennedy and Jakobsson (1993) have also shown how the contingent valuation estimates for Leadbeater's possum could be used in an application of dynamic programming to determining optimal forestry management in the area. As the purpose of the paper was to demonstrate how such a model might be developed, a restricted set of assumptions regarding forestry management was used. The estimates could also be used in a decision analysis framework (Maguire 1986) to assist in estimating payoffs at various decision points.

The contingent valuation estimates of value for Leadbeater's possum could also be of immediate use if applied to the expenditure of public funds. The contingent valuation estimates indicate that citizens of Victoria are prepared to pay up to $80 million per year (with a 'best' estimate of $40 million per year) on a project guaranteeing the survival of Leadbeater's possum.

The estimates of willingness to pay for conservation of endangered flora and fauna and for conservation of Leadbeater's possum are both considerably higher than present expenditure. The estimated values indicate that Victorians derive substantial benefit from the continued existence of endangered species and Leadbeater's possum. These values should be taken into account in the assessment of projects which threaten species survival.

CONTINGENT VALUATION AND POLICY APPLICATION

The theme of this section will be to review the general policy application of contingent valuation results in Australia and New Zealand and relate the performance here to the situation in Europe and the US. Significant reviews and bibliographies of the European contingent valuation situation are found in Navrud (1992), Wibe (1994) and Johansson, Kriström and Mäler (1995) and of the US situation in Carson *et al.* (1994a) and Walsh, Johnson and McKean (1992), and no substantive attempt will be made here to repeat that work. A useful complementary Australian review is to be found in New South Wales Environmental Protection Authority (1995).

The use of contingent valuation in Australia is considered together with its use in New Zealand because the history of use of the technique in both places is similar and there are regular exchanges of information among both academics and the public service. Contingent valuation has not been applied widely in either country. The first studies were reported in the early 1980s, about five years behind the formative US applications. Sinden (1991) and DeLacy and Lockwood (1992) review Australian studies of non-market values using contingent valuation as well as other techniques.

Most of the contingent valuation studies which have been undertaken in Australia and New Zealand to date are summarised in Tables 11.1 to 11.6. Few, if any, of the studies reported in these tables appear to have had a strong impact on public policy. Sinden (1991) suggested that only one study has been applied in a policy context - the Resource Assessment Commission study of the Kakadu Conservation Zone (Imber, Stevenson and Wilks 1991). Bennett (1992) added the studies by Hundloe *et al.* (1990) and a study of the south eastern forests by Carter and Bennett (Resource Assessment Commission 1992 and Carter 1992). However, in all three cases, the contingent valuation results appear to have had little, if any, influence on the decisions made concerning the resources in question (Bennett 1992, Bennett and Carter 1993, Glyde 1992, Hundloe and Blamey 1992 and Sinden 1991). The New Zealand studies have been predominantly academic research.

One recent Australian study which used contingent valuation estimates of benefit does appear to have had some policy application. This study did not elicit values itself, but collated the results from about 80 Australian, New Zealand and US studies to estimate the use and conservation benefits of a number of rivers and catchments being considered for listing as heritage rivers and natural catchments (Dumsday, Jakobsson and Ransome 1992).

The social and economic appraisal of the candidate rivers and catchments conducted in this study played a major role in the Land Conservation Council's recommendations as to which river segments and catchments should be given protection. Most of the rivers and catchments for which environmental values were estimated to be greater then the resource use values (for example, timber, water supply and hydro-electric development) were recommended for protection. These recommendations have now been written into legislation (*Heritage Rivers Act,* 1992 Victoria).

In general, however, there has been considerable scepticism about the results of contingent valuation studies in Australia. The Resource Assessment Commission study of the Kakadu Conservation Zone (Imber, Stevenson and Wilks 1991) is the most widely publicised Australian application. This study attracted much criticism from Australian sources, in particular because of the implied high level of willingness to pay for the conservation of an area that many respondents were probably unlikely to visit (Australian Bureau of Agricultural and Resource Economics 1991, Brunton 1991, Moran 1991 and Stone 1991).

Bennett and Carter (1993) have grouped the major criticisms in four categories; communication aspects, embedding effects, strategic bias and validation. The ability and willingness of respondents to truthfully reveal their values in a hypothetical market situation is also questioned (Australian Bureau of Agricultural and Resource Economics 1991). The main concern with communication aspects was whether people understood what they were valuing. For the Kakadu Conservation Zone, 'the critics' hypothesis was that respondents believed they were paying to preserve the whole of Kakadu National Park, not just the small area to be mined which lay outside park boundaries' (Bennett and Carter 1993, p. 81). Similar criticisms have been made of other Australian studies.

Table 11.1 Australian and New Zealand contingent valuation studies

Author	Good valued	Population surveyed	Type of survey	Payment vehicle	Method of elicitation	Mean WTP estimate[1]
Bennett 1981[2] 1984a	Existence values Nadgee Nature Reserve NSW	544 residents of Canberra ACT	Personal interview	Once only payment, increase in taxes OR donation to conservation organisation	Open-ended	Once off payment of $27.08
Sinden *et al.* 1982[2]	Eucalypt dieback research	Two surveys of farmers in NSW	NR[6]	1.Willing to travel to obtain stock shelter, firewood and construction material 2.Once only payment for purchase or preservation of a tree	NR	*Travel* Stock shelter; eucalypt 5.3km; radiata 5.7km Firewood; eucalypt 14.6km; radiata 4.1km Construction; eucalypt 15.4km; radiata 3.9km. *Payment* Preserve tree; eucalypt $28.80; radiata $20.50 Purchase tree; eucalypt $23.70; radiata $16.30
Johnston 1982[2]	Fly control	537 residents of Canberra ACT	Personal interview	Local taxes paid to research fund	Split samples, bidding game and open-ended	$13.40
Scott and Co. 1982[2]	Clean air in NSW and SA	501 people Sydney and 251 people Adelaide	Personal interview	Increase in the price of goods and services	Payment card and open-ended	Sydney - $17.66 Adelaide - $10.44
Economic Associates 1983[3]	Recreation value, Green Island, Qld	Visitors	NR	NR	NR	$29 per visitor day
Sinden *et al.* 1983[2]	Eucalypt dieback in NSW	Households in New England	NR	NR	NR	$6.84
Waikato Valley Aty 1983[4], Harris 1984	Water pollution control in New Zealand	Households in WVA area	Personal interview	Yearly charge added to electricity account	Iterative bidding	NZ$21 per person

Table 11.2 Australian and New Zealand contingent valuation studies

Author	Good valued	Population surveyed	Type of survey	Payment vehicle	Method of elicitation	Mean WTP estimate
Bennett 1984b[2]	Bushfire cost to users of National Parks	Visitors at Ben Boyd (127) Moreton (130); Kosciusko (127)	Personal interview	Entrance fee for vehicles to the park	Iterative bidding	Average loss per visit; Ben Boyd - $0.06 Moreton - $0.80 Kosciusko - $0.80
Majid *et al.* 1983	Increment to park system	140 households Armidale NSW	Personal interview	NR	Iterative bidding	$1.50 to $5.30 per household
Ekanayake and Sinden 1985[2], Ekanayake 1987	Rare eucalypts, dieback, heritage loss	136 households, Armidale NSW	Personal interview	Once only payment for a fund to buy woodland	Open-ended	Once off payment; 1. Knowledge to prevent dieback $12.40 2. Woodland area for local school $4.80 3. Health benefits from scientific discoveries $3.70
Mattinson and Morrison 1985[3]	Recreational water quality, WA	Residents and visitors	NR	NR	NR	Residents $41-62 per person
Delforce *et al.* 1986[2]	Recreation benefits, Flinders Ranges SA	97 tourist groups in 1st survey 77 tourist groups in 2nd	Personal interview Mail survey	Additional travel costs	NR	Cost per trip of $35.88
Sinden 1987[2]	Community backing for soil conservation	Residents of Sydney and 5 country centres in NSW	Phone survey	Increase in the price of bread	Open and closed-ended	Payment of $0.106 per loaf of bread yielding a total of $15.00 per year per household
Sloan 1987[3]	Recreation value, Heron Island	Visitors	NR	Cost per visit	NR	$54 per visitor day
Hundloe *et al.* 1987[3]	Recreation value, Great Barrier Reef.	Visitors	NR	NR	NR	WTP per visitor: Australian $281; overseas $170; use of coral sites $10.
Kerr 1987	Preservation of Kawarau Gorge New Zealand	371 respondents from 1000 households	Mail survey	Electricity account	Discrete choice	Payment of NZ$68.00 per household

Table 11.3 Australian and New Zealand contingent valuation studies

Author	Good valued	Population surveyed	Type of survey	Payment vehicle	Method of elicitation	Mean WTP estimate
Carter 1987[2], Carter *et al.* 1988	Crown of thorns starfish control for reef preservation	130 non-users in 1st survey and 305 visitor groups in the 2nd	Mail survey Personal interview	Once only donation to a trust to manage the reef OR an increase in entrance fee to be paid to a trust to manage the reef	Open-ended Iterative bidding	*Non-users* $4.13 for reef management; $1.63 for starfish control *Visitors* $9.77 for reef management; $2.66 for starfish control
Roberts *et al.* 1988[2]	Weed and pest control policies in farming areas	126 wheat belt farmers in WA	Personal interview	Not specified	Payment card and closed-ended	$1486.00 per farm
Thomas and Syme 1988[2]	Price elasticity of demand for residential water	312 households in Perth WA	Personal interview	Increase in water price	Closed-ended	A price increase of 41 cents induces 31% of households to reduce water use
Kirkland 1988	Whanga-marino wetland preservation	659 respondents from 1289 NZ households	Mail survey	Payment to special trust fund	Open-ended	NZ$12.68 per household for preservation NZ$6.31 per household for improvement to wetland
Young and Carter 1990.[2]	Forest research benefits	1031 residents NSW-ACT & sub sample of 400 Eden-Monaro	Mail survey	Donation to a research fund OR an increase in tax to be paid to a research fund	Payment card	$4.23 per respondent for South East forests $17.19 for Australian forests
Sinden[2]	Recreational benefits of river management	658 visitor groups in 1st survey and 95 anglers in Victoria	Personal interview Mail survey	Additional travel costs	Open-ended	$8.90 to $16.00 per group per visit - depending on site and availability of substitute sites

Table 11.4 Australian and New Zealand contingent valuation studies

Author	Good valued	Population surveyed	Type of survey	Payment vehicle	Method of elicitation	Mean WTP estimate
Hundloe *et al.* 1990 Blamey 1991	Forest preservation benefits Fraser Island Qld	1188 recreators at Fraser Island and 800 national non-users	Mail survey	Annual taxes	Discrete choice - referendum	Total annual payment; users $11.4m; non-users $534.6m; Total $664.8m Median payment; users $316; non-users $187; Total $205
Cause 1990	Deer hunting. Increased numbers	1468 members of Australian deer hunting association	Mail survey	Hunting trip costs	Open-ended	$15.66 million for present hunting conditions $36.54 million for 2X deer numbers
Greer and Sheppard 1990	Preservation of NZ native forest	2805 adult NZers	Mail survey	Once only tax payment to research fund	Discrete choice	NZ$46 per individual
Dragovich 1990[3]	Prevention of soil erosion	704 Sydney residents	NR	Increase in price of bread	NR	9.3 cents per loaf (loaf=$1.40)
Dragovich 1991[3]	Prevention of soil erosion	104 Singleton, Muswellbrook residents	Personal interview	Increase in price of bread	NR	7.3 cents per loaf
Yapp, Young, Sinden 1991[3]	Prevention of soil erosion	150 Sydney residents	Phone survey	Increase in price of bread	NR	20.6 cents per loaf
Weber *et al.* 1991	Value of instream river flows	650 Ashburton households; 350 Canterbury households	Phone survey	Income reduction in relation instream water adjustment	Iterative bidding (350 households) Discrete choice (650 households)	Per h/hold Iter bid; Ashbton; NZ$84 Cantbury; NZ$63 Discrete choice; Ashbton; NZ$118 Cantbury; NZ$57
Imber *et al.* 1991	Enviro related costs of mining at Kakadu NT	2034 residents AUS & 502 residents of Northern Territory	Personal interview	Reduction in income	Double bounded discrete choice	Median value/year for 10 years; major impact scenario $123.80 - $143.20/hhold $52.80-$80.30 for the minor impact scenario/hhold

Table 11.5 Australian and New Zealand contingent valuation studies

Author	Good valued	Population surveyed	Type of survey	Payment vehicle	Method of elicitation	Mean WTP estimate
Carlos 1991[3]	Improved domestic water quality	100 Yass, NSW households	NR	NR	NR	Value/person: Mean $23 Median $10 Mean (informed) $40; Median (informed) $38
Dwyer Leslie 1991[3]	Preservation of domestic water quality	Sydney households	NR	NR	NR	$51-64 per household
Walpole 1991[3]	Recreation sites Ovens-Kings rivers	Site visitors	NR	NR	NR	$8-33 per visitor day
Carter 1992; RAC 1992; Reark Research 1991	Preservation value of forests in SE NSW	5000 residents of ACT, NSW and Victoria	Mail survey	Higher costs of paper and timber products and also tax increases	Referendum on - logging or preservation - preservation involving a specific cost	Median value of $22 per person Mean not reported
Pitt 1991 Pitt 1992 Pitt 1993	Preservation of north coast dunes, NSW	544 visitor groups	Personal interview	Not clear - additional weekly accommodation costs??	Choice of values from a limited range (small payment card)	27 cents per visitor night OR $8.33 per visitor group per week
Rogers 1992a Rogers 1992b, Rogers and Sinden 1993	Protection of old growth forests in NSW	160 h/hold from (Armidale) & 50 from (Dorrigo)	Personal interview	Annual donation for protection - further allocated to specific issues	Open-ended	Conservation:[5] Armidale $126.30 Dorrigo $77.40 Protect native vegetation: Armidale $35.70 Dorrigo $8.30 Protect native forests: Armidale $16.40 Dorrigo $8.30 [5]
Sappideen 1992	Recreational benefits of wetlands at Sale Victoria	600 residents living near the wetlands	Mail survey	Additional entrance fee paid to a trust fund	Closed ended question with option of offering own bid	Mean WTP/visit of $2.58; & avge of 2 visits. Yields annual WTP of $5.16
Stone 1992	Preservation of wetlands at Barmah forest Victoria	122 people Melbourne and 81 rural Victoria	Personal interview	Donation to a non-government organisation	Two stage open-ended question	$23.65 to $30 per adult Victorian (NB: small pilot study)

Table 11.6 Australian and New Zealand contingent valuation studies

Author	Good valued	Population surveyed	Type of survey	Payment vehicle	Method of elicitation	Mean WTP estimate
Tracey 1992, Lockwood and Tracey 1993	Cattle grazing and cessation of cattle grazing on Bogong High Plains Victoria	1110 persons listed in the Victorian telephone listings - half in each questionnaire	Mail survey	Payment to Australian Heritage Commission trust fund	Discrete choice followed by open-ended question	Median WTP for both goods = 0 No significant difference in the two means
Sheppard et al. 1993	Improved water quality in Lower Waimakariri River	2630 adult residents of the Canterbury Region and 400 adults in Canterbury and 512 users	Mail survey Telephone survey Mail survey	Regional Council rate increase	Discrete choice	NZ$72 to $153
Lockwood et al. 1993, Lockwood 1992, Lockwood et al. 1992, 1994	Protection of national estate forests which are outside National Parks	525 persons listed on the Victorian electoral roll and 200 respondents from the division of Gippsland	Mail survey	Payment to a Australian Heritage Commission trust fund	Discrete choice followed by open-ended question	Open-ended mean of $100 for all unprotected national estate forests in SE Australia
Tracy 1993, Lockwood and Tracey 1995	Keeping urban recreation park	250 Sydney residents	Mail survey	Payment to trust fund	Open-ended	Users $25.81, Non-users $12.10

Notes:
1. All values are per year unless indicated otherwise, usually in dollars pertaining to the year of the report.
2. Indicates that some of this information was derived from Wilks 1990; otherwise information was derived from the original source.
3. Information was derived from New South Wales Environment Protection Authority. All values are expressed in 1990 Australian dollars.
4. Noted in Kerr and Sharp 1987.
5. Results are complex - consult original source.
6. Not reported.

Much of the criticism of the Resource Assessment Commission study was ably rebutted by Carson (1991) and generally the Kakadu study was regarded highly by leading contingent valuation practitioners in the US (Hanemann 1991b). However, Australian decision makers were not convinced and the final decision not to mine the area was made on other grounds.

Sinden (1991) discusses the kind of information and level of accuracy that is required for policy choices. Precise estimates of welfare changes are often unnecessary if the information is adequate to say with reasonable certainty that one course of action makes a substantially greater contribution to welfare than another. There are difficulties in getting precise estimates of value from contingent valuation studies (Chapters 5 and 6), but it is usually possible to be fairly confident about the range within which the value falls or at least the order of magnitude of benefits (Dumsday, Jakobsson and Ransome 1992 and Sinden 1991). However, Bennett and Carter (1993) note that even order of magnitude estimates do not appear to be accepted by the Australian policy makers.

Widespread use of the contingent valuation technique is also relatively recent in Europe (Navrud and Strand 1992). Since the 1980s, numerous studies have been done. Navrud (1992) provides an overview of many studies, Dubgaard, Bateman and Merlo (1994) review studies of countryside valuation and Wibe (1994) lists studies on non-wood benefits from forests. Other reviews include Hanley (1987), Hoevenagel (1990 and 1994) and Opschoor (1986).

What impact, if any, contingent valuation studies have had on policy in Europe is not yet clear. Navrud and Strand (1992) note that in Norway few of the studies have had any influence on policy making although they have provided support for decisions made on other grounds. They suggest the main reason for this is general scepticism towards the method and the lack of convincing evidence as to the validity of the method. Römer and Pommerehne (1992) comment that in Germany the main sponsor of contingent valuation studies is the Federal Environment Agency, so it is possible that results of some studies may influence policy setting within the Agency.

Bennett and Carter (1993) and Hundloe and Blamey (1992) suggest that validation experiments may need to be carried out in Australia to convince Australian policy makers to use the results of contingent valuation experiments. Navrud and Strand (1992) and Glyde (1992) speculate that part of the problem is that the decision makers within government agencies and in the government have little training in environmental economics and find it very difficult to argue in favour of the use of contingent valuation estimates when faced with critical comments about the use of the method.

An additional avenue to explore may be the existing policy setting and decision making processes. Glyde (1992) points out that economic analysis of any kind has rarely played a major role in decision making in Australia at either the political or bureaucratic level. Hundloe (1990 p. 11), in reviewing various environmental controversies in Australia, notes that most were 'ultimately settled in the political arena'.

Most environmental and resource legislation gives no indication as to how specific economic considerations might be incorporated into particular issues of management. This was a theme that emerged in the discussion of the *Flora and Fauna Guarantee Act* (Chapter 2). Navrud and Strand (1992) identify the lack of a formal legal basis for doing cost benefit analyses of projects with environmental impacts as an additional obstacle to the use of non-market valuation methods in Norway.

The situation in the US appears to contrast with the Australian, New Zealand and European experience. Contingent valuation is widely accepted and extensively used in the US, although it is also widely criticised (Chapter 6). The technique has been given legitimacy in the US courts (Knetsch 1993). It is also a required procedure by some US federal agencies as part of their project evaluations (Arrow *et al.* 1993, Bennett and Carter 1993, DeLacy and Lockwood 1992, Eberle and Hayden 1991, Imber, Stevenson and Wilks 1991, Mitchell and Carson 1989 and Wilks 1990). Contingent valuation has also been used by the World Bank to evaluate projects in Latin America, Africa and Asia (Carson 1991).

It may be necessary, as Bennett and Carter (1993) suggest, to undertake further research into contingent valuation in Australia to convince Australian decision makers of the potential usefulness of the contingent valuation method. Legislative requirements for social and economic evaluations of projects, in the *Flora and Fauna Guarantee Act*, may promote the use of the technique as there is no other way to assess non-use values.

SPECIES VALUATION SURVEYS

In leading to a conclusion it is proposed to place the species conservation estimates obtained in this study in context relative to other significant species valuation research. However, there have been no other contingent valuation studies specifically concerning conservation of endangered species in Australia and relatively few studies elsewhere. A selection of these studies are reviewed briefly here (Tables 11.7 to 11.9), focussing on those that value non-consumptive use values and non-use values. Most contingent valuation studies of species have been for single species and almost entirely for animal species.

Boman and Bostedt (1995) conducted a mail survey of the Swedish population to ascertain their willingness to pay for four different population levels of wolf, with each population level being sent to a different sample. They found a positive willingness to pay to preserve a viable Swedish wolf population, with a mean per year of SEK 700-900 and a median of SEK 100-200, but there were no significant differences between the estimates from the different population levels of wolf.

Table 11.7 Comparison of single species valuation surveys

Author	Species - Biodiversity	Value
Boman and Bostedt (1995)	Wolf preservation in Sweden	Mean of SEK 700-900; median of SEK 100-200 per year
Fredman (1995)	Preserving the white-backed woodpecker in Sweden	Mean value of SEK 406 as a once off payment (about SEK 20 per year)
Loomis and Larson (1994)	Increasing gray whale populations by 50% and by 100%	Mean willingness to pay/household/yr (for visitors) of US$25 for a 50% increase; US$29.73 for a 100% increase The values for (general) households were US$16.18 and US$18.14
Hagemann (1985)	Avoiding a 90% reduction (from 16,000 to 1300) in gray whale population	US$36 (1992 dollars) per household per year
Samples and Hollyer (1990)	Conservation of humpback whales and monk seals	Once only payments of; US$125-142 for whales, US$62-103 for monk seals
Hagen, Vincent and Welle (1992)	Preservation of old growth forest and the northern spotted owl	US$47.93 lower bound estimate US$144.28 upper bound estimate per household per year
Rubin, Helfand and Loomis (1991)	Preservation of the northern spotted owl	WTP of US$34.84 per household per year
Navrud and Mungatana (1994)	Recreational value of wildlife viewing in Lake Nakuru National Park in Kenya	Total use value of US$7.5 to US$15 million per year (in 1991 dollars); flamingoes at the park account for a third of the value: Mean WTP values per visitor were $53.25 for the park overall and about $20 for the flamingoes. A willingness to accept value of $87 was estimated for the flamingoes

Author	Species - Biodiversity	Value
Kay, Brown and Allee 1987, cited in Stevens *et al.* (1991)	Atlantic salmon conservation	Mean WTP $10 to $30 existence value
Loomis and Helfand (1993)	Conservation of various species	$25 for bald eagles; $16 for grey whales; $40 for blue whales; $25 for sea otters; $13 for sea turtles and $31 for whooping cranes per household per year
Boyle and Bishop (1987)	Conservation of bald eagles and conservation of striped shiner	Annual WTP values (US dollars) of $10.62 to $75.31 for bald eagle and $1 to $5 for the striped shiner
Whitehead (1993)	Benefits for non-game wildlife	$1 to $75 per household or individual per year depending on the wildlife species
Loomis and White (1995)	Contingent valuation studies in the US for the conservation of 18 different species	Annual mean WTP values per household (1993 US$); from $6 for the striped shiner to $95 for northern spotted owl and its habitat
Jakobsson (1994)	Conservation of Leadbeater's possum	A$29 per household per year for Leadbeater's possum

Fredman (1995) estimated the value of preserving the white-backed woodpecker in Sweden at a mean value of SEK 406 as a once off payment (about SEK 20 per year). Fredman valued three different population levels of the woodpecker and also found no additional benefits from increasing the population size of the species above that of a viable population.

Loomis and Larson (1994) used a personal visitor survey and a household mail survey to estimate the total economic value of increasing gray whale populations by 50 per cent and by 100 per cent over the existing level. Unlike Fredman (1995) and Boman and Bostedt (1995), Loomis and Larson did find a positive willingness to pay to increase the population of gray whales, and a diminishing marginal valuation as population increased. Fredman (1995) argues that this result is expected for use values (such as whale watching) but not for existence values.

Loomis and Larson's estimates of mean willingness to pay per household per year by visitors were US$25 for a 50 per cent population increase and US$29.73 for a 100 per cent population increase. The corresponding figures for households were US$16.18 and US$18.14. Hagemann (1985) valued avoiding a 90 per cent reduction (from 16,000 to 1300) in the gray whale population at US$36 per household per year (1992 dollars). However, the survey had a response rate of only 21 per cent.

Samples and Hollyer (1990) valued humpback whales and monk seals in an experiment on sequencing and subaddivity effects. They obtained estimates of once only payments in the order of US$125-142 for humpback whales and US$62-103 for monk seals when they were valued individually.

Hagen, Vincent and Welle (1992) surveyed 1000 US households by mail to value the preservation of old growth forest and the northern spotted owl. Their conservative estimate of willingness to pay is US$47.93 and the upper bound estimate is US$144.28 per household per year. They calculate a conservative benefit cost ratio of 3.53 for preserving the forest and owl. Rubin, Helfand and Loomis (1991) surveyed 1200 Washington households and estimated a willingness to pay of US$34.84 per household per year to preserve the northern spotted owl.

Navrud and Mungatana (1994) applied travel cost and contingent valuation methods independently to estimate the recreational value of wildlife viewing in Lake Nakuru National Park in Kenya. They estimated total use value to be about US$7.5 to US$15 million per year (in 1991 dollars), with the flamingoes at the park accounting for a third of the value. Mean willingness to pay values per visitor were $53.25 for the park and about $20 for the flamingoes. A willingness to accept value of $87 was estimated for flamingoes.

Other species studies are reviewed in a number of papers. Stevens *et al.* (1991) cite average annual willingness to pay values (US dollars) from Boyle and Bishop (1987) of $10.62 to $75.31 for bald eagle conservation and $1 to $5 for the striped shiner, and existence values of $10 to $30 for Atlantic salmon (from Kay, Brown and Allee 1987). Loomis and Helfand (1993) report annual per household values from contingent valuation studies of $25 for bald eagles, $16 for grey whales, $40 for blue whales, $25 for sea otters, $13 for sea turtles and $31 for whooping cranes.

Whitehead (1993, p. 119) reviewed values from many studies and derives annual benefit estimates (in US dollars) for non-game wildlife ranging from 'about $1 to $75 per household or individual depending on the wildlife species, characteristics of the conservation policy and the type of survey'. Wibe (1994) includes several species valuation studies (particularly recreational hunting values) in a review of the non-wood benefits of forestry.

Loomis and White (1995) report the results of contingent valuation studies in the US for 18 different species. Annual mean willingness to pay values per household (in 1993 US dollars) range from $6 for the striped shiner to $95 for the northern spotted owl and its habitat. The conservative best estimate from the Leadbeater's possum survey (Jakobsson 1994 and Chapter 9) of $29 Australian (roughly US $20) per household per year falls well within the range of values reported for other endangered species in the studies reviewed above.

Loomis and White (1995) analysed the 18 species studies they reviewed and found that 68 per cent of the variation in willingness to pay for species could be explained by change in the size of population, whether the respondent was a visitor or non-user, whether payment is once only or annual and whether the species is a marine animal or a bird. These findings support the contention that contingent valuation studies can provide valid estimates of the benefits of individual species.

Single species estimates are useful in contexts where benefit cost analysis may be required (for example the Leadbeater's possum) to compare the costs and benefits of conservation. However, single species values tend not to account for substitution effects, and they may or may not include habitat and ecosystem values. For example, preserving Leadbeater's possum would also preserve old growth forests which have value in themselves as well as providing habitat for other endangered species. Thus, in many contexts it may be preferable to attempt to value a complement of species, a habitat area or biodiversity as a whole.

Few multiple-species valuation studies or studies of biodiversity value have been done, although the need for such studies is being more widely recognised (Hampicke *et al.* 1991, Loomis and Helfand 1993 and Loomis and White 1995). Biodiversity studies are, however, difficult to do because of problems in defining and measuring biodiversity (Solow, Polasky and Broadus 1993) in order to explain it to respondents. In addition, Spash and Hanley (1995) found that understanding of the biodiversity concept amongst both the general population and students was very limited. Multiple-species studies may face similar problems in presenting complex information in an understandable form.

Hampicke *et al.* (1991) obtained values in the order of 140 to 250 DM per household per year (about $160 to 290 Australian) for programmes to preserve endangered species in West Germany. Various contingent valuation designs were used and a range of programmes was valued. Seventy-seven per cent of respondents preferred the most far reaching programme, although only 57 per cent were prepared to pay for this programme. Veisten *et al.* (1993) used contingent valuation to value biodiversity in Norwegian forests.

Whitehead (1993) obtained a value of around US$15 per household per year for a conservation programme for coastal nongame wildlife and Johansson (1989) obtained an average value of SEK 1,275 (about $220 Australian) as a once only payment for a programme to preserve 300 endangered species in Sweden. If a 4 per cent discount rate is used the once only payment results in an annual payment of about $10 Australian.

Table 11.8 Comparison of multiple species valuation surveys

Author	Species - Biodiversity	Value
Hampicke et al. (1991)	Preserving endangered species in West Germany	Values in the order of 140 to 250 DM per household per year
Jakobsson (1994)	Preservation of all endangered species in Victoria	$118 Australian per household per year
Whitehead (1993)	Conservation programme for coastal nongame wildlife	US$15 per household per year
Johansson (1989)	Once only payment for a programme to preserve 300 endangered species in Sweden	Average value of SEK 1,275

Table 11.9 Comparison of non-contingent valuation species surveys

Author	Species - Biodiversity	Value
Pina (1994)	Spending of ecotourists in Mexico	US$60 to 100 per day for ecotourists
	Debt-for-nature swaps, for the existence of Mexican forests	People are willing to pay US$10 per hectare, debt-for-nature
Filion (1994)	Enjoyment received by participants in wildlife related activities	Total WTP of $6.1 billion; of which $5.1 billion is actual expenditure
Tobias and Mendelsohn (1991)	Tourism and ecotourism based on non-consumptive uses of wildlife in Costa Rica	Net present value of ecotourism is estimated at US$1250 per hectare
Ruitenbeek (1989)	Tourism and ecotourism based on non-consumptive uses of wildlife in Cameroon	Net present value of ecotourism is estimated at US$19 per hectare
Aylward (1993)	Value of private returns to pharmaceutical prospecting in Costa Rica	Net present value of US$4.81 million per product
Norton-Griffiths and Southey (1995)	Opportunity costs of biodiversity conservation in Kenya in terms of forgone agricultural production	Net return of $203 million (opportunity cost), compared with $42 million in net revenues from wildlife tourism and forestry

The conservative best estimate for preservation of all endangered species in Victoria of $118 Australian per household per year (Jakobsson 1994 and Chapter 9) is in the same order of magnitude as that obtained by Hampicke *et al.* (1991).

There have been a number of other studies which have not used the contingent valuation method. Pina (1994) estimates that ecotourists in Mexico spend in the order of US$60 to 100 per day. Using debt-for-nature swaps, Pina calculates that people are willing to pay US$10 per hectare for the existence of Mexican forests. Filion (1994) reports a total willingness to pay for enjoyment received by participants in wildlife related activities of $6.1 billion, of which $5.1 billion is actual expenditure. Barbier and Schulz (1995) report on several studies valuing tourism and ecotourism based on non-consumptive uses of wildlife. For example, the net present value of ecotourism in Costa Rica is estimated at US$1250 per hectare (Tobias and Mendelsohn 1991) and in Cameroon at US$19 per hectare (Ruitenbeek 1989).

There have also been various attempts at estimating returns from pharmaceutical prospecting (Aylward 1993, Principe 1989 and Reid *et al.* 1993). Aylward (1993), for example, estimated the net present value of private returns to pharmaceutical prospecting in Costa Rica at US$4.81 million per product.

Norton-Griffiths and Southey (1995) calculate the opportunity costs of biodiversity conservation in Kenya in terms of forgone agricultural production at a net return of $203 million, compared with $42 million in net revenues from wildlife tourism and forestry. They argue that as much of the benefit of Kenya's wildlife accrues to people living outside Kenya, the international community should be prepared to help fund conservation in the country.

An area of future research in which contingent valuation could play a major role is to investigate the values the international community holds for conservation of biodiversity in countries such as Kenya. It is in extending the consideration of the contingent valuation methodology to this international setting that this book now turns and concludes.

FROM CONTINGENT VALUATION
TO SPECIES CONSERVATION

This study has demonstrated some of the strengths and weaknesses of the contingent valuation method. The main methodological problems identified during the course of this study include the following;

1. the issue of whether to use willingness to pay or willingness to accept welfare measures,

2. the problem of scope effects,
3. the issue of the payment mechanism most appropriate for public goods in the given application setting, and
4. how to deal with uncertainty and the crucial problem of external validation.

Some suggestions for improvements to survey design to overcome some of these problems and proposals for further research have been made.

The contingent valuation method allows the explicit identification and valuation of the non-use values associated with many species in a way that has not been possible before. The evidence which is accumulating from many contingent valuation studies of environmental goods in general and species conservation in particular, shows such goods have considerable value.

Although the values estimated in contingent valuation studies may not be used directly in decision making in many cases, they add considerable support to the contention that environmental services can have significant social value and need to be explicitly considered in comparison to other marketed alternatives and the evaluation of development projects. This increases the pressure on developers to show that projects generate sufficient surpluses to cover environmental costs rather than putting the onus on 'conservationists' to argue the case that environmental impacts should be considered. Explicit recognition of environmental values will improve the allocation of society's total resources.

The strength of the contingent valuation approach probably is in the form of 'enriching the information base' in process of 'value formation public discussion' which Sen recognises as 'an important part of democracy' (1995, p. 18). Such a view may have much substance in a developed country national setting where citizens might consider the 'give and take' and equity-efficiency tradeoff of a range of policy possibilities, but might be more contentious in a developing country setting where many of the world's endangered species reside. The problem in many developing country situations is that the social consideration of such issues as environmental conservation, just does not occur as a function of political and institutional impediments but most significantly as a function of oppressive poverty. In this setting species conservation becomes very much a luxury good out of the reach of many citizens on the edge of starvation.

The key issues for long run species conservation in the face of the day-to-day survival in the developing countries, focus on the need to translate the very high interest and value for species conservation in the rich developed countries to an improvement in the way of life in the developing countries which removes the threat of untimely species extinction. Contingent valuation demonstrates that there is significant value *within* developed countries for species conservation and there is no reason to believe that this valuation would not extend to the conservation of species in less developed countries.

Conventional welfare economics also establishes the principles whereby such conservation might be socially desirable. However, given the very large disparities in income between rich countries - where all the value is - and poor countries - where all the species are - a conventional Kaldor-Hicks compensation test will lead to fundamental contradictions of equity. This could be greatly magnified in that many poor countries do not have the property rights structures in biological species to enable a transfer of wealth from the residents of the rich countries to their poor citizens. In this setting, species conservation based on the large values for conservation in the rich countries, would appear to need a welfare test which requires *actual* compensation to the poor countries rich in endangered species, to enable their citizens to better consider the longer term benefits of species conservation, as part of a broader international community.

References

Abramovitz, J.N. 1991. 'Investing in biological diversity: US research and conservation efforts in developing countries,' World Resources Institute, March.

Adamowicz, W.L. and Graham-Tomasi, T. 1991. 'Revealed preference tests of non-market goods valuation methods,' *Journal of Environmental Economics and Management*, 20, 29-45.

Adamowicz, W.L., Bhardwaj, V. and Macnab, B. 1993. 'Experiments on the difference between willingness to pay and willingness to accept,' *Land Economics*, 69(4), 416-427.

Amacher, R.C., Tollison, R.D. and Willett, W.D. 1972. 'The economics of fatal mistakes: Fiscal mechanisms for preserving endangered predators,' *Public Policy*, 20, 411-441.

Arrow, K.J. 1950, 'A difficulty in the concept of social welfare,' *Journal of Political Economy*, 58: 328-346.

Arrow, K.J. and Fisher, A.C. 1974. 'Environmental preservation, uncertainty and irreversibility,' *Quarterly Journal of Economics*, 88, 312-319.

Arrow, K., Solow, R., Portney, P.P., Leamer, E.E., Radner, R. and Schuman, H. 1993. 'Report of the National Oceanic and Atmospheric Administration Panel on Contingent Valuation,' *Federal Register*, 58(10), January 15, 4602-4614. US.

Auditor-General's Office, Victoria. 1993. *Timber industry strategy*. Special Report No 22. Melbourne: Government Printer.

Australian Bureau of Agricultural and Resource Economics. 1991. 'Valuing conservation in the Kakadu Conservation Zone,' Submission 91.2 to the Resource Assessment Commission. Canberra: Australian Government Printing Service.

Ayer, M., Brunk, H.D., Ewing, G.M. and Silverman, E. 1955. 'An empirical distribution function for sampling with incomplete information,' *Annals of Mathematical Statistics*, 26, 641-47.

Aylward, B.A. 1993. 'The economic value of pharmaceutical prospecting and its role in biodiversity conservation,' LEEC Discussion Paper 93-05, London Environmental Economics Centre, London.

Bachmura, F.T. 1971. 'The economics of vanishing species,' *Natural Resources Journal*, 11, 674-692.

Barbier, E.B., Burgess, J.C., Swanson, T.M. and Pearce, D.W. 1990. *Elephants, economics and ivory*. Earthscan Publications, London.

Barbier, E.B., Burgess, J.C., Bishop, J.T. and Aylward, B.A. 1994. *The economics of the tropical timber trade*. Earthscan Publications, London.

Barbier, E.B. and Schulz, C.E. 1995. 'Wildlife, biodiversity and trade,' Paper presented at the European Association for Environmental and Resource Economics Annual Meeting, Umeå, Sweden, 19-21 June.

Barrett, S. 1988. 'Economic guidelines for the conservation of biological diversity,' Paper prepared for Economics Workshop at IUCN General Assembly, San Jose, Costa Rica, Feb.

Bateman, I.J. 1993. 'Evaluation of the environment: A survey of revealed preference techniques,' GEC Working Paper 93-06. Centre for Social and Economic Research on the Global Environment, University of East Anglia and University College London.

Bateman, I.J., Langford, I.H., Willis, K.G., Turner, R.K. and Garrod, G.D. 1993. 'The impacts of changing willingness to pay question format in contingent valuation studies: An analysis of open-ended, iterative bidding and dichotomous choice formats,' GEC Working Paper 93-05. Centre for Social and Economic Research on the Global Environment, University of East Anglia and University College London.

Bateman, I.J., Langford, I.H., Turner, R.K., Willis, K.G. and Garrod, G.D. 1995. 'Elicitation and truncation effects in contingent valuation studies,' *Ecological Economics* 12, 161-179.

Bateman, I.J. and Willis, K.G. (eds) (forthcoming). *Valuing environmental preferences: Theory and practice of the contingent valuation method in the US, EC and developing countries.* Oxford, UK: Oxford University Press.

Bennett, J.W. 1981. Evaluation of the benefits of natural ecosystem preservation with special reference to existence values. Unpublished PhD thesis. Australian National University, Canberra.

Bennett, J.W. 1984a. 'Using direct questioning to value the existence benefits of preserved natural areas,' *Australian Journal of Agricultural Economics*, 28(2-3), 136-52.

Bennett, J.W. 1984b. 'The cost of bushfires to national park users,' A report prepared for the CSIRO Division of Forest Research.

Bennett, J.W. 1992. 'Assessing the prospects for contingent valuation in Australia,' In Lockwood, M. and DeLacy, T. (eds) *Valuing natural areas: Applications and problems of the contingent valuation method,* Johnstone Centre, Charles Sturt University, Albury, pp. 183-192.

Bennett, J.W. and Carter, M. 1993. 'Prospects for contingent valuation: Lessons from the south-east forest,' *Australian Journal of Agricultural Economics*, 37(2) 79-94.

Berck, P. 1979. 'Open access and extinction,' *Econometrica*, 47, 877-882.

Bergstrom, J.C., Stoll, J.R. and Randall, A. 1989. 'Information effects in contingent markets,' *American Journal of Agricultural Economics*, August, 685-691.

Bishop, R.C. 1978. 'Endangered species and uncertainty: The economics of a safe minimum standard,' *American Journal of Agricultural Economics*, 60(1), 10-18.

Bishop, R.C. 1979. 'Endangered species, irreversibility and uncertainty: A reply,' *American Journal of Agricultural Economics*, 61(2), 376-379.

Bishop, R.C. 1980. 'Endangered species: An economic perspective,' *Transactions of the 45th North American Wildlife and Natural Resources Conference.* Published by the Wildlife Management Institute, Washington D.C.

Bishop, R.C. 1982. 'Option value: An exposition and extension,' *Land Economics*, 58(1), 1-15.

Bishop, R.C. 1986. 'Resource valuation under uncertainty: Theoretical principles for empirical research,' In Smith, V.K. (ed). *Advances in Applied Microeconomics*, Vol. 3. Greenwich, Ct: JAI Press.

Bishop, R.C. 1988. 'Option value: Reply,' *Land Economics*, 64(1), 88-93.

Bishop, R.C. and Heberlein, T.A. 1979. 'Measuring values of extramarket goods: Are indirect measures biased?' *American Journal of Agricultural Economics*, 61(5), 926-930.

Bishop, R.C. and Heberlein, T.A. 1980. 'Simulated markets, hypothetical markets and travel cost analysis. Alternative methods of estimating outdoor recreation demand,' Staff Paper Series No. 187, Department of Agricultural Economics, University of Wisconsin.

Bishop, R.C. and Boyle, K.J. 1985. 'The economic value of Illinois Beach State Nature Preserve,' Final Report to Illinois Department of Conservation. University of Wisconsin, Madison.

Bishop, R.C. and Heberlein, T.A. 1986. 'Does contingent valuation work?' Chapter 9 in Cummings, R., Brookshire, D. and Schulze, W. (eds) *Valuing environmental goods: An assessment of the contingent valuation method.* Totowa, New Jersey: Rowman and Allanheld, pp. 123-147.

Bishop, R.C. and Heberlein, T.A. 1987. 'The contingent valuation method,' In Kerr, G.H. and Sharp, B.M.H. (eds) *Valuing the environment: Economic theory and applications.* Studies in Resource Management No. 2. Centre for Resource Management, University of Canterbury and Lincoln College.

Bishop, R.C. and Heberlein, T.A. 1990. 'The contingent valuation method,' In Johnson, R.L. and Johnson, G.V. (eds) *Economic valuation of natural resources: Issues, theory and applications.* Social Behaviour and Natural Resources Series, Boulder and Oxford. Westview Press, pp. 81-104.

Bishop, R.C. and Welsh, M.P. 1992. 'Existence values in benefit cost analysis and damage assessment,' *Land Economics*, 68(4), 405-17.

Bishop, R.C., Heberlein, T.A. and Kealy, M.J. 1983. 'Contingent valuation of environmental assets: Comparisons with a simulated market,' *Natural Resources, Journal*, 23(3), 619-33.

Bishop, R.C., Boyle, K.J. and Welsh, M.P. 1987. 'Toward total economic valuation of Great Lake fishery resources,' *Transactions of the American Fisheries Society*, 116, 339-345.

Blamey, R.K. 1991. 'Contingent valuation and Fraser Island,' Invited paper. Twentieth Conference of Economists. Economic Society of Australia Hobart, October. 1991.

Blamey, R.K. and Common, M. 1992. 'Sustainability and the limits to pseudo market valuation,' In Lockwood, M. and DeLacy, T. (eds) *Valuing natural areas: Applications and problems of the contingent valuation method*, Johnstone Centre, Charles Sturt University, Albury, pp. 117-146.

Boadway, R. and Bruce, N. 1984. *Welfare Economics.* Oxford, New York: Blackwell.

Bohm, P. 1972. 'Estimating demand for public goods. An experiment,' *European Economic Review*, 3, 111-130.

Boman, M. and Bostedt, G. 1995. 'Valuing the wolf in Sweden: Are benefits contingent upon the supply?' In Bostedt, G. 1995. Benefits of amenities in the forest environment: Four papers based on contingent valuation. Swedish University of Agricultural Sciences, Department of Forest Economics, Umeå. Report No. 110.

Bostedt, G. and Boman, M. 1995. 'Respondents and nonrespondents in contingent valuation surveys - reducing uncertainty in value inference,' In Bostedt, G. 1995. Benefits of amenities in the forest environment: Four papers based on contingent valuation. Swedish University of Agricultural Sciences, Department of Forest Economics, Umeå. Report No. 110.

Bowker, J.M. and Stoll, J.R. 1988. 'Use of dichotomous choice non-market methods to value the whooping crane resource,' *American Journal of Agricultural Economics*, May, 372-381.

Boyle, K.J. 1985. 'Essays on the valuation of non-market resources. Conceptual issues and empirical case studies,' PhD dissertation. Department of Agricultural Economics, University of Wisconsin, Madison.

Boyle, K.J. 1989. 'Commodity specification and the framing of contingent valuation questions,' *Land Economics*, 65(1), 57-63.

Boyle, K.J. and Bishop, R.C. 1984. 'A comparison of contingent valuation techniques,' Staff Paper No. 222, Department of Agricultural Economics, University of Wisconsin.

Boyle, K.J. and Bishop, R.C. 1985. 'The total value of wildlife resources. Conceptual and empirical issues. Invited paper,' Association of Environmental and Resource Economists workshop on recreational demand modelling. Boulder, Colorado, May.

Boyle, K.J. and Bishop, R.C. 1987. 'Valuing wildlife in benefit cost analyses: A case study involving endangered species,' *Water Resources Research*, 23(5), 943-950.

Boyle, K.J. and Bishop, R.C. 1988. 'Welfare measurements using contingent valuation: A comparison of techniques,' *American Journal of Agricultural Economics*, 70(1), 20-28.

Boyle, K.J. and Bishop, R.C. 1989. 'The economic valuation of endangered species of wildlife,' *Transactions of the 51st North American Wildlife and Natural Resources Conference.* Wildlife Management Institute, Washington, D.C. 153-161.

Boyle, K.J., Welsh, M.P. and Bishop, R.C. 1988. 'Validation of empirical measures of welfare change: Comment,' *Land Economics*, 64(1), 94-98.

Boyle, K.J., Desvousges, W.H., Johnson, F.R., Dunford, R.W. and Hudson, S.P. 1994. 'An investigation of part-whole biases in contingent valuation studies,' *Journal of Environmental Economics and Management*, 27, 64-83.

Brookshire, D.S. and Coursey, D.L. 1987. 'Measuring the value of a public good: An empirical comparison of elicitation procedures,' *American Economic Review*, 77, 555-566.

Brookshire, D.S., Randall, A. and Stoll, J.R. 1980. 'Valuing increments and decrements in natural resource service flows,' *American Journal of Agricultural Economics*, 62(3), 478-488.

Brookshire, D.S., Eubanks, L.S. and Randall, A. 1983. 'Estimating option prices and existence values for wildlife resources,' *Land Economics*, 59, 1-15.

Brookshire, D.S., Thayer, M.A., Schulze, W.W. and d'Arge, R.L. 1982. 'Valuing public goods: A comparison of survey and hedonic approaches,' *American Economic Review*, 72, 165-177, March.

Brown, G.M. Jr. 1985. 'Valuation of genetic resources,' Paper prepared for workshop on conservation of genetic resources. Lake Wilderness, US. June 12-16.

Brown, G.M. Jr. 1986. 'Preserving endangered species and other biological resources,' *The Science of the Total Environment*, 56, 89-97.

Brown, G. M. Jr. and Goldstein, J.H. 1984. 'A model for valuing endangered species,' *Journal for Environmental Economics and Management*, 11(4), 303-309.

Brown, G.M. Jr. and Swierzbinski, J. 1985. 'Endangered species, genetic capital and cost reducing research and development,' Chapter 15 in Hall, D.O., Myers, N. and Margaris, N.S. (eds) *Economics of ecosystem management*. Dordrecht: Dr. W. Junk Publishers, pp. 111-127.

Brown, G.M. Jr. and Henry, W. 1989. 'The economic value of elephants,' International Institute for Environment and Development and UCL London Environmental Economics Centre. London Environmental Economics Centre Paper 89-12, Nov.

Brown, G.M. Jr. and Henry, W. 1993. 'The viewing value of elephants,' In E.B. Barbier (ed.) *Economics and ecology: New frontiers and sustainable development*. Chapman and Hall, London.

Brown, K. and Moran, D. 1993. 'Valuing biodiversity: The scope and limitations of economic analysis,' GEC Working Paper 93-09. Centre for Social and Economic Research on the Global Environment, University of East Anglia and University College London.

Brunton, R. 1991. 'Will play money drive out real money? Contingent valuation surveys and Coronation Hill,' *Environmental Backgrounder*, 2, 1-9.

Buchanan, J.M. 1959. 'Positive economics, welfare economics and political economy,' *Journal of Law and Economics*, 124 .

Buchanan, J.M. and W.J. Samuels. 1975. 'On some fundamental issues in political economy: An exchange of correspondence'. *Journal of Economic Issues*, 9: 15-38, March.

Buchanan, J.M. and Stubblebine, W.C. 1962. 'Externality,' *Economica*, 29, 371-84.

Buchanan, J.M. and Tullock, G. 1962. *The calculus of consent*. Ann Arbor: University of Michigan Press.

Cambridge Economics, Inc. 1992. *Contingent valuation: A critical assessment*. A symposium. Cambridge, Ma: Cambridge Economics Inc., April 1992.

Cameron, T.A. 1988. 'A new paradigm for valuing non-market goods using referendum data. Maximum likelihood estimation by censored logistic regression,' *Journal of Environmental Economics and Management*, 15, 355-379.

Cameron, T.A. and James, M.D. 1987. 'Efficient estimation methods for use with "closed-ended" contingent valuation survey data,' *Review of Economics and Statistics*, 69, 269-276.

Carlos, C. 1991. 'What is town water worth?' *Australian Journal of Soil and Water Conservation*, 4(3), 32-36.

Carson, R.T. 1991. 'The Resource Assessment Commission's Kakadu Conservation Zone contingent valuation study. Remarks on the Brunton, Stone and Tasman Institute critiques,' Department of Economics, University of California, San Diego, March. In *Commentaries on the Resource Assessment Commission's contingent valuation survey of the Kakadu Conservation Zone*, Canberra.

Carson, R.T. 1994. 'Contingent valuation surveys and test of insensitivity to scope,' Paper presented at the International Conference on Determining the value of non-marketed goods: Economic, psychological and policy relevant aspects of the contingent valuation method, Bad Homburg, July 27-29. Forthcoming in Kopp R. and Schwarz, N. *Determining the value of non-marketed goods: Economic, psychological and policy relevant aspects of the contingent valuation method.* Werner Reimer Stiftung, Bad Homburg, Germany.

Carson, R.T. and Mitchell, R.C. 1995. 'Sequencing and nesting in contingent valuation surveys,' *Journal of Environmental Economics and Management,* 28, 155-173.

Carson, R.T., Hanemann, W.M. and Mitchell, R.C. 1986. 'The use of simulated political markets to value public goods,' Economics Department, University of California, San Diego. Cited in Hanemann, W.M. 1994a.

Carson, R.T., Flores, N.E. and Hanemann, W.M. 1992. 'On the creation and destruction of public goods: The matter of sequencing,' Paper presented at the European Association of Environmental and Resource Economists Meeting, Cracow, Poland. Working paper 690, Agricultural and Resource Economics, University of Berkeley, California.

Carson, R.T., Wright, J., Carson, N., Alberini, A. and Flores, N. 1994a. *A bibliography of contingent valuation studies and papers.* Natural Resource Damage Assessment Inc., La Jolla, California.

Carson, R.T., Flores, N.E., Martin, K. and Wright, J. 1994b. 'Contingent valuation and revealed preference methodologies: Comparing the estimates for quasi-public goods,' Discussion paper 94-07, University of California, San Diego.

Carter, M. 1987. 'The economic impacts of the crown of thorns starfish on the Great Barrier Reef,' Paper presented at ANZAAS, James Cook University, Queensland University, August.

Carter, M. 1992. 'The use of contingent valuation in the valuation of national estate forests in south-east Australia,' pp. 89-100. In Lockwood, M. and DeLacy, T. (eds) *Valuing natural areas: Applications and problems of the contingent valuation method,* Johnstone Centre, Charles Sturt University, Albury.

Carter, M., Vanclay, F.M. and Hundloe, T.J. 1988. 'Economic and socio-economic impacts of the crown of thorns starfish on the Great Barrier Reef,' A report to the Great Barrier Reef Marine Park Authority. Institute of Applied Environmental Research, Griffith University, Brisbane.

Cause, M. 1990. 'Social and economic value of recreational deer hunting in Australia,' Unpublished MSc Thesis, Griffith University, Brisbane.

Chisholm, A.G and Moran, A.J. 1993. *The price of preservation.* Melbourne: Tasman Institute.

Chisholm, A.H. 1988. 'Sustainable resource use, uncertainty, irreversibility and rational choice,' In Tisdell, C. and Maitra, P. (eds) *Technological change, development and the environment: Socio-economics perspectives.* London: Routledge.

Chisholm, A.H. and Clarke, H.R. 1992. 'Natural resource management and the precautionary principle,' LaTrobe University, Agricultural Economics Discussion Paper 16/92.

Christoff, P. and Blakers, M. 1986. *Jobs in East Gippsland: A transitional economic strategy.* Melbourne: Conservation Council of Victoria.

Cicchetti, C.J. and Freeman, A.M. 1971. 'Option demand and consumer's surplus: Further comment,' *Quarterly Journal of Economics.* 85(3), 528-539.

Cicchetti, C.J. and Wilde, I.L. 1992. 'Uniqueness, irreversibility and the theory of non-use values,' *American Journal of Agricultural Economics,* Dec. 1121-1125.

Ciriacy-Wantrup, S.V. 1947. 'Capital returns from soil-conservation practices,' *Journal of Farm Economics,* 29, 1188-90.

Ciriacy-Wantrup, S.V. 1952. *Resource Conservation. Economics and Policies,* 3rd edition 1968. Berkeley: University of California Press.

Clark, C.W. 1973. 'Profit maximisation and the extinction of animal species,' *Journal of Political Economy,* 81, 950-961.

Clarke, H.R. and Dragun A.K. 1989. *Natural resource accounting: East Gippsland case study,* Canberra: Australian Environmental Council.

Coase, R.H. 1960. 'The Problem of Social Cost'. *Journal of Law and Economics.* Vol III, Oct, 368-391.

Commonwealth of Australia. 1991. *Ecologically sustainable development, working groups final report - Agriculture,* Canberra: AGPS.

Conrad, J.M. 1980. 'Quasi-option value and the expected value of information,' *Quarterly Journal of Economics*, 94, 813-820.

Cooper, J.C. 1993. 'Optimal bid selection for dichotomous choice contingent valuation surveys,' *Journal of Environmental Economics and Management*, 24(1), 25-37.

Cooper, J.C. and Loomis, J.B. 1992. 'Sensitivity of willingness to pay estimates to bid design in dichotomous choice contingent valuation models,' *Land Economics*, 68(2), 211-24.

Cory, D.C. and Saliba, B.C. 1987. 'Requiem for option value,' *Land Economics*, 63(1), 1-10.

Council of Nature Conservation Ministers. 1989. *List of Australian endangered vertebrate fauna*, Australian National Parks and Wildlife Service Canberra.

Crosthwaite, J.M. and McMahon, I. 1992. 'Economic issues and the protection of endangered species,' Paper presented at 36th Annual Conference, Australian National University, Canberra, Feb. 10-12.

Crosthwaite, J.M., Dragun, A.K., Edmonds, S.A. and Jakobsson, K.M. 1992. 'The *Flora and Fauna Guarantee Act*: Pioneering conservation legislation in Australia. Paper to the Second meeting of the International Society for Ecological Economics, Stockholm August 1992.

Cummings, R.G. and Harrison, G.W. 1992. 'Identifying and measuring non-use values for natural and environmental resources. A critical review of the state of the art,' Washington DC: American Petroleum Institute.

Cummings, R.G. and Harrison, G.W. 1995. 'The measurement and decomposition of nonuse values: A critical review,' *Environmental and Resource Economics*, 5, 225-247.

Cummings, R.G., Brookshire, D. and Schulze, W. (eds) 1986. *Valuing environmental goods. An assessment of the contingent valuation method*. Totowa, New Jersey: Rowman and Allanheld.

Cummings, R.G., Ganderton, P.T. and McGuckin, T. 1994. 'Substitution effects in CVM values,' *American Journal of Agricultural Economics*, 76, 205-214.

Cummings, R.G., Harrison, G.W. and Rutström, E.E. 1995. 'Homegrown values and hypothetical surveys: Is the dichotomous choice approach incentive compatible?' *American Economic Review*, 85(1), 260-266.

Dalecki, M.G., Whitehead, J.C. and Blomquist, G.C. 1993. 'Sample non-response bias and aggregate benefits in contingent valuation: An examination of early, late and non-respondents,' *Journal of Environmental Management*, 38, 133-143.

Davis, R.K. 1963. 'The value of outdoor recreation: An economic study of the Maine Woods,' PhD dissertation, Harvard University. Cited in Mitchell, R.C. and Carson, R.T. 1989.

DeLacy, T. and Lockwood, M. 1992. 'Economic valuation of natural areas,' In Lockwood, M. and DeLacy, T. (eds) *Valuing natural areas: Applications and problems of the contingent valuation method*. Johnstone Centre, Charles Sturt University, Albury, pp. 1-16.

Delforce, R., Sinden, J.A. and Young M.D. 1986. 'Policy preferences and social economic values to resolve pastoralism conflicts,' *Landscape Planning* 12, 387-401.

Department of Conservation and Resources. 1993. Financial accounts.

Department of Conservation, Forests and Lands. 1986. Discussion paper on the programme for a native flora and fauna conservation guarantee with particular reference to a proposal for new legislation. Department of Conservation, Forests and Land, Melbourne, Victoria.

Department of Conservation, Forests and Lands, Community Education and Information Branch (undated). Conservation in Victoria 1. Plants and animals at risk.

Desvousges, W.H., Gable, A.R., Dunford, R.W. and Hudson, S.P. 1993a. 'Contingent valuation. The wrong tool to measure passive-use losses,' *Choices*, Second Quarter, 9-11.

Desvousges, W.H., Johnson, F.R., Dunford, R.W., Boyle, K.J., Hudson, S.P. and Wilson, K.N. 1993b. 'Measuring natural resource damages with contingent valuation: Tests of validity and reliability,' In Hausman, J.A. (ed.) *Contingent valuation: A critical assessment.* North-Holland, Amsterdam.

Desvousges, W.H, Smith, V.K. and McGivney, M.P. 1983. 'A comparison of alternative approaches for estimating recreation and related benefits of water quality improvements,' EPA-230-05-83-001. Washington, DC, Office of Policy Analysis, US Environmental Protection Agency. Cited in Mitchell, R.C. and Carson, R.T. 1989.

De Vaus, D.A. 1985. *Surveys in social research.* Sydney: Allen and Unwin.

Diamond, P.A and Hausman, J.A. 1993. 'On contingent valuation measurement of non use values,' In Hausman, J.A. (ed.) *Contingent valuation: A critical assessment.* Contributions to economic analysis. Amsterdam: North Holland.

Dickie, M., Fisher, A. and Gerking, S. 1987. 'Market transactions and hypothetical demand data: A comparative study,' *Journal of American Statistical Association,* 82, 67-75.

Dillman, D. 1978. *Mail and telephone surveys: The total design method,* New York: John Wiley and Sons.

Domencich, T.A. and McFadden, D. 1975. *Urban Travel Demand,* Amsterdam: North-Holland.

Dragovich, D. 1990. 'Does soil erosion matter to people in metropolitan Sydney?' *Australian Journal of Soil and Water Conservation,* 3(1), 29-32.

Dragovich, D. 1991. 'Who should pay for soil conservation? Community attitudes about financial responsibility for land repair,' *Australian Journal of Soil and Water Conservation,* 4(1), 4-7.

Dragun, A.K. 1994. 'Structures of governance and the political resolution of forest use entitlements: Equity and sustainability in the old growth forests of the Central Highlands of Victoria,' Paper presented to the Third Biennial Meeting of the International Society for Ecological Economics. San José, Costa Rica, October.

Dubgaard, A. 1994. 'Valuing recreation benefits from the Mols Bjerge area, Denmark,' In Dubgaard, A., Bateman, I. and Merlo, M. (eds) *Economic Valuation of Benefits from Countryside Stewardship.* Proceedings of a Workshop organised by the Commission of the European Communities Directorate General for Agriculture, Brussels 7-8 June 1993. Wissenschaftsverlag Vauk Kiel KG.

Dubgaard, A., Bateman, I. and Merlo, M. (eds) 1994. *Economic Valuation of Benefits from Countryside Stewardship.* Proceedings of a Workshop organised by the Commission of the European Communities Directorate General for Agriculture, Brussels 7-8 June 1993. Wissenschaftsverlag Vauk Kiel KG.

Duffield, J.W. and Patterson, D.A. 1991. 'Inference and optimal design for a welfare measure in dichotomous choice contingent valuation,' *Land Economics,* 67(2), 225-39.

DuMouchel, W.H. and Duncan, G.J. 1983. 'Using sample survey weights in multiple regression analysis of stratified samples,' *Journal of the American Statistical Association,* 78, 535-543. Cited in Loomis, J.B. 1987a.

Dumsday, R.G. Jakobsson, K.M. and Ransome, S. 1992. 'State-wide assessment of protection of river segments in Victoria, Australia, paper to a symposium on the Management of Public Resources, Resources Policy Consortium, Washington, D.C., May 1992.

Dwyer Leslie 1991. *Cost-benefit analysis of the drinking water quality program: A contingent valuation approach.* Report prepared in conjunction with the Sydney Water Board, Sydney.

Eberle, W.D. and Hayden, F.G. 1991. 'Critique of contingent valuation and travel cost methods for valuing natural resources and ecosystems,' *Journal of Economic Issues,* 25(3), 649-687.

Economic Associates Australia 1983. *Green Island Economic Study.* Great Barrier Reef Marine Park Authority, Townsville.

Ehrlich, P.R. and Daily, G.C. 1993. 'Population extinction and saving biodiversity,' *Ambio,* 22(2-3), 64-68.

Ehrlich, P.R. and Ehrlich, A. 1981. *Extinction: The causes and consequences of the disappearance of species.* New York: Random House.

Ekanayake, R. 1987. 'Preferences and choices for preserving eucalypt woodland in the northern New South Wales,' Contributed paper to the 31st Annual Conference of the Australian Agricultural Economics Society, University of Adelaide, Adelaide, Feb.

Ekanayake, R. and Sinden, J.A. 1985. 'Identification of needs and preferences of a rural community for indigenous woodland,' Paper presented to the Australian and New Zealand Institute of Foresters Conference, 20-24 May 1985, Hobart.

Feenberg, D. and Mills, E.S. 1980. *Measuring the benefits of water pollution abatement.* New York, Academic Press. Cited in Hoehn, J.P and Randall, A. 1987.

Filion, F. 1994. 'Estimating the economic value of biodiversity,' In 'Incentives for Protecting North American Biodiversity,' *Different Drummer*, 1(3), 20-23.

Fischhoff, B. and Furby, L. 1988. 'Measuring values: A conceptual framework for interpreting transactions with special reference to contingent valuation of visibility,' *Journal of Risk and Uncertainty*, 1, 147-184.

Fisher, A.C. and Hanemann, W.M. 1985. 'Endangered species: The economics of irreversible damage,' Chapter 16 in Hall, D.O., Myers, N. and Margaris, N.S. (eds) *Economics of ecosystem management*. Dordrecht: Dr W. Junk Publishers. pp. 129-138.

Fisher, A.C. and Hanemann, W.M. 1986. 'Option value and the extinction of species,' In Smith, V.K. (ed.) *Advances in Applied Microeconomics*, Vol. 4, Greenwich, Ct: JAI Press.

Fisher, A.C. and Hanemann, W.M. 1987. 'Quasi-option value: Some misconceptions dispelled,' *Journal of Environmental Economics and Management*, 14(2) 183-190.

Fisher, A.C. and Hanemann, W.M. 1990. 'Option value: Theory and measurement,' *European Review of Agricultural Economics*, 17, 167-180.

Folke, C., Perrings, C., McNeely, J.A. and Myers, N. 1993. 'Biodiversity conservation with a human face: Ecology, economics and policy,' *Ambio*, 22(2-3), 62-63.

Fredman, P. 1995. 'Endangered species: Benefit estimation and policy implications,' Swedish University of Agricultural Sciences, Department of Forest Economics, Umeå. Report No. 109.

Freeman, A.M. 1979. *The benefits of environmental improvement: Theory and practice.* Baltimore: Johns Hopkins University Press.

Freeman A.M. 1984. 'The quasi-option value of irreversible development,' *Journal of Environmental Economics and Management*, 11(3), 292-295.

Freeman, A.M. 1985. 'The sign and size of option value,' *Land Economics*, 60(1), 1-13.

Freeman, A.M. 1986. 'On assessing the state of the arts of the contingent valuation method of valuing environmental changes,' Chapter 10 in Cummings, R., Brookshire, D. Schulze, W. (eds) *Valuing environmental goods. An assessment of the contingent valuation method*. Totowa, New Jersey: Rowman and Allanheld, pp. 148-161.

Frykblom, P. 1994. 'Statistical bias functions: The alchemy of contingent valuation?' Working paper series 1994:1, Department of Economics, Swedish University of Agricultural Sciences, Uppsala.

Galapitage, D.C. 1992. 'Optimal management of mountain ash forests for water and timber harvesting: A case study of the Maroondah catchment of the Melbourne water supply system,' PhD thesis, Department of Economics, La Trobe University, Melbourne.

Gallagher, D.R. and Smith, V.K. 1985. 'Measuring values for environmental resources under uncertainty,' *Journal of Environmental Economics and Management*, 12(2), 132-143.

Glyde, P. 1992. 'Difficulties of integrating contingent valuation results into decision making processes,' In Lockwood, M. and DeLacy, T. (eds) *Valuing natural areas: Applications and problems of the contingent valuation method*, Johnstone Centre, Charles Sturt University, Albury, pp. 175-182.

Goodland, R.J.A. 1988. 'A major new opportunity to finance the preservation of biodiversity,' Chapter 49 in Wilson, E.O (ed.) *Biodiversity*. Washington DC: National Academy Press pp. 437-445.

Goodland, R.J.A. and Ledec, G. 1987. 'Neoclassical economics and principles of sustainable development,' *Ecological Modelling*, 38(1), 19-46.

Graham, D.A. 1981. 'Cost-benefit analysis under uncertainty,' *American Economic Review*, 71, 715-725.

Greer, G. and Sheppard 1990. 'An economic evaluation of the benefits of research into biological control of *Clematis vitalba*,' Report No. 203, Agribusiness and Economics Research Unit, Lincoln University.

Gregory, R. 1986. 'Interpreting measures of economic loss. Evidence from contingent valuation and experimental studies,' *Journal of Environmental Economics and Management*, 13, 325-337.

Gregory, R. and Bishop, R.C. 1986. 'Willingness to pay or compensation demanded,' Paper presented at the workshop on integrating psychology and economics in valuing public amenity resources, Estes Park, Colorado.

Gregory, R., Lichtenstein, S. and Slovic, P. 1993. 'Valuing environmental resources: A constructive approach,' *Journal of Risk and Uncertainty*, 7, 177-197.

Gregory, R., Mendelsohn, R. and Moore, T. 1989. 'Measuring the benefits of endangered species: From research to policy,' *Journal of Environmental Management*, 29, 399-407.

Groves, R.H. and Ride, W.D.L. (eds) 1982. *Species at risk. Research in Australia.* Proceedings of a symposium on the biology of rare and endangered species in Australia, sponsored by the Australian Academy of Science, 25-26 Nov. 1981. Canberra: Springer-Verlag.

Hageman, R. 1985. 'Valuing marine mammal populations: Benefit valuations in a multi-species ecosystem,' Administrative Report LJ-85-22. Southwest Fisheries Center, National Marine Fisheries Service, La Jolla, California. Cited in Loomis, J.B. and White, D.S., forthcoming and in Stone, A. 1992.

Hagen, D.A., Vincent, J.W. and Welle, P.G. 1992. 'Benefits of preserving old-growth forests and the spotted owl,' *Contemporary Policy Issues*, 10, 13-26.

Hammack, J. and Brown, G.M. Jr 1974. *Waterfowl and wetlands: Toward bioeconomic analysis.* Baltimore, John Hopkins University Press for Resources for the Future.

Hampicke, U., Tampe, K., Kiemstedt, H., Horlitz, Th., Walters, U. and Timp, D. 1991. 'Die volkswirtschaftliche bedeutung des arten und biotopschwundes in der Bundesrepublik Deutschland (The economic importance of preserving species and biotopes in the Federal Republic of Germany),' *Berichte des Bundesumweltamtes* 3/91. Berlin, Erich Schmidt Verlag. Cited in Römer A.U. and Pommerehne, W.W. 1992.

Hanemann, W.M. 1984. 'Welfare evaluations in contingent valuation experiments with discrete responses,' *American Journal of Agricultural Economics*, 66, 332-341.

Hanemann, W.M. 1987. 'Welfare evaluations in contingent valuation experiments with discrete responses: Reply,' *American Journal of Agricultural Economics*, 69, 185-86.

Hanemann, W.M. 1989a. 'Information and the concept of option value,' *Journal of Environmental Economics and Management*, 16, 23-37.

Hanemann, W.M. 1989b. 'Welfare evaluations in contingent valuation experiments with discrete response data: Reply,' *American Journal of Agricultural Economics*, 71(4), 1057-1061.

Hanemann, W.M. 1991a. 'Willingness to pay versus willingness to accept: How much can they differ?' *American Economic Review*, 81(3), 635-647.

Hanemann, W.M. 1991b. 'Review of 'A contingent valuation survey of the Kakadu Conservation Zone,' In Imber, D., Stevenson, G. and Wilks, L. 'A contingent valuation survey of the Kakadu Conservation Zone,' Resource Assessment Commission Research Paper No. 3. Volume One.

Hanemann, W.M. 1994a. 'Valuing the environment through contingent valuation,' *Journal of Economic Perspectives*, 8(4), 19-43.

Hanemann, W.M. 1994b. 'Contingent valuation and economics,' Working paper No. 697. Giannini Foundation of Agricultural and Resource Economics, University of California, Berkeley. Forthcoming in Willis, K. and Corkindale, J. (eds) *Environmental valuation: Some new perspectives.* Wallingford, Oxon, UK: CAB International.

Hanemann, W.M., Loomis, J.B. and Kanninen, B.J. 1991. 'Statistical efficiency of double-bounded dichotomous choice contingent valuation,' *American Journal of Agricultural Economics*, 73(4), 1255-1263.

Hanley, H.D. 1987. 'Valuing non-market goods using contingent valuation: A survey and a synthesis,' University of Stirling Discussion Papers in Economics, Finance and Investment, No. 138. August.

Hanley, H.D., Spash, C.L. and Walker, L. 1995. 'Problems in valuing the benefits of biodiversity protection,' *Environmental and Resource Economics*, 5(3), 249-272.

Harris, B.S. 1984. 'Contingent valuation of water pollution control,' *Journal of Environmental Economics and Management*, 19, 199-208.

Harris, C.C., Driver, B.L. and McLaughlin, W.J. 1989. 'Improving the contingent valuation method. A psychological perspective,' *Journal of Environmental Economics and Management*, 17, 213-229.

Harrison, G.W. 1993. 'General reactions to the NOAA report,' Reports for the CVM network newsletter. Stockholm School of Economics, March, pp. 19-24.

Harrison, G.W. and Kriström, B. 1995. 'On the interpretation of responses in contingent valuation surveys,' In Johansson, P-O., Kriström, B. and Mäler, K-G. (eds) *Current Issues in Environmental Economics*. Manchester University Press, Manchester.

Harrison, G.W., Harstad, R.M. and Rutström, E.E. 1995. 'Experimental Methods and the Elicitation of Values,' Seminar Paper, Environmental Economics Seminar Series, Department of Economics, Swedish University of Agricultural Sciences, Uppsala, presented by G.W. Harrison.

Hausman, J.A. (ed.) 1993. *Contingent valuation. A critical assessment.* Contributions to economic analysis. Amsterdam: North Holland.

Heberlein, T.A. and Bishop, R.C. 1986. 'Assessing the validity of contingent valuation: Three field experiments,' *The Science of the Total Environment*, 56, 99-107.

Henry, C. 1974. 'Investment decisions under uncertainty: The irreversibility effect,' *American Economic Review*, 64(6), 1006-1012.

Heritage Rivers Act 1992. Victoria.

Hicks, J.R. 1939. 'Foundations of welfare economics,' *Economic Journal*, 49, 696-712.

Hoehn, J.P and Randall, A. 1987. 'A satisfactory benefit cost indicator from contingent valuation,' *Journal of Environmental Economics and Management*, 14(3), 226-247.

Hoehn, J.P and Randall, A. 1989. 'Too many proposals pass the benefit cost test,' *American Economic Review*, 79(3), 544-551.

Hoevenagel, R. 1990. 'The validity of the contingent valuation method. Some aspects on the basis of three Dutch studies,' Paper presented at the congress 'Environmental Cooperation and Policy in the Single European Market,' Venice, Italy, April 17-20.

Hoevenagel, R. 1994. 'The contingent valuation method: Method and scope,' PhD dissertation, Institute for Environmental Studies, Vrije Universitet, Amsterdam.

Hohl, A. and Tisdell, C.A. 1992. 'How useful are environmental safety standards in economics? The example of safe minimum standards for protection of species,' Discussion Paper No. 97, Dept. of Economics, University of Queensland. Sept.

Hundloe, T. 1990. 'Measuring the value of the Great Barrier Reef,' *Australian Parks and Recreation*, 26(3), 11-15.

Hundloe, T. and Blamey, R. 1992. 'The use of contingent valuation to value natural areas,' In Lockwood, M. and DeLacy, T. (eds) *Valuing natural areas: Applications and problems of the contingent valuation method*, Johnstone Centre, Charles Sturt University, Albury, pp. 17-30.

Hundloe, T., McDonald, G.T., Blamey, R., Wilson, B. and Carter, M. 1990. 'Socio-economic analysis of non-extractive natural resource use in the Great Sandy region,' A report to the Queensland Department of Environment and Heritage. Institute of Applied Environmental Research, Griffith University.

Hundloe, T., Vanclay, F. and Carter, M. 1987. Economic and socioeconomic impacts of the crown of thorns starfish on the Great Barrier Reef. Report to the Great Barrier Reef Marine Park Authority. Institute of Applied Environmental Research. In Hundloe, T. 1990. 'Measuring the value of the Great Barrier Reef,' *Australian Parks and Recreation*, 26(3), 11-15.

Imber, D., Stevenson, G. and Wilks, L.C. 1991. 'A contingent valuation survey of the Kakadu Conservation Zone,' Resource Assessment Commission. Research Paper No. 3, Vol. 1. Australian Government Printing Service, Canberra.

Jakobsson, K.M. 1994. 'Methodological issues in contingent valuation: An application to endangered species,' PhD dissertation. La Trobe University, Melbourne, Australia.

Johansson, P-O. 1989. 'Valuing goods in a risky world: An experiment,' In Folmer, H. and Irland, E. (eds) *Evaluation methods and policy making in environmental economics*. Amsterdam: North Holland, 37-48.

Johansson, P-O. 1990. 'Willingness to pay measures and expectations. An experiment,' *Applied Economics*, 22, 313-329.

Johansson, P-O. 1993. *Cost-benefit analysis of environmental change*. Cambridge; New York and Melbourne: Cambridge University Press.

Johansson, P-O., Kriström, B. and Mäler, K.-G. 1989. 'A note on welfare evaluations with discrete response data,' *American Journal of Agricultural Economics*, 71(4), 1054-1056.

Johansson, P-O., Kriström, B. and Mäler, K.-G. (eds) 1995. *Current Issues in Environmental Economics*. Manchester University Press, Manchester.

Johansson, P-O., Kriström, B. and Nyquist, H. 1994. 'Optimal designs, spikes and risks,' Working Paper, Stockholm School of Economics.

Johansson, P-O. and Zavisic, S. 1989. 'Svenska folkets miljöbudget,' *Ekonomisk Debatt*, 6, 472-474. Cited in Fredman, P. 1995.

Johnston, B.G. 1982. 'External benefits in rural research and the question of who should pay,' Paper presented to the 26th Annual Conference of the Australian Agricultural Economics Society, 9-11 February 1982, University of Melbourne.

Kahneman, D. and Knetsch, J.L. 1992a. 'Valuing public goods. The purchase of moral satisfaction,' *Journal of Environmental Economics and Management*, 22, 57-70.

Kahneman, D. and Knetsch, J.L. 1992b. 'Reply. Contingent valuation and the value of public goods,' *Journal of Environmental Economics and Management*, 22, 90-94.

Kahneman, D. and Tversky, A. 1979. 'Prospect theory: An analysis of decisions under risk,' *Econometrica*, 47(2), 263-291.

Kahneman, D., Slovic, P. and Tversky, A. (eds) 1982. *Judgement under uncertainty: Heuristics and biases*. New York: Cambridge University Press.

Kaldor, N. 1939. 'Welfare propositions of economics and interpersonal comparisons of utility,' *Economic Journal*, 49, 549-52.

Kanninen, B.J. 1993. 'Optimal experimental design for double-bounded dichotomous choice contingent valuation,' *Land Economics*, 69, 128-46.

Kanninen, B.J. and Kriström, B. 1992. 'Welfare benefit estimation and the income distribution,' Beijer Discussion Paper Series No. 20. Beijer International Institute of Ecological Economics, The Royal Swedish Academy of Sciences.

Kanninen, B.J. and Kriström, B. 1992. 'Sensitivity of willingness to pay estimatesto bid design in dichotomous choice valuation models: Comment,' *Land Economics*, 69(2), 199-202.

Kay, D.L., Brown, T.L. and Allee, D.J. 1987. 'The economic benefits of the restoration of Atlantic salmon to New England rivers,' Draft report, Department of Natural Resources, NY State College of Agriculture and Life Sciences, Cornell University. Cited in Stevens, T.H. *et al*. 1991.

Kealy, M.J. and Turner, R.W. 1993. 'A test of the equality of closed ended contingent valuations,' *American Journal of Agricultural Economics*, 75(2), May, 321-31.

Kealy, M.J., Dovidio, J.F. and Rockel, M.L. 1988. 'Accuracy in valuation is a matter of degree,' *Land Economics*, 64(2), 158-171.

Kealy, M.J., Montgomery, M. and Dovidio, J.F. 1990. 'Reliability and predictive validity of contingent values. does the nature of the good matter?' *Journal of Environmental Economics and Management*, 19, 244-263.

Kennedy, J.O.S. 1994. 'Optimal management of multiple-use forest under risk,' Paper to the Australian Agricultural Economics Society, Annual Conference, Wellington, New Zealand, February.

Kennedy, J.O.S. and Jakobsson, K.M. 1993. 'Optimal timber harvesting for wood production and wildlife habitat,' Department of Economics Discussion Paper, 14/93, La Trobe University, Melbourne.

Kennedy, J.O.S., Read, M. and Sturgess, N. 1993. 'Optimal management policies for timber and water output from the Thomson dam in Victoria,' Paper to the Australian Agricultural Economics Society, Annual Conference, Sydney, NSW, February.

Kerr, G. 1987. 'Changes in Kawarau Gorge values with hydro development,' In Kerr, G.N. and Sharp, B.M.H. (eds) *Valuing the environment: Economic theory and applications*. Studies in Resource Management No. 2. Centre for Resource Management, Lincoln College, Canterbury pp. 159-161.

Kerr, G.N. and Sharp, B.M.H. (eds) 1987. *Valuing the environment: Economic theory and applications*. Studies in Resource Management No. 2. Centre for Resource Management, Lincoln College, Canterbury.

Kim, K.C. and Weaver, R.D. (eds) 1995. *Biodiversity and landscapes.* Cambridge University Press.

Kirkland, W.T. 1988. 'Preserving the Whangamarino Wetland - an application of the contingent valuation method,' Unpublished M.Ag.Sc. Thesis, Massey University, Palmerston North, New Zealand.

Knetsch, J.L 1989. 'Preferences and nonreversibility of indifference curves,' *American Economic Review*, 79, 1277-84.

Knetsch, J.L. 1990. 'Environmental policy implications of disparities between willingness to pay and compensation demanded measures of values,' *Journal of Environmental Economics and Management*, 18, 227-237.

Knetsch, J.L. 1993. 'Environmental valuation. Some practical problems of wrong questions and misleading answers,' Occasional Publication Number 5. Resource Assessment Commission, AGPS, Canberra.

Knetsch, J.L. and Davis, R.K. 1977. 'Comparisons of methods for recreation evaluation,' In Dorfman, R. and Dorfman N.S. (eds) *Economics of the environment.* Selected readings. Second edition. W.W. Norton and Co. Inc. New York. Chapter 24, pp. 450-468.

Knetsch, J.L. and Sinden, J.A. 1984. 'Willingness to pay and compensation demanded. Experimental evidence of an unexpected disparity in measures of value,' *Quarterly Journal of Economics*, 94(3), 507-521.

Knetsch, J.L. and Sinden, J.A. 1987. 'The persistence of evaluation disparities,' *Quarterly Journal of Economics*, 97(3), 691-95.

Kriström, B. 1990a. 'Valuing environmental benefits using the contingent valuation method. An econometric analysis,' Umeå Economic Studies No. 219. University of Umeå, Sweden.

Kriström, B. 1990b. 'A non-parametric approach to the estimation of welfare measures in discrete response valuation studies,' *Land Economics*, 66, 135-139.

Kriström, B. 1993. 'Comparing continuous and discrete contingent valuation questions,' *Environmental and Resource Economics*, 3, 63-71.

Kriström, B. 1994. 'Practical problems in contingent valuation,' Invited paper presented at the International Conference on Determining the value of non-marketed goods: Economic, psychological and policy relevant aspects of the contingent valuation method, Bad Homburg, July 27-29. Forthcoming in Kopp R. and Schwarz, N. *Determining the value of non-marketed goods: Economic, psychological and policy relevant aspects of the contingent valuation method.* Werner Reimer Stiftung, Bad Homburg, Germany.

Kriström, B. 1995. 'Spike models in contingent valuation: theory and illustrations. Invited paper presented to 1st Toulouse Conference on Environmental and Resource Economics, Toulouse, France, March 30-31.

Krutilla, J.V. 1967. 'Conservation reconsidered,' *American Economic Review*, 57, 777-786.

Langner, L. and Bishop, R.C. 1982. 'Endangered species: What are the issues?' *Economic Issues*, No 66 March. Department of Agricultural Economics, College of Life Sciences, University of Wisconsin-Madison.

Larson, D.M. 1992. 'Can non-use value be measured from observable behaviour?' *American Journal of Agricultural Economics*, Dec. 1114-1120.

Lawton, J.H. and May, R.M. 1995. *Extinction rates*. Oxford: Oxford University Press.

Ledec, G. and Goodland, R. 1988. 'Wildlands. Their protection and management in economic development,' The World Bank. Washington D.C.

Lehmkubl, J.F. 1984. 'Determining size and dispersion of minimum viable populations for land management planning and species conservation,' *Environmental Management*, 8(2), 167-176.

Leopold, A. 1966. *A Sand County almanac*. New York: Oxford University Press.

Li, C-Z. 1994. 'Welfare evaluations in contingent valuation: An econometric analysis,' PhD dissertation. Umeå Economic Studies 341. Swedish University of Agricultural Sciences, Department of Forest Economics, Umeå.

Li, C-Z. and Fredman, P. 1995. 'On reconciliation of the discrete choice and open-ended responses in contingent valuation experiments,' Manuscript, Swedish University of Agricultural Sciences, Umeå.

Lindenmayer, D. 1989. 'The ecology and habitat requirements of Leadbeater's possum,' PhD thesis, Australian National University, Canberra.

Lindenmayer, D., Cunningham, R.B., Smith, A.P, Tanton, M.T. and Nix, H.A. 1990a. 'The conservation of arboreal marsupials in the montane ash forests of the central highlands of Victoria, South-East Australia: III. The habitat requirements of Leadbeater's possum and the models of the diversity and abundance of arboreal marsupials,' *Biological Conservation*, 54.

Lindenmayer, D., Cunningham, R.B., Tanton, M.T. and Smith, A.P, 1990b. 'The conservation of arboreal marsupials in the montane ash forests of the central highlands of Victoria, south-east Australia: II. The loss of trees with hollows and its implications for the conservation of Leadbeater's possum, *Gymnobelideus leadbeateri*, McCoy (Marsupialia: Petauridae),' *Biological Conservation*, 54, 133-45.

Lindenmayer, D., Cunningham, R.B., Tanton, M.T., Smith, A.P. and Nix, H.A. 1990c. 'Characteristics of hollow bearing trees occupied by arboreal marsupials in the montane ash forests of the central highlands of Victoria, south-east Australia,' *Forest Ecology Management*, 38.

Lindenmayer, D., Nix, H.A., McMahon, J.P. and Hutchinson, M.F. 1990d. 'Bioclimatic modelling and wildlife conservation and management - A case study on Leadbeater's possum, *Gymnobelideus leadbeateri*,' In Clark and Seebeck, (eds) *Conservation and management of small populations,* Chicago: Chicago Zoological Society, pp. 253-74.

Lindgren, B.W. 1962. *Statistical theory*. New York: Macmillan.

Little, I.M.D. 1949. 'The foundations of welfare economics,' *Oxford Economic Papers,* 1, 227-46.

Little, I.M.D. 1957. *A critique of welfare economics*. London: Oxford University Press.

Lockwood, M. 1992. 'Embedding effects in contingent valuation studies and the implications for benefit cost analysis,' In Lockwood, M. and DeLacy, T. (eds) *Valuing natural areas: Applications and problems of the contingent valuation method,* Johnstone Centre, Charles Sturt University, Albury, pp. 101-116.

Lockwood, M. and DeLacy, T.P. (eds) 1992. *Valuing natural areas: Applications and problems of the contingent valuation method,* Johnstone Centre, Charles Sturt University, Albury.

Lockwood, M. and Tracey, P. 1993. 'Assessment of non-market conservation and heritage values related to cattle grazing on the Bogong High Plains, Victoria,' Paper presented to the 37th Annual Conference of the Australian Agriculture Economics Society, Sydney, 9-11 February. 1993.

Lockwood, M. and Tracey, P. 1995. 'Nonmarket economic valuation of an urban recreation park,' *Journal of Leisure Research*, 27(2), 155-167.

Lockwood, M., Loomis, J.B. and DeLacy, T.P. 1992. 'Evidence of a non-market willingness to pay for timber harvesting,' Unpublished manuscript.

Lockwood, M., Loomis, J.B. and DeLacy, T.P. 1993. 'A contingent valuation survey and benefit-cost analysis of forest preservation in East Gippsland, Australia,' *Journal of Environmental Management*, 38, 233-243.

Lockwood, M., Loomis, J.B. and DeLacy, T.P. 1994. 'The relative unimportance of non-market willingness to pay for timber harvesting,' *Ecological Economics*, 9, 145-152.

Loehman, E.T. and De, V.H. 1982. 'Application of stochastic choice modelling to policy analysis of public goods: A case study of air quality improvements,' *Review of Economics and Statistics*, 64(3), 474-480.

Loomis, J.B. 1987a. 'Expanding contingent value sample estimates to aggregate benefit estimates: Current practices and proposed solutions,' *Land Economics*, 63(4), 396-402.

Loomis, J.B. 1987b. 'Importance of net economic values of wildlife in planning and impact assessment,' In Walsh *et al.* 1987. *Issues and technology in the management of impacted Western wildlife*. Boulder Colorado: Thorne Ecological Institute, pp. 72-75.

Loomis, J.B. 1989. 'Test-retest reliability of the contingent valuation method: A comparison of general population and visitor responses,' *American Journal of Agricultural Economics*, 71(1), 76-84.

Loomis, J.B. 1990. 'Comparative reliability of the dichotomous choice and open ended contingent valuation techniques,' *Journal of Environmental Economics and Management*, 17(1), 78-85.

Loomis J.B. and du Vair, P.H. 1993. 'Evaluating the effect of alternative risk communication devices on willingness to pay: Results from a dichotomous choice contingent valuation experiment,' *Land Economics*, 69(3), 287-98.

Loomis, J.B. and Helfand, G. 1993. 'A tale of two owls and lessons for the reauthorization of the Endangered Species Act,' *Choices*, Third Quarter, 21-22, 24-25.

Loomis, J.B. and Larson, D.M. 1994. 'Total economic values of increasing gray whale populations: Results from a contingent valuation survey of visitors and households,' *Marine Resource Economics*, 9(3), 275-286.

Loomis, J.B. and White, D.S. 1995. 'Economic benefits of rare and endangered species: Summary and meta analysis,' Working paper, Department of Agricultural and Resource Economics, Colorado State University.

Loomis, J.B., Lockwood, M. and DeLacy, T.P. 1993. 'Some empirical evidence on embedding effects in contingent valuation of forest protection,' *Journal of Environmental Economics and Management*, 24, 45-55.

Macfarlane M.A. and Seebeck, J.H. 1991. 'Draft management strategies for the conservation of Leadbeater's possum, *Gymnobelideus leadbeateri*, in Victoria,' Department of Conservation and Environment, Melbourne: Victoria.

Madariaga, B. and McConnell, K.E. 1987. 'Exploring existence value,' *Water Resources Research*, 23(5), 936-942.

Maddala, G.S. 1983. *Limited dependent variables and qualitative variables in econometrics*. New York: Cambridge University Press.

Maguire, L.A. 1986. 'Using decision analysis to manage endangered species populations,' *Journal of Environmental Management*, 22, 345-360.

Majid, I., Sinden, J.A. and Randall, A. 1983. 'Benefit evaluation of increments to existing systems of public facilities,' *Land Economics* 59(4), 377-392.

Mattinson, B.C. and Morrison, D.A. 1985. 'A cost-benefit study of alternative strategies for reducing the algae nuisance in the Peel-Harvey estuary,' Western Australian Department of Agriculture.

Mattson, L. and Li, C-Z. 1994. 'Sample nonresponse in a mail contingent valuation survey: An empirical test on the effect on value inference,' *Journal of Leisure Research*, 26(2), 182-188.

McConnell, K.E. 1990. 'Models for referendum data: The structure of discrete choice models for contingent valuation,' *Journal of Environmental Economics and Management*, 18(1), 19-34.

McFadden, D. 1976. 'Quantal choice analysis: A survey,' *Annals of Economic and Social Measurement*, 5, 363-370.

McKenney, D.W. and Lindenmayer, D.B. 1994. 'An economic assessment of a nest-box strategy for the conservation of an endangered species,' *Canadian Journal of Forestry Research*, 24, 2012-2019.

McMichael, D.F. 1982. 'What species, what risk?' In Groves, R.H. and Ride, W.D.L. (eds) *Species at risk. Research in Australia.* Proceedings of a symposium on the biology of rare and endangered species in Australia, sponsored by the Australian Academy of Science, 25-26 Nov. 1981. Canberra: Springer-Verlag.

McNeely, J.A., Miller, K.R., Reid, W.V., Mittermeier, R.A. and Werner, T.B. 1990. *Conserving the world's biological diversity.* Prepared and published by the International Union for Conservation of Nature and Natural Resources, World Resources Institute, Conservation International, World Wildlife Fund-US and the World Bank.

Meier, C.E. and Randall, A. 1991. 'Use value under uncertainty: Is there a "correct" measure?' *Land Economics*, 67(4), 379-89.

Miller, J.R. 1981. 'Irreversible land use and the preservation of endangered species,' *Journal of Environmental Economics and Management*, 8, 19-25.

Miller, J.R. and Menz, F.C. 1979. 'Some economic considerations in wildlife preservation,' *Southern Economic Journal*, 45, 718-729.

Milner-Gulland, E.J. and Leader-Williams, N. 1992. 'A model of incentives for the illegal exploitation of black rhinos and elephants: Poaching pays in Luangwa Valley, Zambia,' *Journal of Applied Ecology*, 29, 388-401.

Milon, J.W. 1989. 'Contingent valuation experiments for strategic behaviour,' *Journal of Environmental Economics and Management*, 17, 293-308.

Mishan, E.J. 1969. *Welfare economics: An assessment.* Amsterdam: North Holland.

Mishan, E.J. 1971. 'The postwar literature on externalities: An interpretative essay,' *Journal of Economic Literature*, 9, 1-28.

Mishan, E.J. 1982. 'Horse and rabbit stew,' Chapter 22 in *Cost benefit analysis,* 3rd edition, London: Allen and Unwin, pp. 149-154.

Mitchell, R.C. and Carson, R.T. 1984. 'A contingent valuation estimate of national freshwater benefits,' Technical report to the US Environmental Protection Agency. Washington, DC, Resources for the Future. Cited in Mitchell, R.C. and Carson, R.T. 1989.

Mitchell, R.C. and Carson, R.T. 1989. *Using surveys to value public goods. The contingent valuation method.* Washington DC: Resources for the Future.

Moran, A. 1991. 'Valuing the Kakadu conservation zone: A critique of the Resource Assessment Commissions contingent valuation study,' Resource Assessment Commission (ed.) 'Commentaries on the Resource Assessment Commission's contingent valuation survey of the Kakadu Conservation Zone,' Resource Assessment Commission, Canberra.

Moser, D.A. and Dunning, C.M. 1986. 'A guide for using the contingent value methodology in recreation studies,' National Economic Development Procedures Manual - Recreation. Vol II. US Army Corps of Engineers, Water Resources Support centre, Institute for Water Resources. IWR Report 86-R-5.

Moyle, B. 1995. 'Valuation of endangered species: Towards a new approach,' PhD dissertation, University of Waikato, Hamilton, New Zealand. 240pp.

Myers, N. 1979. *The sinking ark.* New York: Pergamon.

Myers, N. 1985. 'Endangered species and the North-South dialogue,' Chapter 17 in

Hall, D.O., Myers, N. and Margaris, N.S. (eds) *Economics of ecosystem management.* Dordrecht: Dr. W. Junk Publishers. pp. 139-148.

Myers, N. 1993. 'Biodiversity and the precautionary principle,' *Ambio*, 22, 74-79.

Nape, S., Frykblom, P., Harrison, G.W. and Lesley, J.C. 1995. 'Hypothetical bias and willingness to accept,' Unpublished manuscript, University of South Carolina.

Navrud, S. 1991. 'Willingness to pay for preservation of species - an experiment with actual payments,' Paper presented at the Second Annual Meeting of the European Association of Environmental and Resource Economists, Stockholm, June 11-14.

Navrud, S. (ed.) 1992. *Pricing the European environment.* Oslo: Scandinavian University Press.

Navrud, S. and Mungatana, E.D. 1994. 'Environmental valuation in developing countries: The recreational value of wildlife viewing,' *Ecological Economics* 11, 135-151.

Navrud, S. and Strand, J. 1992. 'Norway,' Chapter 6 in Navrud, S. (ed.) *Pricing the European environment.* Scandinavian University Press.

Neill, H.R., Cummings, R.G., Ganderton, P.T., Harrison, G.W. and McGuckin, T. 1994. 'Hypothetical surveys and real economic commitments,' *Land Economics*, 70(2), 145-154.

New South Wales Environment Protection Authority 1995. NSW EPA Environmental Valuation Database Handbook, EPA 95/34.

Ng, Y.K. 1985. *Welfare economics: Introduction and development of basic concepts.* Revised edition. London: Macmillan Publishers Ltd.

NOAA 1994. *Oil Pollution Act* of 1990: Proposed regulations for natural resource damage assessments. National Oceanic and Atmospheric Administration, US Department of Commerce.

Norgaard, R.B. 1985. 'Environmental economics: An evolutionary critique and a plea for pluralism,' *Journal of Environmental Economics and Management*, 12(4), 382-94.

Norgaard, R.B. and Howarth, R.B. 1991. 'Sustainability and discounting the future,' In Costanza, R. (ed.) *Ecological Economics.* New York: Columbia University Press.

Norton, B.G. 1986. 'On the inherent danger of undervaluing species,' In Norton, B.G. (ed.) *The Preservation of Species. The Value of Biological Diversity.* Princeton University Press.

Norton-Griffiths, M. and Southey, C. 1995. 'The opportunity costs of biodiversity conservation in Kenya,' *Ecological Economics* 12, 125-139.

Norusis, M.J. 1983. *Introductory statistics guide, SPSSX.* New York: McGraw-Hill.

Norusis, M.J. 1985. *Advanced statistics guide, SPSSX.* New York: McGraw-Hill.

Nyquist, H. 1991. 'Optimal designs of discrete response experiments in contingent valuation studies,' Draft paper. Department of Statistics, University of Umeå, Sweden.

Oldfield, M.L. 1981. 'Tropical deforestation and genetic resources conservation,' In Sutlive, V.H, Altschuler, N. and Zamora, M.D. (eds) *Studies in third world societies,* Williamsburg: College of William and Mary.

Opschoor, J.B. 1986. 'A review of monetary estimates of benefits of environmental policy and decision making,' Conference paper, Avignon, France.

Pearce, D.W. 1987. 'Economic values and the natural environment,' Discussion paper No 87-08. Discussion papers on economics, Department of Economics, University College London. Cambridge University press.

Pearce, D.W. and Markandya, A. 1989. *Environmental policy benefits: Monetary valuation.* OECD, Paris.

Pearce, D.W. and Moran, D. 1994. *The economic value of biodiversity.* IUCN. Earthscan Publications Ltd, London.

Perrings, C., Mäler, K,-G., Folke, C., Holling, C.S. and Jansson, B-O. 1995. Biodiversity conservation and economic development: The policy problem and unresolved issues. Beijer Reprint Series No. 42. Reprinted from: Perrings, C. Mäler, K-G., Folke, C., Holling, C.S. and Jansson, B-O. (eds) 1994. *Biodiversity Conservation.* Kluwer Academic Press.

Peterson, G.L. 1992. 'New horizons in economic valuation: Integrating economics and psychology,' pp.193-207. In Lockwood, M. and DeLacy, T. (eds) *Valuing natural areas: Applications and problems of the contingent valuation method,* Johnstone Centre, Charles Sturt University, Albury.

Pina, C.M. 1994. 'The economic value of Mexican biodiversity,' In 'Incentives for Protecting North American Biodiversity,' *Different Drummer*, 1(3), 26-28.

Pindyck, R.S. and Rubinfield, D.L. 1976. *Econometric models and econometric forecasts.* McGraw-Hill Book Co. New York.

Pitt, M.W. 1991. 'Tourism and coastal land management: A survey of visitors on the north coast of New South Wales,' Economic Papers, Department of Conservation and Land Management, New South Wales, Sydney.

Pitt, M.W. 1992. 'The value of beach and dune maintenance to tourism: A contingent valuation study on the north coast of NSW, pp. 71-78. In Lockwood, M. and DeLacy, T. (eds) *Valuing natural areas: Applications and problems of the contingent valuation method*, Johnstone Centre, Charles Sturt University, Albury.

Pitt, M.W. 1993. 'The contingent value of maintaining natural vegetation on beach dunes,' Paper presented to the 37th Annual Conference of the Australian Agricultural Economics Society. Sydney, 9-11 February. 1993.

Polasky, S. and Solow, A.R. (forthcoming). 'On the value of a collection of species,' *Journal of Environmental Economics and Management.*

Principe, P. 1989. *The economic value of biodiversity among medicinal plants.* OECD, Paris.

Rabinowitz, A. 1995. 'Helping a species go extinct: The Sumatran rhino in Borneo,' *Conservation Biology*, 9(3), 482-488.

Ragozin, D. and Brown, G.M. Jr. 1985. 'Harvest policies and non-market valuation in a predator-prey system,' *Journal of Environmental Economics and Management*, 12(2), 155-168.

Randall, A. 1986. 'Preservation of species as a resource allocation problem,' In Norton, B.G. (ed.) *The Preservation of Species. The Value of Biological Diversity*. Princeton, New Jersey: Princeton University Press, pp. 79-109.

Randall, A. 1991. 'The value of biodiversity,' *Ambio*, 20(2), 64-68.

Randall, A. 1993. 'Passive use values and contingent valuation - valid for damage assessment,' *Choices*, Second Quarter, 12-15.

Randall, A. and Stoll, J.R. 1980. 'Consumer's surplus in commodity space,' *American Economic Review* 79(3), 449-455.

Randall, A., Hoehn, J.P. and Brookshire, D.S. 1983. 'Contingent valuation surveys for evaluating environmental assets,' *Natural Resources Journal*, 23(3), 635-48.

Randall, A., Ives, B. and Eastman, C. 1974. 'Bidding games for valuation of aesthetic environmental improvements,' *Journal of Environmental Economics and Management*, 1, 132-149.

Raven, P. 1994. 'Why it matters?' Paper presented at the First Meeting of the Conference of the Parties to the Convention on Biological Diversity, Nassau, The Bahamas, 28 Nov. to 9 Dec.

Reading, R.P., Clark, T.W and Kellert, S.R. 1991. 'Towards an endangered species re-introduction paradigm,' *Endangered Species Update*, 8(11).

Ready, R.C. and Bishop, R.C. 1991. 'Endangered species and the safe minimum standard,' *American Journal of Agricultural Economics*, 73(2), 309-312.

Ready, R.C. and Hu, D. (no date). 'Calculating mean willingness to pay from dichotomous choice contingent valuation data,' Draft manuscript. Dept. of Agricultural Economics, University of Kentucky.

Read Sturgess and Associates. 1992. *Evaluation of the economic values of wood and water for the Thomson catchment.* Consultants report prepared for Melbourne Water and the Department of Conservation and Natural Resources.

Read Sturgess and Associates and Tasman Economic Research Pty Ltd. 1994. *Phase two of the study into the economic evaluation of wood and water for the Thomson catchment.* Consultants report prepared for Melbourne Water and the Department of Conservation and Natural Resources. February.

Reark Research Pty Ltd 1991. 'Contingent valuation study of the south east forests of Australia,' Resource Assessment Commission Consultancy Series. Australian Government Publishing Service, Canberra.

Reid, W.V. and Miller, K.R. 1989. 'Keeping options alive. The scientific basis for conserving biodiversity,' World Resources Institute. Centre for Policy Research. October.

Reid, W.V., Laird, S.A., Meyer, C.A., Gamez, R., Sittenfeld, A., Janzen, D.H., Gollin, M.A. and Juma, C. 1993. *Biodiversity Prospecting.* Washington: World Resources Institute.

Reiling, S.D., Boyle, K.J., Phillips, M.L. and Anderson, M.W. 1990. 'Temporal reliability of contingent values,' *Land Economics*, 66(2), 128-134.

Resource Assessment Commission (ed.) 1991. 'Commentaries on the Resource Assessment Commission's contingent valuation survey of the Kakadu Conservation Zone,' Resource Assessment Commission, Canberra.

Resource Assessment Commission 1992. Forest and Timber Inquiry Final Report. Volume 2B. Australian Government Publishing Service, Canberra.

Roberts, E.J., McLeod, P.B. and Syme, G.J. 1988. 'Contingent valuation analysis of government provision of agricultural protection services,' Paper presented to the Australian Economics Congress, Canberra.

Rogers, M.F. 1992a. 'The allocation of old growth forest between preservation and logging in NSW,' In Lockwood, M. and DeLacy, T. (eds) *Valuing natural areas: Applications and problems of the contingent valuation method*, Johnstone Centre, Charles Sturt University, Albury, pp. 79-88.

Rogers, M.F. 1992b. 'An assessment and allocation of old growth forest preservation in NSW,' Master of Natural Resources Thesis, University of New England, Armidale.

Rogers, M.F. and Sinden, J.A. 1993. 'The safe minimum standard for environmental choices: Old growth forests in NSW,' Paper presented to the Australian Agricultural Economics Conference, Sydney, February.

Römer, A.U. 1992. 'How to handle strategic and protest bids in contingent valuation studies. An application of the two-step Heckman procedure,' Paper presented to the international conference 'Econometrics of Europe 2000' of the Applied Econometric Association, Brussels.

Römer A.U. and Pommerehne, W.W. 1992. 'Germany and Switzerland,' In Navrud, S. (ed.) *Pricing the European environment*, Oslo: Scandinavian University Press.

Rowe, R.D. and Chestnut, L.G. 1983. 'Valuing environmental commodities revisited,' *Land Economics*, 59(4), 404-10.

Rowe, R.D., d'Arge, R. and Brookshire, D. 1980. 'An experiment on the economic value of visibility,' *Journal of Environmental Economics and Management*, 7, 1-19.

Rubin, J., Helfand, G. and Loomis, J. 1991. 'A benefit-cost analysis of the northern spotted owl,' *Journal of Forestry*, 89 (12), 25-30.

Ruitenbeek, H.J. 1989. Social cost-benefit analysis of the Korup project, Cameroon. Report prepared for the World Wide Fund for Nature and the Republic of Cameroon, London. Cited in Barbier, E.B. and Schulz, C-E. 1995.

Saddler, H., Bennett, J., Reynolds, I. and Smith, B. 1980. 'Public choice in Tasmania: Aspects of the lower Gordon river hydro proposal,' Canberra. CRES Monograph, Australian National University.

Sagoff, M. 1988. 'Some problems with environmental economics,' *Environmental Ethics*, 10, 55-74.

Sagoff, M. 1994. 'Should preferences count,' *Land Economics*, 70(2), 127-44.

Salzman, J. 1990. 'Evolution and application of critical habitat under the endangered species act,' *Harvard Environmental Law Review*, 311.

Samples, K.C., Dixon, J.A. and Gowen, M.M. 1986. 'Information disclosure and endangered species valuation,' *Land Economics*, 62(3), 306-312.

Samples, K.C. and Hollyer, J.R. 1990. 'Contingent valuation of wildlife resources in the presence of substitutes and complements,' In Johnson, R.L. and Johnson, G.V. (eds) *Economic valuation of natural resources: Issues, theory and applications*. Social Behaviour and Natural Resources Series, Boulder and Oxford. Westview Press. pp. 177-92.

Samuelson, P.A. 1950. 'Evaluation of real national income,' *Oxford Economic Papers*, 2, 1-29.

Samuelson, P. 1954. 'The pure theory of public expenditure,' *Review of Economics and Statistics*, 36(4), 387-389.

Sappideen, B. 1992. 'Valuing the recreational benefits of the Sale wetlands using the contingent valuation method,' In Lockwood, M. and DeLacy, T. (eds) *Valuing natural areas: Applications and problems of the contingent valuation method*, Johnstone Centre, Charles Sturt University, Albury, pp. 39-46.

Schmalensee, R. 1972. 'Option demand and consumer surplus: Valuing price changes under uncertainty,' *American Economic Review*, 62, 813-824.

Scitovsky, T. 1954 'Two concepts of external economies,' *Journal of Political Economy*, 17, 143-51.

Scott, W.D. and Company 1982. 'Public willingness to pay for clean air: A survey of community attitudes,' Australian Environment Council Report No. 7, Australian Government Publishing Service, Canberra.

Seip, K. and Strand, J. 1992. 'Willingness to pay for environmental goods in Norway: A contingent valuation study with real payments,' *Environmental and Resource Economics*, 2, 91-106.

Sellar, C., Chavas, J.P. and Stoll, J.R. 1986. 'Specification of the logit model: The case of the valuation of non-market goods,' *Journal of Environmental Economics and Management*, 13(4), 382-390.

Sellar, C., Stoll, J.R. and Chavas, J.P. 1985. 'Validation of empirical measures of welfare change. A comparison of non-market techniques,' *Land Economics*, 61(2), 156-175.

Sen, A.K. 1970. 'The impossibility of a Paretian liberal,' *Journal of Political Economy*, 78, 152-7.

Sen, A. 1995. 'Rationality and social choice,' *American Economic Review*, 85(1), 1-24.

Shaffer, M.L. and Samson, F.B. 1985. 'Population size and extinction: A note on determining critical population sizes,' *The American Naturalist*, 125(1), 144-152.

Sheppard, R., Kerr, G., Cullen, R. and Ferguson, T. 1993. 'Contingent valuation of the improved water quality in the Lower Waimakariri River,' Research Report No. 221. Agribusiness and Economics Research Unit, Lincoln University, Canterbury, New Zealand.

Shogren, J.F., Seung, S.Y., Hayes, D.J. and Kliebenstein, J.B 1994. 'Resolving differences in willingness to pay and willingness to accept,' *American Economic Review*, 84(1), 255-270.

Sinden, J.A. 1987. 'Community support for soil conservation,' *Search* 18(4), 188-194.

Sinden, J.A. 1988a. 'Empirical tests of hypothetical bias in consumers' surplus surveys,' *Australian Journal of Agricultural Economics,* 32, 98-112.

Sinden, J.A. 1988b. 'Valuation of unpriced benefits and costs of river management. A review of the literature and a case study of the recreation benefits in the Ovens and King Basin,' Department of Conservation and Environment, Office of Water Resources, Victoria.

Sinden, J.A. 1990. 'Valuation of the recreational benefits of river management: A case study in the Ovens and King Basin,' Report to the Ovens River Management Board, Victoria, July.

Sinden, J.A. 1991. 'An assessment of our environmental valuations,' Invited paper, 20th Conference of Economists, Economic Society of Australia, University of Tasmania, Hobart.

Sinden, J.A., Jones, A.D. and Fleming, P.J. 1983. 'Relationship between eucalypt dieback and farm income, stocking rate and land value in southern New England, New South Wales,' University of New England, Armidale.

Sinden, J.A., Koczanowski, A. and Sniekers, P.P. 1982. 'Public attitudes to eucalypt woodland, eucalypt dieback and dieback research in the New England region of New South Wales,' *Australian Forestry* 45(2), 107-116.

Sloan, K. 1987. 'Valuing Heron Island: Preliminary report,' Paper presented to the 16th Conference of Economists. Surfers Paradise, August.

Smith, A.P. 1982. 'Leadbeater's possum and its management,' In Groves, R.H. and Ride, W.D.L. (eds) *Species at risk. Research in Australia.* Proceedings of a symposium on the biology of rare and endangered species in Australia, sponsored by the Australian Academy of Science, 25-26 Nov. 1981. Canberra: Springer-Verlag, pp. 129-145.

Smith, A.P. 1983. 'Leadbeater's possum,' In Strahan (ed.) *The Australian Museum complete book of Australian mammals.* Sydney: Angus and Robertson, pp. 142-143.

Smith, A.P. 1984. 'Demographic consequences of reproduction, dispersal and social interaction in a population of Leadbeater's possum,' In Smith, A.P. and Hume, I.M. (eds) *Possums and gliders*, Australian Mammal Society: Sydney, pp. 359-373.

Smith, A.P. and Lindenmayer, D. 1988. 'Tree hollow requirements of Leadbeater's possum and other possums and gliders in timber production ash forests of the Victorian central highlands. *Australian Wildlife Research*, 15, 347-62.

Smith, V.K. 1985. 'Supply uncertainty, option price and indirect benefit estimation,' *Land Economics*, 61(3), 303-307.

Smith, V.K. 1990. 'Valuing amenity resources under uncertainty. A skeptical view of recent resolutions,' *Journal of Environmental Economics and Management*, 19, 193-202.

Smith, V.K. 1992. 'Comment. Arbitrary values, good causes and premature verdicts,' *Journal of Environmental Economics and Management*, 22, 71-89.

Smith, V.K. and Desvousges, W.H. 1987. 'An empirical analysis of the economic value of risk changes,' *Journal of Political Economy*, 95(1), 89-114.

Smith, V.K. and Krutilla, J.V. 1979. 'Endangered species, irreversibilities and uncertainty: A comment,' *American Journal of Agricultural Economics*, May, 371-79.

Smith, V.K. and Osborne, L. 1994. 'Do contingent valuation estimates pass a "scope" test? A preliminary meta analysis,' Paper presented at the American Economics Association Annual Meeting, Boston MA, Jan 5.

Smith, V.K., Desvousges, W.H. and Fisher, A. 1986. 'A comparison of direct and indirect methods for estimating environmental benefits,' *American Journal of Agricultural Economics*, 68(2), 280-90.

Solow, A. and Polasky, S. 1994. 'Measuring biological diversity,' *Environmental and Ecological Statistics*, 1(2), 95-107.

Solow, A., Polasky, S. and Broadus, J. 1993. 'On the measurement of biological diversity,' *Journal of Environmental Economics and Management*, 24, 60-68.

Soulé, M.E. (ed.) 1986. *Conservation biology: The science of scarcity and diversity.* Sunderland, MA: Sinauer Associates.

Soulé, M.E. 1987. *Viable populations for conservation.* Cambridge, Cambridge University Press.

Sparrowe, R.D. and Wight, H.M. 1975. 'Setting priorities for the endangered species program,' *Transactions of the 40th North American Wildlife Conference.* Wildlife Management Institute, Washington D.C., pp. 143-156.

Spash, C.L. 1993. 'Economics, ethics and long term environmental damages,' *Environmental Ethics* 15, 117-132.

Spash, C.L. and Hanley, N. 1995. 'Preferences, information and biodiversity preservation,' *Ecological Economics*, 12, 191-208.

SPSS Inc. 1983. *SPSSX Users guide.* New York: McGraw-Hill Book Company.

Squire, R.O., Campbell, R.G., Wareing, K.J. and Featherston, G.R. 1987. 'The mountain ash (*Eucalyptus regnans* F. Muell.) forests of Victoria: Ecology, silviculture and management for wood production. In *Forest management in Australia.* Proceedings of conference of the Institute of Foresters, Perth, Sept., pp. 63-87.

Stevens, T.H., Echeverria, J., Glass, R.J., Hager, T. and More, T.A. 1991. 'Measuring the existence value of wildlife: What do CVM estimates really show?' *Land Economics*, 67(4), 390-400.

Stoll, J. and Johnson, L.A. 1984. 'Concepts of value, non-market valuation and the case of the whooping crane,' *Transactions of the 49th North American Wildlife and Natural Resources Conference.* Wildlife Management Institute, Washington D.C.

Stone, A. 1992. 'Assessing the economic value of wetlands,' In Lockwood, M. and DeLacy, T. (eds) *Valuing natural areas: Applications and problems of the contingent valuation method,* Johnstone Centre, Charles Sturt University, Albury, pp. 47-70.

Stone, J. 1991. 'Holes found in Kakadu mining survey,' In Resource Assessment Commission (ed.) 'Commentaries on the Resource Assessment Commission's contingent valuation survey of the Kakadu Conservation Zone,' Resource Assessment Commission, Canberra.

Streeting, M and Hamilton, C. 1991. *An economic analysis of the forests of south-eastern Australia*. Resources Assessment Commission, Research paper No. 5, Canberra: AGPS.

Sutton, P. 1988. 'Flora and fauna forever - the Flora and Fauna Guarantee and the conserver economy,' *Eingana*, Aug-Sept.

Swaney, J.A. and Olson, P.I. 1992. 'The economics of biodiversity: Lives and lifestyles,' *Journal of Economic Issues*, 26(1), 1-25.

Swanson, T.M. 1994. 'The economics of extinction revisited and revised: A generalised framework for the analysis of the problems of endangered species and biodiversity loss,' *Oxford Economic Papers*, 46, 800-821.

Swanson, T.M. and Barbier, E.B. (eds) 1992. *Economics for the wilds: Wildlife, wildlands, diversity and development*. Earthscan Publications, London.

Terbough, J. 1974. 'Preservation of natural diversity: The problem of extinction prone species,' *Bioscience*, 24(12), 715-722.

Thomas, J.F. and Syme, G.J. 1988. 'Estimating residential price elasticity of demand for water: A contingent valuation approach,' *Water Resources Research* 24(11), 1847-1857.

Throsby, C.D. and Withers, G.A. 1986. 'Strategic bias and demand for public goods. Theory and an application to the arts,' *Journal of Public Economics*, 31, 307-327.

Tisdell, C.A. 1979. 'On the economics of saving wildlife from extinction,' Paper for Section 24, Economics. ANZAAS Conference. University of Auckland, New Zealand. 22-26 January.

Tisdell, C.A. 1990. 'Economics and the debate about preservation of species, crop varieties and genetic diversity,' *Ecological Economics*, 2, 77-90.

Tobias, D. and Mendelsohn, R. 1991. 'Valuing ecotourism in a tropical rain-forest reserve,' *Ambio*, 20(2), 91-93.

Tracey, P.J. 1992. 'An assessment of the non-market conservation and heritage values relating to cattle grazing on the Bogong High Plains, Victoria. Honours Thesis, Charles Sturt University, Albury.

Tracy, K. 1993. 'A non-market economic evaluation of three urban parks in Sydney,' Honours dissertation, Charles Sturt University, Albury.

Tversky, A. and Kahneman, D. 1981. 'The framing of decisions and the rationality of choice,' *Science*, 211, 1124-1131.

Veisten, K., Hoen, H-F., Navrud, S. and Strand, J. 1993. 'Valuing biodiversity in Norwegian forests: A contingent valuation study with multiple bias testing,' Memorandum, Dept. of Economics, University of Oslo, No. 7.

Viscusi, W.K. 1993. 'The value of risks to life and health,' *Journal of Economic Literature*, 31(4), 1912-1946.

Waikato Valley Authority 1983. 'An application of contingent valuation to water pollution control in the Waikato Basin,' Waikato Valley Authority Technical Publication No. 27. Cited in Kerr, G.N. and Sharp, B.M.H. 1987.

Walpole, S.C. 1991. 'The recreational and environmental benefits of the Ovens-Kings river systems,' *Australian Parks and Recreation*, 33-37.

Walsh, R.G., Bjonback, D., Rosenthal, D. and Aiken, R. 1987. 'Public benefits of programs to protect endangered wildlife in Colorado,' In *Issues and technology in the management of impacted Western wildlife*. Boulder Colorado: Thorne Ecological Institute, pp. 65-71.

Walsh, R.G., Gillman, R.A. and Loomis, J.B. 1982. 'Wilderness resource economics: Recreation use and preservation values,' American Wilderness Alliance, Denver, Colorado.

Walsh, R.G., Johnson, D.M. and McKean, J.R. 1989. 'Issues in non-market valuation and policy application: A retrospective glance,' *Western Journal of Agricultural Economics*, 14(1), 178-188.

Walsh, R.G., Johnson, D.M. and McKean, J.R. 1992. 'Benefit transfer of outdoor recreation demand studies, 1968-1988,' *Water Resources Research*, 28(3), 707-713

Weber, J.A., Lynch, R.J. and Halverson, P.B. 1991. 'Allocating water in the Ashburton River: Irrigation versus instream flows,' Paper for the New Zealand Agricultural Economics Society Annual Meeting. August.

Weitzman, M.L. 1992. 'On diversity,' *Quarterly Journal of Economics,* 102(2), May, 363-405

Whitehead, J.C. 1992. '*Ex ante* willingness to pay with supply and demand uncertainty. Implications for valuing a sea turtle protection program,' *Applied Economics,* 24, 981-988.

Whitehead, J.C. 1993. 'Total economic values for coastal and marine wildlife: Specification, validity and valuation issues,' *Marine Resource Economics,* 8, 119-132.

Whitehead, J.C., Groothuis, P.A. and Blomquist, G.C. 1993. Testing for non-response and sample selection bias in contingent valuation: Analysis of a combination phone/mail survey,' *Economics Letters,* 41, 215-220.

Wibe, S. 1994. 'Non-wood benefits in forestry: Survey of valuation studies,' Swedish University of Agricultural Sciences, Department of Forest Economics, Umeå. Working paper No. 199.

Wilcox, B.A. 1988. *1988 IUCN red list of threatened animals.* Gland, Switzerland: International Union for Conservation of Nature and Natural Resources. Cambridge, UK.

Wilkinson, H.E. 1961. 'The rediscovery of Leadbeater's possum,' *Victorian Naturalist,* 78, 97-102.

Wilks, L.C. 1990. 'A survey of the contingent valuation method,' Resource Assessment Commission. Research Paper No. 2. Canberra: Australian Government Publishing Service.

Willig, R. 1976. 'Consumer's surplus without apology,' *American Economic Review,* 66(4), 587-597.

Willis, K.G. and Garrod, G.D. 1993. 'Valuing landscape: A contingent valuation approach,' *Journal of Environmental Management,* 37, 1-22.

Wilson, E.O. (ed.) 1988. *Biodiversity,* Washington, DC: National Academy Press.

Wohlers, A.C. and Vlastuin, C. 1990. 'The decision to fund a research proposal. Some results for wool production,' Paper presented to the 34th Annual Conference of the Australian Agricultural Economics Society. University of Queensland, Brisbane.

Yapp, T.P., Young, L.J. and Sinden, J.A. 1991. 'Trends in community support for soil conservation,' Paper presented to 35th Annual Conference of the Australian Agricultural Economics Society, University of New England, Armidale.

Yagerman, K.S. 1990. 'Critical habitat under the endangered species act,' *Environmental Law,* 811.

Young, R. and Carter, M. 1990. 'The economic evaluation of environmental research: A case study of the south east forests,' Presented to the 34th Annual Conference of the Australian Agricultural Economics Society, University of Queensland, February.

Zeckhauser, R. 1973. 'Voting systems, honest preferences and Pareto optimality,' *American Political Science Review,* 67, 934-946.

SUBJECT INDEX